"Dr. Schmidt has produced an informative, instructive, insightful, and very inspiring book. Any reader will be rewarded by this well written, scholarly, and timely book on the subject every American needs to understand."

Anis Shorrosh, D. Phil.
Author of *Islam Revealed*

"Rather than either reciting the 'religion of peace' mantra or muttering that Muslims murder all infidels, we can use the help of Alvin Schmidt in surveying the forests rather than obsessing about individual trees" (From the Foreword)

Marvin Olasky, Ph.D.
University of Texas at Austin
Editor-in-chief of *World* magazine
Author of *The Religions Next Door*

"Alvin J. Schmidt's *The Great Divide: The Failure of Islam and the Triumph of the West* elegantly delineates the differences between the Christian and Muslim worldviews. In a world of obfuscation and "can't-we-all-just-get-along" indifferentism, this book is a much-needed beacon of theological and moral clarity—as well as common sense"

Robert Spencer
Author of *Islam Unveiled* and *Onward Muslim Soldiers*

"In *The Great Divide: The Failure of Islam and the Triumph of the West*, Alvin Schmidt addresses many issues concerning the perception of Islam promoted in the United States. Christians should reach out to Muslims and present Christ's love to them, yet they cannot remain ignorant about the spiritual and physical threat that Islam is to the West."

Tom White
Executive Director, *The Voice of the Martyrs*

Professor Schmidt has not just written an important book—he has written an essential book. Written with passion, this book is a clear defense of our Lord, without becoming mean-spirited. In addition, it is written with a scholar's eye for accuracy and research. It is well worth your time. It will greatly affect your witness.

Ergun Mehmet Caner, Th.D.
Liberty University
Author of *Unveiling Islam*

The Great Divide

The Failure of Islam and the Triumph Of The West

The Great Divide

The Failure of Islam and the Triumph Of The West

Alvin J. Schmidt

Regina Orthodox Press Inc.

Boston, Massachusetts

ISBN 1-928653-19-7

Regina Orthodox Press Inc.

www.reginaorthodoxpress.com

ACKNOWLEDGEMENTS

No scholar ever writes a book without receiving assistance from number of individuals. This was also true in regard to writing this book. The library staff of Illinois College, especially Laura Sweatman, was exceptionally helpful in obtaining dozens of books for me for a number of months via inter-library loan. There were times, I am sure, the staff was wondering when I would stop requesting so many books as I did my research. For their kind assistance I sincerely want to say: "Thank You." I would be quite remiss if I did not thank my dear wife, Carol, who once again put up with my social isolation, as she did in my previous writing ventures. And last, but certainly not least, I appreciate the time Marvin Olasky took out of his busy schedule to read the galley pages so he could write the book's foreword. In a similar vein, I also appreciate the efforts of Erget Mehmet Caner, Anis Shorrosh, Robert Spencer, and Tom White, who took time to read the manuscript and write endorsements for the book. May God bless you all!

Dedicated to all who have wondered what the differences are between the West and Islam but were afraid to ask.

CONTENTS

FOREWORD

These days, the hills are alive with the sound of musings about Islam. *Publisher's Weekly* reported this spring that a spate of new books on the religion are hitting the bookstores, and they're unlike the critical books that came out after September 11; the new tomes assure readers that Islam is a religion of peace. That, as Alvin Schmidt points out in *The Great Divide*, is wishful thinking. Muslims are right to point out that the Bible has its parts (such as the book of Joshua) that sound bloodthirsty to modern readers, but the Quran is Joshua all the way through, without its contextualization in the peace-emphasizing prophetic and New Testament books.

On the other hand, the Internet is replete with accounts (probably urban legends) of Christians routing Muslims in debate by asking a few easy questions. Here's one such account:

> I directed my question to the Imam and asked: "Please, correct me if I'm wrong, but I understand that most Imams and clerics of Islam have declared jihad [holy war] against the infidels of the world. And, that by killing an infidel, which is a command to all Muslims, they are assured of a place in heaven. If that's the case, can you give me the definition of an infidel?"

> There was no disagreement with my statements and, without hesitation, he replied, "Non-believers!" I responded, "So, let me make sure I have this straight. All followers of Allah have been commanded to kill everyone who is not of your faith so they can go to Heaven. Is that correct?" The expression on his face changed from one of authority and command to that of a little boy who had just got his hand caught with his hand in the cookie jar. He sheepishly replied, "Yes."

... I continued, "I also have a problem with being your friend when you and your brother clerics are telling your followers to kill me. Let me ask you a question. Would you rather have your Allah who tells you to kill me in order to go to Heaven or my Jesus who tells me to love you because I am going to Heaven and He wants you to be with me?" You could have heard a pin drop as the Imam hung his head in shame. Please pass this on to all your email contacts. This is a true story.

If only it were that easy. That's not the way these discussions go, unless the Imam is an idiot. Many Muslims contest the critical definition of jihad. Many say that Muslims fight and are rewarded only when defending Muslim lands. Many say that only renegade Muslims murder civilians, and that those who do have no place in heaven. It's time to peel back layers of an onion: What is a Muslim land? (Islam occupied Spain for nearly eight centuries. Perhaps all lands are or should be Muslim lands.) Who is a civilian? (Is it an Israeli non-soldier who has military training and could be called into active service at any time? Is it a worker at the Pentagon? How about those at the World Trade Center who advance the capitalism that undergirds U.S. military efforts?)

Most American Muslims stop after one or two layers. Muslim terrorists peel away all of them, all the way down to killing pregnant women and their children, even making sure that unborn children are blasted away. After all, the unborn could eventually become soldiers occupying land that belongs to Islam. Should all Muslims be blamed for such brutality? Clearly not. Many Muslims are pro-life concerning the unborn. Should Islam be exonerated? No. Muslims should take responsibility for what is typical in Islamic history and the culture that grows out of the Quran. Rather than either reciting the "religion of peace" mantra or muttering that Muslims murder all infidels, we can use the help of Alvin Schmidt in surveying the forests rather than obsessing about individual trees.

Professor Schmidt does not hack away at Islam, nor does he attack Christianity because of headlined abuses that arise in it. He doesn't hyperventilate about the Abu Ghraibs of Christianity—the misogyny of some church fathers, the bloody entry of the Crusaders into Jerusalem, the pro-slavery rhetoric of some antebellum fire-eaters. Instead, he compares the normal practice of Christianity and Islam. He shows how Christianity grew by the blood of its martyrs, but Islam grew by killing those who opposed it. He compares the view of women in the New Testament and the Quran, showing how Christ's teaching eventually led to the development of complementary roles for men and women but Muhammad's teaching led to subservience. He shows how Christians looked at slavery critically over the centuries and how many fought for its abolition; Islam, though, has no intrinsic anti-slavery position, so it's no surprise that some Islamic countries today still allow it.

Do you want to know whether beheading is part of traditional Muslim practice? Professor Schmidt's book notes that Muhammad himself ordered such killings, and that when Ottoman Muslims finally captured Constantinople in 1453 the embalmed head of Emperor Constantine XI became part of a traveling exhibit. Do you want to know the difference between Christ's and Muhammad's attitudes toward the needy? Schmidt points out that Jesus had compassion on the lame, the deaf, and the sick, but Muhammad in Sura 80 "frowned and turned his back" on a blind man. Do you remember what Jesus told those accusing an adulterous woman without sufficient evidence, "Let him who is without sin cast the first stone"? Professor Schmidt notes that when a prostitute confessed to Muhammad, he participated in her execution by throwing the first stone.

Christians who understand these specific differences, delineated in Schmidt's book, will strengthen their own faith and be ready to enter into discussions with Muslims without offering either appeasement or shotgun-blast aggression.

———————————————

Marvin Olasky, PhD., is the editor-in-chief of *World*, a professor at The University of Texas at Austin, and the author of over fifteen books, including *The Religions Next Door*.

INTRODUCTION

In A.D. 622, Muhammad founded the religion of Islam when he made his *hijra* (flight) from Mecca to Medina. The Meccans had rejected him and his group of about 70 followers (Muslims), so he fled to Medina.

Most Westerners, especially North Americans, have until recently had little or no contact with Muslims or with the religion and culture of Islam. But now that Muslims comprise about 20 percent of the world's approximately six billion people, together with increasing numbers of Muslim immigrants to Western countries, Westerners, including Americans, are becoming aware that Islam is not just a different religion, but interwoven with it is also a very different culture. Compared to the Judeo-Christian influence, and especially Christianity's impact, on the West, the culture and religion of Islam is on the other side of a great divide, so to speak. It is this great divide that the present book documents, portrays, and analyzes.

Since the West has especially been greatly influenced and shaped by Christian values, the first chapter begins by comparing the life of Jesus Christ with Muhammad. The comparison is based on reliable, scholarly records. A lot of the information revealed in this chapter cites highly unfavorable, but corroborated facts about Muhammad, facts that Muslims are not permitted to hear, read, or talk about in Islamic countries, where he is above all criticism. To criticize him is equivalent to an act of religious apostasy.

All historical accounts revealed in this book intend to inform both Westerners and Muslims. "Facts," as John Adams once said, "are stubborn things." But they are necessary to understand what is true or not true. Life is improved when people know the facts and try to learn from them. Thus, in noting the numerous uncomplimentary facts of Muhammad, for

1

instance, vis-à-vis Jesus Christ, the intent is not to offend or anger any Muslims, but to help them see what history does indeed reveal. Hopefully, truth-seeking Muslims will benefit from reading and reflecting upon those facts, especially since many now reside in the West, where they have the opportunity to examine facts of history in the context of political and religious freedom.

The second chapter focuses on how early Christianity grew and expanded during its first 300 years without resorting to any form of violence, even when countless numbers of Christians were severely persecuted, as opposed to Islam, which from the time of its inception in 622 frequently and widely employed the sword to expand and grow both geographically and numerically. This chapter discusses this component of the great divide.

The third chapter surveys the role of women in the West versus the role of women in Islamic countries. It shows that the treatment women receive in Islamic and Western countries is the result of the gulf-wide differences between Christianity and Islam. Jesus Christ's views of women, which greatly influenced the West's view and treatment of women, differed remarkably from those of Muhammad. Most of those pronounced differences are still present in Islam today. Many of them are highly significant.

Chapter 4 concentrates on the moral issue of slavery. It shows that slavery was first outlawed in the West, where Christianity had its greatest presence. Unknown to many, this chapter also documents and shows that slavery still exists today in some Islamic countries in Africa.

In the fifth chapter the Christian concept of charity is compared with the Islamic practice of *Zakat*. The latter is often loosely translated as "charity." But the chapter shows that the two are not the same, especially not in terms of what charity originally meant when Christians in the West practiced it as a

2

gesture of altruistic love for those in need. The chapter also discusses the difference between charity and governmental welfare.

The sixth chapter, "The Crusades and the Rest of the Story," shows how the Crusades of the Middle Ages have commonly been presented in the West with an anti-Christian or anti-Western bias in school textbooks, a bias that is the result of historians having overlooked some very significant historical facts. The chapter provides evidence that the Crusades really began as defensive (just) war as a result of the West having experienced numerous military attacks and invasions from Islamic forces for several centuries before the Crusades were launched.

The differences regarding liberty and justice between the West and Islamic countries are significant and prominent. They reflect another aspect of the great divide. In the West, liberty and justice are by-products of Judeo-Christian beliefs and values. In most Islamic countries a very different concept of liberty, rights, and justice prevails. For example, frequently laws, privileges, and rights are not the same for men and women. Chapter 7 discusses those differences.

Chapter 8 explores the question of which religion, Christianity or Islam, has provided the most favorable conditions to the growth and development of modern science. The chapter reveals information not commonly found in textbooks relative to the role Christianity's theological presuppositions played in making modern experimental science in the West possible. In addition, Appendix B also provides portraits of scientists whose Christian beliefs motivated them to study, explore, and understand their God-given natural environment. The pre-modern (13th century) thoughts and contributions of Islam's natural philosophers are contrasted to this Western background.

The ninth chapter discusses the differences between Islam and the West in regard to the relationship between religion and the state. The Western concept of the separation of church and state is traced back to Jesus Christ (Matthew 22:21). To Muslims the separation of religion from the state conflicts with Islam's doctrine that religion is the state and the state is religion. The West's separation of the two violates Islamic theology and theory of government.

The tenth chapter examines the question of whether Islam is a peaceful religion, as is often heard today. To answer this question, the chapter looks at Islam's 1,400-year history, including what the Koran and the Hadith reveal on this matter.

The final chapter discusses the effects Islam's apologists (Muslims and non-Muslims) are having in the West today. It notes that apologists in the West's current environment of political correctness not only are disallowing discussion regarding anything unfavorable to Islam, regardless of the facts, but also, knowingly or unknowingly, are posing a major threat to the Judeo-Christian culture of the Western world.

Quotations from the Koran are taken from the translation by M. H. Shakir and published by Tahrike Tarsile Qur'an, Inc., 1997. Quotations from the Koran are referenced by noting the Sura (chapter) and the appropriate verse(s) of a given Sura.

In addition to citations from the Koran, references are also cited from the Hadith. The Hadith are authentic statements or actions of Muhammad. Some scholars use the word Hadith in a singular sense; others see the word Hadith as a plural. In the citations, the first numeral, following the designation of *Sahih Al-Buhkari,* refers to a given book in the Hadith; the second figure refers to the chapter, and on occasion the third figure appears that refers to the verse in the chapter. All Hadith references are taken from *The Translation of the Meanings of Sahih Al-Bukhari*, sixth revised edition, Kazi Publications,

Lahore, Pakistan, 1983. This nine-volume work ranks next to the Koran in terms of authority for Muslims.

Shariah citations are from the manual known as *Reliance of the Traveller*. This is the manual of the Sunni Muslims, who comprise approximately 85 percent of the world's Muslims, and it reflects the Shafi'i school of jurisprudence. The first symbol in a citation is a lower-case letter of the alphabet, which refers to a given book in this manual. The second symbol, a numeral, refers to a particular chapter, and the third symbol, also a numeral, indicates the verse.

References cited from the Bible, unless otherwise indicated, are from the English Standard Version. Thus, if a citation is from the New International Version, the abbreviation "NIV" follows the chapter and verse notation. If a passage is taken from the New King James Version, the abbreviation "NKJV" is used.

Finally, throughout the book, except when a quotation is cited in the text or in a footnote that uses the word "Qur'an," I opted for the spelling of "Koran." Either spelling is used by respectable scholars.

1

JESUS AND MUHAMMAD: POLAR OPPOSITES

"Facts do not cease to exist because they are ignored" (Aldous Huxley)

Those who know something about the history of Muhammad's numerous warmongering activities may wonder why this book begins with a chapter that compares Muhammad with Jesus Christ, for most people know that no greater nonviolent and morally upright man of love, peace, and justice than Jesus Christ has ever lived. In comparing Jesus with Muhammad, I am mindful of the words spoken by Philip Schaff, the renowned 19th-century church historian: "To compare such a man [Muhammad] with Jesus is preposterous and even blasphemous. ... He falls far below Moses, or Elijah, or any of the prophets and apostles in moral purity."[1] I am also aware of what George Sale, an 18th-century British scholar of Muhammad who first translated the Koran into English in 1734, said with regard to Jesus and Muhammad:

> No two personages ever appeared in the world more perfect and absolute contrasts to each other than the founder of the Turkish [Islam] and Christian religion. Christ was pure and Unspotted in the whole of his deportment ... but Mohammad was a sink of iniquity, lust, and ambition, if we listen to his friends. Jesus employed no weapons in defense of his mission but the artillery of reason and argument, joined to the impetuous influence of stupendous miracles, while Mohammad could do nothing without the energy of the sword.[2]

Nevertheless, because Muslims see Jesus as a prophet, though really inferior to Muhammad, I deem it appropriate to compare the two. Objectively minded readers of the Bible, the Koran, and historically reliable books about the lives of Jesus and Muhammad will see that Jesus was a prophet not inferior but far superior to Muhammad. In thought, word, and deed he was more than a prophet. To say this is not in tune with today's multiculturalist code of political correctness. "These days," says Robert Spencer, "it's considered in bad taste ... that Muhammad of Islam and the Jesus of Christianity are not interchangeable."[3]

There is clearly a double standard in today's public media in regard to their portrayals of Jesus Christ compared to Muhammad. Publications unfavorable to Muhammad or Islam are avoided; however, uncomplimentary and often undocumented articles about Jesus Christ are frequently aired. This double standard that exists in the secular media is unfortunate and not supportive of the truth. As Robert Spencer has noted, "Muhammad cannot be judged; rather, he is the standard by which all others are judged."[4]

By citing numerous historical incidents in the following chapter regarding Muhammad's life, many of which are not laudatory, I am not primarily trying to counter the existing pro-Muhammad bias but merely providing an honest look at what history reveals about him and Jesus Christ.

The Births of Jesus and Muhammad

Jesus of Nazareth was born about 5 or 6 B.C., when Caesar Augustus ruled the Roman Empire. He was born of a Jewish mother named Mary (Miriam in Greek), a virgin who had not known a man sexually. His birth was foretold by some of the Old Testament prophets, including Moses: "I will raise up for them a prophet like you from among their brothers. And I will put my words in his mouth, and he shall speak to them all

8

that I command him" (Deuteronomy 18:18). Some 700 years before Christ was born, Isaiah the prophet declared: "Behold the virgin shall conceive and bear a Son, and shall call his name Immanuel" (Isaiah 7:14). The prophet Micah, a contemporary of Isaiah, even foretold the town (Bethlehem) of his birth (Micah 5:2).

Unlike the birth of Jesus, the birth of Muhammad (about A.D. 570 in Mecca) was not a miraculous event. Muhammad's father died before his mother gave birth to him. In his infancy he was nourished by a wet nurse. At age six his mother died, requiring his maternal grandfather to provide for him until he was eight years old. At this age his grandparent died. Then his uncle reared him. Also unlike Jesus, his birth was not foretold by any prophet in the Old Testament, or elsewhere, although some Muslims have for some time tried to make such claims by arguing that Moses predicted the birth of Muhammad by citing the same passages (e.g., Deuteronomy 18:18) that Christians used five centuries before Muhammad was born.

For instance, the Gospel of John quotes Philip, one of Jesus' disciples, saying to Nathaniel: "We have found him of whom Moses in the Law and also the prophets wrote, Jesus of Nazareth ... " (John 1:45). Luke, the writer of the book of Acts, stated: "Moses said, 'The Lord God will raise up for you a prophet like me from your brothers. You shall listen in whatever he tells you' " (Acts 3:22). Both of these passages have reference to Deuteronomy 18:18. Moreover, Jesus himself said, "If you believed Moses, you would believe me, for he wrote of me" (John 5:46).

There is also plenty of extra-biblical evidence that cites the Deuteronomy passage as referring to the coming of Jesus Christ. In the second century, Clement of Alexandria (ca. 150–213), an early church father, cited Deuteronomy 18:15 (which is virtually identical to verse 18) as evidence that predicted the birth of Jesus Christ (*Pedagogus* 1:7). Tertullian (ca. 150–ca.

220), a contemporary of Clement of Alexandria, did so as well in his work *Against Marcion* 4:32. Similarly, Origen (185-254), another church father, also noted the Deuteronomy verse as a prophecy that predicted Christ's birth (*Contra Celsus* 4:95).

Genesis 49:10 is another passage that some Muslims cite as predicting Muhammad's birth. It reads: "The scepter shall not depart from Judah, nor the ruler's staff from between his feet, until he comes to whom it belongs; and to him shall be the obedience of the peoples." Again, as most biblical scholars know, Christians, hundreds of years before the birth of Muhammad, had seen this reference as another Messianic prophecy predicting the birth of Jesus Christ.

To cite Moses' prophecy in Deuteronomy 18:18 and Genesis 49:10 as pointing to the coming of Muhammad is not only a specious claim, but it also contradicts the Muslim argument that says the Bible is not a reliable book because the Jews and Christians had corrupted it. The Shafi'i Shariah manual, *Reliance of the Traveller*, regarding the Torah and New Testament, says, "the Jews and Christians have altered the texts and interpolated spurious material ..." (k30.6).[5] Thus, if the Bible has been corrupted, what evidence is there that Deuteronomy 18 and Genesis 49 are not part of corruption?

It is probably safe to say that when Muslims cite Deuteronomy 18 and Genesis 49, it is done to persuade biblically uninformed Christians that Muhammad, similar to Jesus Christ, has a biblical legitimacy. However, between Muslims, these passages mean very little, for Muslims have no need to cite the Bible in support of Muhammad's legitimacy because the Koran is seen as superior to the Bible. It is also helpful to know that although Muhammad said he was a prophet, he himself did not say his birth was predicted in the Old Testament.

Some Muslims try to argue that Muhammad's birth is predicted in the words Jesus spoke in John 15:26: "But when the Helper comes, whom I will send to you from the Father, the Spirit of truth, who proceeds from the Father, he will bear witness about me. ... " The Greek word for "Counselor" in this passage is *parakletos*. It can also mean "Advocate," "Comforter," or "Helper." Muslims believing the Bible to be corrupted say this Greek word should really be *periklutos*, meaning the "praised one," that is, Muhammad. However, as the scholar John Gilchrist has shown, "There is not a shred of evidence in favour of the assertion that the original word was '*periklutos.*' " Gilchrist continues: "We have thousands of New Testament manuscripts pre-dating Islam and not one of these contains the word '*periklutos.*' "[6]

Finally, it is interesting to know how and when Muslims started using the same Old Testament references to prove Muhammad's birth was foretold. Reliable evidence shows it began as the result of a statement made by John of Damascus (d. ca.750), a Christian monk who lived among Muslims near Jerusalem. He told some Muslims that many biblical prophecies foretold the birth of Christ, but none foretold the coming of Muhammad. Gustave von Grunebaum, reputed scholar of Islam, said the comments by John of Damascus shamed and silenced his Muslim acquaintances.[7] Ever since that time, more than a century after Muhammad's death, Muslims have been trying to show that Muhammad's birth, similar to Christ's, was also foretold in the Old Testament. But the evidence does not support their belated argument.

Religious Callings

Biographers of Muhammad note he had a favorite retreat—a cave at Mount Hira, a couple of miles from Mecca—where he would retire for days to pray and meditate, often to struggle with doubts about his self-confidence and with temptations to commit suicide. While suffering one of these psychological/mental traumas, the angel Gabriel (in A.D. 610) reportedly appeared to him at Mount Hira. Holding up some written words, the angel told Muhammad to read them. He replied, "I cannot read." After being told a second time to read, he asked: "What shall I read?" The angel responded by reading the words to him, which reportedly are the words of Sura 96:1–2 in the Koran. After the reading Gabriel told Muhammad he was Allah's Prophet.[8]

But his mental traumas and terrifying thoughts did not end quickly after his experience with the angel Gabriel. Returning from the cave, he said to his wife Khadija, "I am afraid of becoming mad ... I see all the signs of madness in myself."[9] He even thought he might be "possessed by a jinn."[10] Thoughts of committing suicide plagued him.[11]

After his encounter with the angel Gabriel, it took another three years for him to believe he was a prophet. Apparently consolations from his wife Khadija helped change his mind. She, who was Muhammad's first convert to Islam, comforted and assured him that he was not going mad or possessed by demons.[12] Three years after his unusual cave experience, he began preaching his new religion in about A.D. 613/614, hoping to gain converts.[13]

At first converts were few in number, only about 15 in a period of about three years. His new converts (Muslims) were not well received in Mecca, whose residents, especially the Quraish tribe, were incensed at him for preaching against the numerous idols housed in the Kaaba, the pagan shrine to which various Arabic tribes came to worship a variety of gods and goddesses. So, in about A.D. 617, this small number of Muslims fled to the west, across the Red Sea, to Abyssinia (Ethiopia). This flight has sometimes been called Muhammad's first flight, his first *hijra*.

From Abyssinia, Muhammad soon made his way back to Mecca, where, in order to appease the Meccans, he made a religious compromise. He agreed to recognize some of their

12

idols by saying that Allah had three daughter goddesses: Al-Lat, Al-Uzza, and Manat (Sura 53:19–20). According to Sir William Muir, a 19th-century scholar of Islam, Muhammad added: " 'These are the exalted goddesses whose intercession with the Deity is to be sought. ... ' " (*MI*, 40). These words elated the Meccans, for they thought he had finally compromised his anti-polytheistic posture. Meanwhile, the Abyssinian refugees, hearing false rumors that the Meccans had converted to Islam, returned to Mecca. Upon returning, however, they found the Meccans (many of them of the Quraish clan) were persecuting Muhammad and his followers anew because Muhammad had retracted his earlier statements favorable to the female goddesses, saying that Satan had deceived him. The retracted or abrogated verses are now known as the "Satanic Verses."

Things did not improve for Muhammad in Mecca. People ridiculed and derided him.[14] Some reports say that Quraish thugs even beat him.[15] "He was almost murdered in his bed, but escaped and took to the caves while his pursuers ranged the desert, seeking for his tracks."[16] In A.D. 622, Muhammad, together with about 70 of his followers, "slipped secretly out of town,"[17] and made their *hijra* to Medina. Thus, contrary to common impression, the *hijra* to Medina was more than a migration—it was a flight for survival.

After he arrived in Medina, Muhammad changed his manner of gaining converts to Islam, largely as a result of having received a revelation from Allah while still in Mecca that told him to use force and violence to advance Islam.[18] Previously, in Mecca he had used peaceful methods in trying to get Meccans to convert to Islam, but since that approach had brought him no real success, he now embarked on a radically new philosophy by resorting to violent methods, as discussed below in greater detail. In fact, "The whole life of Mohammed after his flight to Medina was one continued scene of butchery and rapine. He and his associates and followers plundered every caravan of its valuable commodities."[19]

This change in Muhammad's behavior is noted by both non-Muslim and some scholarly Muslim historians. For instance, Al Dashti, an Iranian Muslim and a scholar of Islam and Muhammad, is one such honest writer. He states: "After the move to Medina ... he [Muhammad] became a relentless warrior, intent on spreading his religion by the sword, and a scheming founder of a state."[20]

When we look at the call Jesus received from God, in comparison to Muhammad, we find many differences. Jesus' ministry began with his baptism by John the Baptist, at which time a voice from heaven said: " 'You are my beloved Son; with you I am well pleased' " (Luke 3:22). Jesus is called God's Son, conveying a personal Father-Son relationship, a relationship absent in the words that the angel Gabriel addressed to Muhammad.

Comparing Muhammad's results in terms of gained converts to those of Jesus, we do find some similarities. Like Muhammad's numbers, Jesus' three-year ministry also yielded a low number of converts. Moreover, most of Jesus' followers were fickle with little or no commitment. The Gospel of John states that when they heard the "hard teachings" of Jesus, "many of his disciples [followers] turned back and no longer walked with him" (John 6:66). But, unlike Muhammad, this did not prompt him to change his methodology by resorting to violence to support his cause. Undeterred, he steadfastly continued teaching and preaching, trying to persuade people with his love-directed words and actions, even when his enemies at times tried to stone him.

Nor did Jesus ever try to gain converts by compromising or retracting any of his teachings or blaming the devil for misleading him, as Muhammad did with the Satanic Verses. Instead, Jesus withstood the devil when tempted by him on

14

three occasions.   Jesus as the Son of God met the test.
Muhammad did not. They were polar opposites.

Their View of Human Life

When we compare Jesus and Muhammad regarding their
value of human life, we again find major differences. Jesus
came so human beings might have life: "I came that they may
have life, and have it abundantly" (John 10:10).   He
demonstrated the genuineness of this claim by miraculously
healing the lame, the deaf, and the sick, because "he had
compassion on them" (Matthew 14:14). On one occasion, when
a large crowd rebuked two blind men who were calling out to
Jesus, "Lord, have mercy on us, Son of David," he stopped and
healed both (Matthew 20:29–34). This was only one of several
healings of the blind Jesus performed. This act of compassion
stands in stark contrast to Muhammad's behavior. When a poor
blind man desiring religious instruction called out to him for his
attention, the Koran says that Muhammad "frowned and turned
(his) back, because there came to him a blind man" (Sura 80:1–
2).

Christ ministered to the downtrodden, the outcast, and
the poor. He himself was the poorest of the poor, as he
reminded us: "Foxes have holes, and birds of the air have nests,
but the Son of Man has nowhere to lay his head" (Luke 9:58).
He was a homeless man. Again, the life of Muhammad stands
in marked contrast to the man from Nazareth, for at the age of
25 (some say 28) he married Khadija, a 40-year-old, well-to-do
Arabic widow. Later, when he began leading armed expeditions against various tribal groups, he amassed considerable
wealth, much of it in the form of booty, of which he commonly
took one-fifth.[21]

The account of the adulterous woman in John's Gospel
is a well-known example of Jesus' value of human life. When a
group of self-righteous men were about to stone to death a

woman accused of adultery, Jesus, coming upon the scene, told the would-be executioners: "Let him who is without sin among you be the first to throw a stone at her" (John 8:7). Knowing they were hypocrites, the accusers dispersed. Then, in order that the woman might now live a God-pleasing life, Jesus told her, "from now on sin no more" (John 8:11). When we compare this incident to another involving a wayward woman, namely, one who confessed to Muhammad and his men that she was a prostitute, we find a very different response. Muhammad participated in her execution by throwing the first stone.[22]

Their View of Human Violence

The night before Christ's crucifixion, when the Roman soldiers and servants of the chief priest in Jerusalem came to apprehend him in the Garden of Gethsemane, his brash disciple Peter wielded his sword at one of the high priest's servants, cutting off his right ear. It was a tempestuous act that Jesus firmly rebuked, saying, "Put your sword back into its place. For all who take the sword will perish by the sword" (Matthew 26:51, 52). With these words Jesus told his disciples—and the world—that although he came to redeem the world, he did not come to do it through violence, even though, as he said, he could have summoned 12 legions of angels (72,000) to truly fight off his arrest. Philip Yancey notes that, had Jesus done so, it would have been truly a "Holy War."[23] Following his arrest, Jesus told Pontius Pilate, the Roman governor: "My kingdom is not of this world. If my kingdom were of this world, my servants would have been fighting ... " (John 18:36). The ways of the world were not his ways.

In addition to what we have already seen regarding Muhammad's acceptance of violence, we find him engaged in many bloody battles, too numerous to cite in this chapter. One scholar maintains Muhammad "conducted twenty-seven battles and planned thirty-nine others."[24]   Many of his battles were brutally inhuman. What follows are a few examples.

When Muhammad and his 3,000 Muslims in the Medina area in about A.D. 627 conquered the Banu Qurayza, a Jewish clan, and had taken about 2,000 prisoners, the women and children were separated from the men, leaving about 700 male prisoners (some sources say 800). Muhammad ordered trenches be dug. The next day, five to six male prisoners at a time were brought to the trenches and forced to go to the edge, where his men then decapitated them. The slaughter began in the morning and ended with the last prisoner massacred by torchlight.[25] Another time, Muhammad ordered one of his men to decapitate Kab ibn al-Ashraf (a half Jew from Medina), one of 80 accompanying assassinations.[26]   Then Kab's severed head was cast "at Mohammad's feet with the loud cry: 'Allah is great,' and the Prophet heartily agreed."[27]

After the Battle of Bedr two prisoners were singled out for execution. One of them, Okba, asked Muhammad why he was to be executed. Muhammad told him it was because of his enmity to Allah and his prophet. The concerned prisoner also asked what would happen to his little daughter after his execution. " 'Hell-fire!' answered the Prophet, as the victim was hewn to the ground. 'Wretch and persecutor!' he continued, 'scorner of God, of his Prophet, and of His Word. I thank the Lord, who hath comforted mine eyes by thy death' " (*MI*, 100).

Numerous other acts of bloody violence and butchery were carried out by Muhammad. He strongly hated most poets, and so he had four of them executed, three in Medina and one on his return to Mecca (*JW*, 57). He was "the first Arab who dared make war during the sacred months. ..."[28] For instance, when all the tribes had agreed to a truce during the sacred month of Rahab, he "commanded his followers to attack one of the Meccan caravans, which they did, shedding blood."[29] By acts such as these, "Mahomet demonstrated that cruelty was not incompatible with Islam."[30] Clearly, acts such as these distinguished him from Jesus Christ, the prince of peace.

Any discussion of Muhammad's brutally violent acts would not be complete if one failed to consider his advocacy of jihad. In the Koran, he gave specific reasons for why and how jihad should be part of a faithful Muslim's life. For example, Sura 2:191 states: "And kill them wherever you find them, and drive them out from when they drove you out. ... " The Koran contains many other such examples (see Appendix A). These jihad passages show how Muhammad favored and advocated the practice of violence. They also show that either he never heard or tried to follow Jesus' admonition of "love your enemies."

In recent years some apologists for Islam, especially in America, have been trying to say that jihad is unrelated to violence, but that it is "The way an individual can be a better Muslim and be of service to society."[31] Expressed another way, it is a Muslim's personal fight to improve himself by endeavoring to conquer temptations and other tendencies that keep him from being a good citizen. This attempt to redefine jihad is undoubtedly designed to put a good face on Islam during the present time of terrorism. But is such revisionism true to the etymology of the term or to the contexts in which jihad is spelled out in the Koran? *Reliance of the Traveller* says: "*Jihad* means to war against non-Muslims, and is etymologically derived from the word *mujahada,* signifying warfare to establish the religion" (o9.0).

Two former Muslims, Ergun Mehmet Caner and Emir Fethi Caner, in their book, *Unveiling Islam* (2002), refute the attempt to redefine jihad: "Strictly speaking, *jihad* means a continuing *warfare* [sic] against them [unbelievers]."[32] The Caner brothers further say: "Despite the explanations of Islamic apologists after the terrorist attack, jihad does not primarily

18

refer to a 'struggle of personal piety.' Jihad is combat on the fronts of politics, warfare, and culture. Muhammad exemplified this principle when he authorized the slaughter of thousands of men throughout the Arabian Peninsula in the name of Allah."[33] Neither does the Hadith, Islam's second source of authority after the Koran, support that kind of revisionism, for it states, "according the statement of Allah's Apostle, 'Whoever changed his Islamic religion, then kill him' "(*Sahih Al-Bukhari* 84:2:57).

In light of Muhammad's many violent battles, George Sale somberly stated in the 18th century: "But when the character of Mohammed is attentively surveyed, whether delineated by friends or enemies, the picture is so shocking that it is a wonder the place of his nativity has not been buried in oblivion. Any country might blush to have produced such a monster."[34] It was this kind of knowledge concerning the founder of Islam that prompted Alighieri Dante in his *The Divine Comedy* (14th century) to picture Muhammad weeping in the lowest circle of hell (Canto 28). Today, Dante's book, largely because of Muslim pressures, supported by political correctness, is on the shunned list of textbooks for students in many American and European colleges and universities. Unlike today's Western appeasers of Islam, Dante saw Muhammad as the ultimate false prophet who was given to violence and other ungodly behavior.

Their View of Women

From the time in which Jesus lived to the time of Muhammad in Arabia 600 years later, the cultural view of women had changed very little. Women had to be veiled and silent, they had very few rights, and they were seen as creatures to satisfy men's sexual desires. Muhammad saw nothing amiss with this *Weltanschauung,* as was evident with his taking multiple wives and concubines; often the latter were slave women.

Not only did he have numerous wives (one Muslim scholar says 20)[35] and some concubines, but the manner in which he acquired some of them shows that a lust for sex was a predominant force in Muhammad's life. His sixth wife, Juwariyah, captured from one of the tribes, was already married when Muhammad ransomed her and took her as his wife. One biographer says: "he was struck with her beauty."[36] Another time, while in Medina, he was impressed by the beauty of Zainab, a married woman. In response, Muhammad said: "Praise be Allah who changeth the hearts of men."[37] Tor Andrae, a biographer highly favorable to Muhammad, says these words appealed to Zainab, whereupon her husband volunteered to divorce her so that Muhammad could marry her. But there was a problem. Zainab was the wife of Muhammad's adopted son. In order for Muhammad to marry her and not be guilty of incest, he needed a heavenly revelation to approve of such a marriage. That desired "revelation" soon came to justify Muhammad's desire for Zainab. The message, now recorded in the Koran, said in part: "We gave her to you as a wife, so that there should be no difficulty for believers in respect of wives of their adopted sons, when they have accomplished their want of them, and Allah's command shall be performed" (Sura 33:37).

After Muhammad had defeated the Jewish tribe of Banu Qurayza and ordered the execution of about 700 prisoners (noted earlier), he caught a glimpse of Rihana, a beautiful Jewish woman whose husband was one of the men massacred. Muhammad asked her to become his wife. She refused. So he took her as his unwilling slave concubine (*LM*, 318–319).

These acts on the part of Muhammad again reveal him to be the polar opposite of Jesus Christ. Not only did Jesus never lust after women, but he warned all red-blooded males that, "Everyone who looks at a woman with lustful intent has already committed adultery with her in his heart" (Matthew 5:28).

20

Their View of Marriage

Jesus descended from the lineage of King David, who, like some other Hebrews in the Old Testament, was a polygamist or, more accurately, a polygynist (poly=many + gynos=woman), that is, a man who is married to more than one woman at the same time. David had six wives and some concubines. His son Solomon out did him by far, for he had 700 wives and 300 concubines (I Kings 11:3). Gideon, before David and Solomon, also had many wives, from whom he had 70 sons.

Nor were Gideon, David, and Solomon the only Hebrew men who had multiple wives and concubines. For unknown reasons, God tolerated polygynous marriages in the Old Testament, even among some of the heroes of faith. This polygynous ethic was not confined to Palestine. It was also part of the culture in Arabia at the time of Muhammad, hundreds of years later.

How widespread polygyny was among the Jews at Jesus' time is not known. That polygynous marriages, however, still occurred is certain, for Josephus (A.D. 37–ca.100), the Jewish historian and friend of the Romans, wrote: "It is the ancient practice among us [Jews] to have many wives at the same time" (*Jewish Antiquities* 17:1,2,15). But Jesus never lent any support to the Mid-Eastern culture of polygyny. Whenever he spoke about marriage, or used a marriage illustration, it was always in the context of monogamy. "Therefore a man shall leave his father and mother and hold fast to his wife [not three or four wives] and they shall become one flesh" (Matthew 19:5). Another time he said if anyone wished to follow him, he would have to choose him over his brothers, sisters, mother, and wife (Luke 14:26). He did not say "wives."

Christ's view of marriage as a monogamous institution complemented his high regard for women because polygyny invariably demeans women, a topic discussed below in Chapter 3. His concept of monogamous marriage became the norm among Christians. Thus, St. Paul, some 30 years after Christ, enjoined bishops of the church to be "the husband of one wife" (I Timothy 3:1–2).

Muhammad did not become a polygynist until after his first wife died. As already noted, the fact that a woman was already married did not stop him from marrying her. In the light of Christ's teachings, Muhammad was not only a polygynist, but, as we have seen, he was also an adulterer who broke up existing marriages. This lifestyle made him entirely different in comparison to Jesus Christ, who neither lusted after women, nor disrupted any marriage by yielding to sexual temptation.[38]

The Role of Miracles

During his three-year ministry, Jesus performed about 30 recorded miracles, depending on how they are counted. They included instantaneous healings of individuals who were deaf, blind, leprous, and crippled. He also performed non-healing miracles: he calmed the stormy Sea of Galilee; cast out demons; walked on water; made wine out of water at a wedding; fed 5,000 people with five loaves of bread and two fish; and most, astounding of all, he raised three individuals from the dead.

Although Jesus performed numerous miracles, he did not perform any to satisfy people's curiosity. He once said: "A wicked and adulterous generation seeks for a miraculous sign" (Matthew 12:39, NIV). He performed miracles when he saw they would benefit given individuals and glorify his Father in heaven. Another time he told an audience: "Do not believe me unless I do what my Father does. But If I do it, even though you do not believe me, believe the miracles, that you may learn and understand that the Father is in me, and I in the Father" (John 10:37–38, NIV).

At least twice Jesus said his miracles were evidence of his deity. He did so when he linked the divine act of forgiving the sins of a paralytic man with another divine act of healing him (Mark 2:8-11). He did so again when the disciples of the imprisoned John the Baptist came to find out for sure whether he really was the promised Messiah, or whether they were to look for another. Jesus told them: "Go and tell John what you hear and see: the blind receive their sight and the lame walk, lepers are cleansed and the deaf hear, and the dead are raised up ... " (Matthew 11:2–5). In short, he argued that his miracles demonstrated he was the incarnate Son of God.

Today, many modern skeptics, influenced by the 18th century's Age of Reason, deny the reality of Christ's miracles, but people of his day did not. True, some accused Jesus of having demonic powers, but they did not—and could not—deny what they saw. In fact, even decades later, pagan Romans, such as Tacitus (d. 120) and Celsus (d. ca. 250) did not accuse the writers of the four New Testament Gospels of fabricating tales with regard to the miracles of Jesus. Nor did Muhammad deny Christ's miracles, even though he admitted he was not able to perform any himself.

In the Koran Muhammad says: "And they swear by Allah with the strongest of their oaths, that if a sign came to them they would most certainly believe in it. Say: Signs are only with Allah; and what should make you know that when it comes they will not believe?" (Sura 6:109). In another verse the question is asked: "And they say: Why are not signs sent down upon [Muhammad] from his Lord? Say: The signs are only with Allah, and I am only a plain warner" (Sura 29:50). These are just two passages in the Koran that show Muhammad had no miraculous powers.

In the Old Testament, Moses, Isaiah, Jeremiah, Ezekiel, and other prophets performed miracles. Thus, given that Muhammad admitted he himself had not performed any miracles, some have asked whether Muhammad even qualifies as a prophet. Perhaps that is why some Muslims in later Islamic tradition credit him with some miracles.

Those who say he performed some miracles commonly point to four: the clefting of the moon, his mystical night journey to heaven, his victory in the Battle of Bedr in A.D. 624 (the turning point in Muhammad's battles), and producing the Koran. Regarding the Battle of Bedr, it has been said that if Muhammad had lost this battle, "the whole Islamic movement might have come to a violent end."[39]

Why do some Muslims now say Muhammad performed miracles? There is no certain answer, but it seems to have something to do with wanting to make him as credible and significant as the miracle-performing prophets in the Bible and also Jesus. Although Muslims present their Islamic beliefs as superior to the Bible, and even say the Bible has been corrupted, they often use the Bible as a point of comparison to present their beliefs in a positive light.

As with the Koranic verses just cited, those who assign miracles to Muhammad ignore or dismiss another revealing remark he made—a remark that the miracles of Moses and Jesus had been ineffectual. So, not to be similarly ineffectual, Muhammad said: " 'I therefore, the last of the prophets am sent with the sword.' "[40] He also said: "The sword is the key of heaven and hell."[41] That Islam is a religion of the sword, not of peace, is an idea that is explored further in Chapters 2 and 10.

Their Concepts of God

The current perception in the West, especially among those who favor the ideological phenomenon of political correctness or those who are religiously indifferent, is that the nature of God is substantially the same whether it is described by Muhammad in the Koran or by Jesus in the New Testament. But when we examine and compare what Jesus said about God with Muhammad's utterances about Allah, we find the differences could not be greater.

When Muhammad came to Mecca in the early seventh century, Allah was but one god in a pantheon with many other gods. *The Encyclopedia of Islam*, a highly authoritative source favorable to Islam, corroborates this by saying that Allah "was known to the pre-Islamic Arabs; he was one of the Meccan deities."[42] These Meccan deities included a moon god and a sun god. This is underscored by Malise Ruthven, a respected authority on Islam, when he refers to Mas'udi, a 10th-century Muslim writer: "The historian Mas'udi (896–956) stated that certain people had regarded the Ka'ba as a temple dedicated to the Sun, Moon, and the five visible planets. ..."[43] Given this kind of evidence, some have argued that Allah was a moon god.

The argument that Allah among Arabs and other tribes in Mesopotamia initially was seen as *the* god among several other gods also has etymological support. The name Allah is derived from the Arabic compound of *Al-'ilah* (*Al* meaning "the" and *ilah* meaning "god"). This indicates Allah was *the* god among other gods, but he was *not* the only god.

Some scholars argue that in Arabian paganism, "Allah, the moon god, was married to a sun goddess. Together they produced three goddesses who were called 'the daughters of Allah.' These three were called Al-Lat, Al-Uzza, and Manat."[44] As shown earlier, Muhammad even mentions these three female goddesses in the Koran in what are now known as the "Satanic Verses."

Some archaeological artifacts show that "in ancient Syria and Canna, the Moon-god Sin was usually represented by the moon in its crescent phase."[45] Hence, it is interesting to note Islam's continued use of the crescent moon symbol, which is conspicuously visible on flags and mosques in Islamic countries. Even the scimitar resembles the moon's crescent. So do the sickle knives. Apparently, the crescent symbol harks back to the era when *Al-'ilah* was the pagan moon god. Some argue that the Islamic calendar, based on the phases of the moon, is another example of Islam's moon-cultic ties. It is also helpful to know that "The cult of the Moon-god was the most popular religion throughout ancient Mesopotamia."[46] Moreover, as already noted, the Arabian moon god was depicted by the moon's crescent phase.[47] But whether it will ever be definitively known that Islam's use of the crescent moon stems from the moon-god remains to be seen.[48]

One scholar of Islam, B. D. MacDonald, has said the name Allah is applicable only to the Arabic understanding of "their peculiar God."[49] He also stated: " 'Allah' is not a common name meaning 'God' (or a god)."[50] This fact, however, is not widely known by Westerners. But informed Muslims do seem to know Allah and the God of the Bible are not the same. Here is one example. In speaking about Islam in a public gathering, Ergun Mehmet Caner, a former Muslim, had a Muslim in the audience challenge him. In the course of their exchange, Caner asked the challenger: "Is Allah the same god as Jehovah?" The challenger replied: "No, of course not."[51]

That many Muslims know Allah is not the same as God in the Bible is usually evident when an imam offers a public prayer. For instance, following the Muslim terrorist bombing of the World Trade Center in New York on September 11, 2001, an interreligious gathering took place a few days later in the Washington Cathedral in Washington, DC. At this gathering the Muslim imam, who offered a prayer, did not invoke God, but rather he called upon Allah. When an informed Muslim uses the name God, he most likely does so deliberately to give the impression that God and Allah are the same, and thereby he deceives non-Muslims, especially Christians, so that they would not see Islam as a radically different religion. The names of God and Allah are not synonymous or interchangeable. This also means that Muslims and Christians do not pray to the same God, as is often said erroneously today.

The error of seeing Allah as synonymous with the God of the Bible goes back at least to the first Arabic translation of the Bible in the ninth century. This translation used the word Allah for God, because the translators did not want to experience harm at the hands of zealous, politically minded Muslims by not making this equation.[52] Equating Allah with God of the Bible was then (and still is) only advantageous to Muslims, especially when they use this equation to enhance their efforts to convert uninformed Christians to Islam.[53]

Although Muhammad is credited with having moved Arabs away from polytheism to strict monotheism, his concept of God as delineated in the Koran differs significantly from what Jesus taught about God. Jesus taught that God was a loving Father, whom we could know personally through his Son, Jesus Christ.

The concept of God as a personal Father was repugnant to Muhammad, and hence Muslims still see it as blasphemous to speak of God in such a personal manner. Such language, according to Muhammad, contradicts Allah's transcendent and exalted nature. But not so with Jesus who wanted believers to address God as "Father." Not only is this evident in the Lord's Prayer, but also when he spoke to his disciple Philip: "Whoever has seen me has seen the Father" (John 14:9).

It is equally blasphemous to avowed Muslims to say Jesus Christ is the Son of God, for the Koran denies that he is the Son of God who entered the world arena in human flesh. In fact, the Koran uses strong condemnatory language concerning this cardinal Christian doctrine. "Christians say: The Messiah is the son of Allah; these are words of their mouths; they imitate the saying of those who disbelieved before; may Allah destroy them … " (Sura 9:30).

Muhammad, via the Koran, also taught that Allah leads individuals morally astray. Here is how he expressed it: "What is the matter with you, then, that you have become two parties about the hypocrites, while Allah has made them return to unbelief for what they have earned? Do you wish to guide him whom Allah has caused to err? And whomever Allah causes to err, you shall by no means find a way for him" (Sura 4:88). No such words were ever uttered by Jesus.

Jesus Christ taught that he, the incarnate Son of God, "must be delivered into the hands of sinful men and be crucified and on the third day rise" (Luke 24:7). But Muhammad, as stated in the Koran, firmly denied the crucifixion of Christ. Sura 4:157 declares: "And their saying: we have killed the Messiah, Isa [Jesus] son of Marium, the apostle of Allah; and they did not kill him nor did they crucify him, but it appeared to them so (like Isa) and most surely those who differ therein are only in a doubt about it; have no knowledge respecting it, but only follow a conjecture, and they killed him not for sure." Moreover, if Jesus' crucifixion is denied, his bodily resurrection is *ipso facto* also denied.

Finally, Jesus taught that he was God: "Anyone who has seen me has seen the Father" (John 14:9); "I tell you the truth, Jesus answered, before Abraham was born, I am" (John 8:58, NIV). Muhammad denied and rejected these claims of Christ's deity, saying: "the Messiah, Isa [Jesus] son of Marium is only an apostle of Allah … " (Sura 4:171).

Their Portrayals of Heaven

Both Jesus and Muhammad spoke about heaven, but what they said differed remarkably. Jesus said there was only one way to heaven, namely, through him alone: "No one comes to the Father except through me" (John 14:6). In addition, he made it known that mere pious ritualism does not get anyone through its portals: "Not everyone who says to me, 'Lord, Lord,' will enter the kingdom of heaven, but only he who does the will of my Father who is in heaven" (Matthew 7:21).

On the other hand, Muhammad taught that a Muslim enters heaven (paradise) by performing good deeds: "And whoever does good deeds whether male or female ... shall enter the garden [heaven] ... " (Sura 4:124). The Koran further says: "Surely (as for) those who believe and do good, their Lord will guide them by their faith; there shall flow from beneath them rivers in gardens of bliss" (Sura 10:9).

The two men also differed notably in terms of what they said about the nature of heaven. Jesus pointed out that heaven was a place prepared for all who believe in him. Heaven was the realm of his Father, where angels sang jubilantly at his birth, where angels rejoice over one sinner who repents, where believers in Christ reside, where people neither marry nor are given in marriage, where Christ sits at the right hand of the Father in glory and power, and from where he will come on Judgment Day to judge the living and the dead.

While Muhammad mentions some aspects of heaven that allude to its non-sensual qualities, for instance, one verse says, "They shall not hear therein [paradise] any vain discourse, but only Peace ... " (Sura 19:62), he also highlights the sensual and carnal. Sura 52:20 states: "Reclining on thrones set in lines and We will unite them to the large-eyed beautiful ones [virgins]." Another Koranic verse, Sura 55:56, assures Muslim men that in paradise there will be "those who restrained their eyes; before them neither man nor jinn shall have touched them [virgins]."

Their Prayers

Mention has already been made that Muhammad prayed and meditated in a cave at Mount Hira. In Medina he prayed standing by a post "planted on the floor of the Mosque" (*MI*, 84). Biographers note that he prayed often, although most of his prayers have not been recorded. In the evenings he would commonly retire for his devotions in the quarters of Aisha, his third and favorite wife (*MI*, 85). And, of course, he left a prayer legacy to all Muslims by commanding them to observe five prayer periods each day: at dawn, noon, mid-afternoon, sunset, and two hours past sunset. He reportedly received these five appointed periods while he was in the so-called seventh heaven, which was part of his mystical night journey to heaven where he met Allah, who was veiled.[54]

Along with the five daily prayer periods, Muhammad left another prayer legacy to Muslims: the *kibla*, a niche in every mosque and Muslim home that points in the direction of Mecca. At first, he and his early followers prayed facing Jerusalem in honor of where Solomon's temple once stood. But approximately one year after his *hijra*, Muhammad commanded all Muslims to pray facing Mecca, the site of the Kaaba, a religious shrine that predates Muhammad. He made the *kibla* change as an angry response when the Jews, whom he tried to gain as converts, rejected him as a prophet. Since this change, all Muslims, whether they are in Iran or in America, pray facing in the direction of Mecca in Saudi Arabia.

There were many times Muhammad's prayers were an integral part of his nefarious behavior of killing and doing violence to his enemies, perceived or real. For instance, Muir recounts the execution of Kab ibn Ashraf, mentioned earlier, as one example. Kab first followed Muhammad, but later, when he forsook him and returned to Mecca to encourage the Quraishites to resist Muhammad's religion, Muhammad prayed for his destruction: " 'O Lord, rid me of the son of Ashraf in whatever way that Thou wilt, because of his sedition and evil verses.' " Following this prayer, he asked some of his followers: "Who will ease me of this pestilent fellow?" Muir says after one volunteer came forth, "Four others joined him, and the plot was soon matured. ... Mahomet accompanied them to the outskirts of the town, and as they went on their deed of darkness, bade them god-speed." When the henchmen returned from murdering Kab, Muhammad greeted them: " 'I see your faces beam with victory.' " " 'And thine too,' they added" (*MI*, 106–107).

Although the prayers of Muhammad and Jesus differed greatly, there are two points of similarity. Like Muhammad, who went to a cave in the hills of Mount Hira to pray, Jesus on occasion also retired "up on the mountain by himself to pray" (Matthew 14:23). The second similarity is that Jesus left his followers the legacy of a model prayer, the Lord's Prayer, and, as already noted, Muhammad left his followers the legacy of the five prayer periods. But this is where the similarities end. Unlike Muhammad, Jesus did not retreat from society to pray in order to cope with doubts of his sanity or to struggle with suicidal temptations. Instead, he prayed to commune with his Father in heaven, with whom he was united as his only begotten Son. Nor did he pray to annihilate his enemies as Muhammad did. Instead, he taught his followers: "Love your enemies ... pray for those who persecute you" (Matthew 5:44).

He not only taught that his followers should love their enemies, but he himself also practiced it. When people falsely accused him of having a demon, of uttering blasphemy, or of breaking the Sabbath, he did not seek to punish them. Even as he hung suspended on the cross, he did not ask God to avenge his crucifiers. Instead, he prayed: "Father, forgive them, for they know not what they do" (Luke 23:34).

That kind of prayer did not come from the lips of Muhammad. For instance, one day a poetess Asma bint Marwan, who disliked him and Islam, composed a poem that criticized Arab men from Medina for gathering around a stranger [Muhammad] who fought against his own people.

Upon hearing her poem, Muhammad asked whether no one would rid him of this woman. A sycophantic follower, Umayr ibn Adi, took it upon himself to carry out Muhammad's wishes, so one night he crept into the poetess' home while she lay asleep, in the presence of her small children. One child was sleeping on the mother's chest. Umayr removed this child and then thrust the sword into the mother's breast. The next morning, while Muhammad and others were worshiping at the mosque, Muhammad asked Umayr whether he had slain the poetess. When Umayr said "yes," Muhammad praised him in the presence of others in the mosque "for his services to God and his Prophet."[55]

Apologists for Muhammad would argue not all of his prayers portrayed anger and revenge, and that he did say some altruistic prayers. True, one can find some of his prayers that were not vengeful. For example, a few days before he died, he went to a cemetery on one of his restless nights and prayed an altruistic prayer: " 'O Lord, have mercy upon them that lie buried here' " (*LM*, 483). But altruistic prayers were not his habit. For as already noted, often at the slightest suspicion or provocation he sought revenge, frequently by invoking the name of Allah.

There is another difference between Muhammad and Jesus in regard to prayer. One biographer, favorable to Muhammad, says Muhammad did not see prayers as petitions. He once said Allah "knows the needs of mankind. It would therefore be impertinence to tell him. So the prayers are praises and thanks and begging forgiveness."[56] But is begging forgiveness not a petition?

Not only was Jesus' prayer life exemplary, but he also taught his disciples and us how to pray in the Lord's Prayer. He taught that prayer is to be accomplished with a believing heart, and that one should not make an outward show of his prayers. Finally, he taught that acceptable prayers are to be addressed to

God through his (Jesus') name: "Whatever you ask in my name, this I will do, that the Father may be glorified in the Son" (John 14:13). Thus, when we look at Christ's prayer life vis-à-vis Muhammad, we find Jesus to be a categorically different person—a polar opposite.

As Messengers of God

Both Jesus and Muhammad said they were God's messengers. To make it known to his followers that he was indeed God's messenger, Muhammad chose the word Koran, which means "recitation," or more specifically, a recitation from God. Thus, every time he or others said "Koran," it was a reminder that he wanted to be seen as the prophet who recited God's messages.

Muhammad believed he was the conduit for Allah's revelations. In receiving what he called revelations, he sometimes sat back, so to speak, and waited for a message from Allah. On one occasion he waited for a "revelation" from Allah to determine whether his wife Aisha, who was accused of adultery, was guilty or not. After some waiting, he told Aisha that Allah had told him she was innocent of the charge. As a result of this incident he put forth the rule requiring four men to be eye witnesses in order for a woman to be found guilty of adultery (*Sahih Al-Bukhari* 82:7:805).

In contrast to Muhammad, Jesus did not have to wait for revelations from God because he was God's revelation. He knew God's will and had no need to wait for revelations to help him cope with personal exigencies. Even in moments of great duress—for instance, at his trial and on the day of his crucifixion—he did not ask God to give him any special revelation. That is why he told his disciples, "I and the Father are one" (John 10:30) and "I am in the Father and the Father is in me" (John 14:10).

33

There is still another major difference between Jesus and Muhammad regarding their role as messengers from God. As noted earlier, before Muhammad's *hijra* (flight) to Medina in A.D. 622, he admitted the devil deceived him by having him reveal a couple of verses, reputedly from Allah, to appease the polytheistic Quraish tribe in Mecca, but later, when these verses caused problems, he retracted them. In contrast, Jesus never uttered any false messages from the devil that he had to retract, for as he said, "I am the way, and the truth, and the life" (John 14:6). And moments before his crucifixion, he told Pontius Pilate: "I have come into the world—to bear witness to the truth" (John 18:37). He did, and he never faltered.

Their Deaths

As already indicated, Muhammad, after his *hijra* to Medina, became a drastically changed man. Even Karen Armstrong, a British apologist for Muhammad, admits: "After his *hijra* to Medina, the Qur'an changes as Muhammad begins to take more and more decisions of a political or social nature."[57] He now also showed a great deal of ill-will to any person or group that did not accept him or the things he did, no matter how evil they were. At times he wantonly had people killed and massacred.

This disposition stayed with him to the end of his life. For instance, as he lay dying in the presence of some of his wives, he overheard two of them talking about what beautiful pictures and decorations they had seen in a Christian cathedral while they were in exile in Abyssinia. Given his dislike for pictures of art, he verbally chastised those who built such churches and beautified them with artistic decorations. Throwing off his bed-clothes, perhaps in delirium, he angrily said: " 'The Lord destroy the Jews and Christians. Let His anger kindle against such as turn their prophets' tombs into places of worship. Let there be but one faith throughout all Arabia' " (*MI*, 230).

Also while he lay dying, the women at his bedside prepared a physic for him and then forced some of it into his mouth, thinking it would help him. He angrily responded: "You have given me physic." They confessed. Then he commanded them to drink the concoction themselves. As obedient Muslims, they did (*LM*, 489). Whether he suspected the mixture to be poisonous is not known, for he was once given poisoned meat of a kid goat by a Jewish woman whose husband, father, and brothers had been killed by him (LM, 379).

Just before he expired, according to one report, he uttered: " 'O Lord [Allah], I beseech thee assist me in the agonies of death.' " Following these words, he called three times: " 'Gabriel, come close to me' " (*LM*, 494). Soon he died with his head on Aisha's breast.

The death of Christ was very different. Suspended on the cross, blood dripping from his head and body, he showed no anger for what was being done to him. Instead, he prayed; "Father, forgive them, for they know not what they do" (Luke 23:34). They were words consistent with his knowing that he was the "Son of Man [who] came ... to give his life as a ransom for many" (Matthew 20:28).

In light of Jesus' forgiving behavior, even on the cross, one must ask: How would Muhammad, who tolerated no criticism of himself, or of his actions during the last 10 years of his life, have responded had he been nailed to a cross? We need to recall the angry words he spoke to his wives, who wanted to help him, when they gave him a physic just before he died.

After Jesus died on the cross, Joseph of Arimathea laid his body in the tomb he had acquired for himself. His disciples had fled. Then on the third day, some of the women who had gone to the tomb told Jesus' disciples that the grave was empty.

Moreover, they said they had seen and spoken to the resurrected Jesus in person.

Clearly, with Christ's rising from the dead, the contrast between Jesus and Muhammad defies comparison, for Muhammad still lies in the grave, awaiting the fulfillment of Jesus' words: "an hour is coming when all who are in the graves will hear his [Jesus] voice and come out, those who have done good to the resurrection of life, and those who have done evil to the resurrection of judgment" (John 5:28–29).

Conclusion

This chapter's comparison of the life and acts of Jesus Christ with those of Muhammad shows them to be polar opposites. No two men could differ more. Christ was the epitome of the perfect man, without an evil thought or act, always ready to forgive, whereas Muhammad, especially during the last 10 years of his life, often manifested the basest qualities of mankind. He was full of suspicious thoughts and often quick to put those thoughts into action, sometimes massacring people either with his own sword or having others do it for him.

When Muhammad is portrayed and believed to have been God's prophet and even seen as superior to Jesus Christ, one wishes every Muslim would, with an open mind, read the authentic historical accounts of Muhammad's life, some of which were cited in this chapter. Countless Muslims, it seems, do not know about the trail of blood Muhammad left behind him. Hence, one wishes that all would read the four Gospels in the New Testament to see the great divide between Jesus Christ and Muhammad. They would see that Jesus came to suffer, die, and rise from the dead so that all who believe in him as God's only Son will receive eternal life (John 3:16). Muhammad neither could nor did accomplish anything remotely similar.

2

SWORD OF THE SPIRIT VS. SCIMITAR OF STEEL

"Not by might, nor by power, but by my spirit, says the Lord" (Zechariah 4:6)

In addition to the great divide between the persons of Jesus Christ and Muhammad, there are many other pronounced differences that divide Christianity and Islam. One of those differences involves how each religion grew and expanded geographically.

Growth and Geographical Expansion of Christianity

When Christ in his Great Commission told his disciples, "Go therefore and make disciples of all nations, baptizing them in the name of the Father and of the Son and of the Holy Spirit, teaching them to observe all that I have commanded you" (Matthew 28:19–20), he sent them on a spiritual mission. He did not tell his disciples to arm themselves, or to form an army, or to coerce anyone to accept his teachings. Jesus was not a political figure; he had no connection with the Roman emperor, King Herod, or the Sanhedrin; and his disciples were relatively uneducated. Yet, he changed millions more than Alexander the Great, Napoleon, and Muhammad put together.[1]

Soon after Christ had risen from the dead, the book of Acts states that on Pentecost (50 days after Christ's physical resurrection) 3,000 converts were baptized and added to the Christian church in Jerusalem (Acts 2:41). Soon after this event, as stated in Acts 4:4, another 5,000 were added. This growth was entirely voluntary, with no coercion. These were joyful occasions, prompted solely by the disciples preaching God's word, the "sword of the spirit," an expression used later by the apostle Paul (Ephesians 6:17).

The euphoria of the early church's embryonic growth in Jerusalem, however, was soon interrupted when in about A.D. 35 the enemies of Christianity falsely accused and executed Stephen, making him the first Christian martyr. At this point, it is necessary to make a parenthetical observation regarding the word "martyr," derived from the Greek meaning "witness."

For the longest time the term martyr in history referred to a Christian who, in the early church under the Romans, was persecuted and often executed for bearing witness to Christ's life, death, and resurrection. Martyrs died for their convictions without resisting or resorting to any form of violence. But now, Muslims, and many in the mass media, have turned the meaning of martyr on its head. Now it is commonly used to refer to an individual who sacrifices himself as an Islamist suicide bomber when he, for example, blows up a bus load of innocent people.

Stephen's martyrdom was followed by a severe persecution in Jerusalem, compelling Christians to scatter and migrate to various regions of the world. As they fled, they also tried to gain more disciples, as Jesus had commanded his disciples in Matthew 28:19–20. Thus, they spread the message of Christ's resurrection, along with the spiritual benefits it imparted to all who through faith in him accepted this message.

As the disciples, apostles, and other early Christians fled to other parts of the world, the persecutions that began in Jerusalem followed them, too. Hence, during the first 300 years of the early church's existence, Christians were often imprisoned, tortured, and even executed because they reflected the mindset of Peter and John who, when arrested, said: "[W]e cannot but speak of what we have seen and heard" (Acts 4:20).

Even during the most severe periods of persecution, the Christians never once used any violent means to defend themselves or to expand their numbers. They let the sword of the spirit do its work, both in keeping them faithful and calm as well as bringing more converts into the Christian fold. In spite of the persecutions, during the Christian church's first 300 years, the number of converts continued to grow, prompting the North African theologian Tertullian (d. ca. 220) to say: "The blood of the martyrs is the seed of the church." When Tertullian made this remark, Christians had already established numerous congregations in Africa and Europe in addition to those that had already been organized in the first century, for example, in Ephesus, Thessalonica, Antioch, Philippi, Sardis, Philadelphia, and other cities mentioned in the New Testament.

Then, in the early fourth century (A.D. 313), Emperor Constantine legalized Christianity. Whether Constantine was a Christian at this time is not certain. That he was considerably influenced by Christian teachings, however, is beyond doubt, for soon after he legalized Christianity he implemented a number of laws reflecting Christian beliefs and values. Other emperors after Constantine, except Julian the Apostate (361–363), also showed they were positively affected by the teachings, beliefs, and practices of Christianity as they issued laws supportive of Christian values. For instance, as a result of Christians having long argued and worked for the sanctity of human life, Emperor Valentinian, a Christian, in 374 outlawed abortion, infanticide, and child abandonment, which had previously been legal and widespread among the pagan Romans. Valentinian also repealed the old Roman law of *patria potestas,* a practice that was highly incongruous with Christ's wholesome views of women, for he saw and treated them as human beings worthy of freedom and dignity. Under *patria potestas* (further detailed in the Chapter 3), the Roman father had absolute power—even of life and death—over any family member, including his wife. Such revolutionary changes in many ways turned the pagan Roman world upside down, a consequence of Christian beliefs and behavior that was already angrily acknowledged in Thessalonica in about A.D. 50 (Acts 17:6).

Elevating the sanctity of human life, giving freedom and dignity to women, and other salutary social changes (such as Christians introducing hospitals in the fourth century), together with the increase in the Christian population, were all brought about by employing the sword of the spirit, not the sword of steel. On the other hand, as shown below, Muslims, beginning with their leader Muhammad, used the sword of steel to spread and expand Islam in the seventh century and in centuries following. In its first 100 years of existence, Islam expanded with "lightning-like rapidity," whereas Christianity in its first 300 years made only "slow progress."[2] Thus, in light of these historical differences between Christianity and Islam, the inevitable question arises: What accounts for the difference?

The difference lies in the nature and the spirit of Christianity, which stems from the motivating effects that Christ's life, death, and resurrection had on his followers. He lived a completely sinless life; he showed love and compassion never seen before; and he taught his disciples not to resort to violence but to turn the other cheek. After he had risen from the dead, his disciples, who had seen him a number of times in his resurrected state, were convinced beyond all doubt that he had indeed conquered death. These profound experiences inspired them to proclaim not only Christ's love and compassion, but also his resurrection and the spiritual benefits realized through faith in him.

So convinced were his disciples and apostles that well-attested tradition says they spread their message peacefully wherever they went. All, except John, signed their testimony in blood, so to speak, by dying without physical resistance for what they preached and wrote. Doing so, they demonstrated that men do not die for stories they contrive.

Following the death and martyrdom of the disciples, countless other Christians were equally convinced by what they heard from the lips of his disciples and apostles. During the first three centuries of the church's existence, thousands of Christians suffered imprisonment, torture, and even death rather than deny the historical facts of Christianity. Despite the numerous persecutions that took place before Constantine had legalized Christianity in A.D. 313, the Gospel of Jesus Christ had made its way into most of Asia Minor, northern Africa, and much of Europe. The size of the Christian population by the time Constantine legalized Christianity is not certain. Rodney Stark estimates that about 16 percent (about 10 million) of the Roman Empire's approximate 60 million inhabitants were Christians.[3] It is especially noteworthy that this growth and expansion occurred without a single Christian taking up the sword. The early Christians unwaveringly took Christ at his word when he said: "My kingdom is not of this world. If it were, my servants would fight … " (John 18:36).

Forced Conversions to Christianity

Unfortunately, some time after Christianity had attained legal status in A.D. 313, some emperors and other leaders who were either nominal or pseudo-Christians tried to expand Christianity's numbers by involuntary, anti-Christian methods. These leaders, of course, were no better than the Muslim caliphs who forced people to become Muslims. It is well known that Emperor Justinian in the sixth century compelled people in the East to accept Christianity, as did Charlemagne (d. 814) who forced the Saxons in Germany to accept Christianity by the power of his sword. King Cnut in Denmark "forcibly rooted out paganism from his dominions."[4] King Stephen of Hungary (d. 1038) during the 11th century, Clovis of France (d. 511), and King Haroldsson (d. 1030) also compelled pagans to become "Christians" in Norway.

Those leaders who forced non-Christians to "convert" either did not know—or did not care—that forced conversion to Christianity is an oxymoron. For being a Christian means a person's heart and mind voluntarily accepts the truthfulness and the benefits of Jesus Christ's redemptive work. Mere outward conformity does not make one a Christian, and faithful Christians have never advocated such "conversions." Moreover, the leaders who forced people to accept Christianity also violated the spirit and love of Jesus Christ, who neither coerced nor urged anyone to follow him or to bear his name involuntarily. As Richard Wurmbrand, who spent 18 years in a Communist prison in Rumania for being a Christian, has stated, these forced converts changed only their name. And he says, what mattered to these rulers of enforced conversions, however, is not what the converts believed in their hearts; "what counted was the act of homage."[5]

Homage apparently is all that leaders like Charlemagne, Justinian, King Stephen, Clovis, and others like them had on their minds. They paid no attention to Jesus' words: "These people honor me with their lips, but their heart is far from me" (Matthew 15:8). While forcing people to become Muslims is acceptable to Islam, it is totally out of sync with the teachings of Jesus Christ and with biblical Christianity. The New Testament does not contain the slightest allusion to forcing non-Christians to become Christians by force or against their will. Thus, whenever individuals were forced to accept Christianity, it was not the fault of Christianity or its teachings, but the fault of leaders who falsely paraded as Christians.

Growth and Geographical Expansion of Islam in the Middle East

Muhammad died in A.D. 632. The first successor (caliph) to Muhammad was Abu Bekr, the right-hand associate of Muhammad in his many bellicose ventures. Under Abu Bekr (632–634) the caliphate became a sovereign divine institution, or, in the words of Ibn Warraq, it became "God's shadow on Earth" (*WI*, 183). Similar to Muhammad, Abu Bekr lost no time in taking up the scimitar to expand Islam. In 633, he invaded Palestine.

In 634 Omar, an associate of Muhammad, succeeded Abu Bekr to become the second caliph. Under his rule Damascus was conquered in 635, and the next year the Byzantines were attacked and defeated at Yarmouk, east of the Sea of Galilee. In 638 he captured Jerusalem, where he prohibited Christians from building new churches, whereas Muslims were free to take over any churches they desired.[6] Jerusalem, until its fall to Omar's Muslim forces, had been under the control of the Byzantine Patriarch Sophrinus, who died soon after his surrender. He said Muslim invaders were "godless barbarians" who destroyed churches and monasteries and profaned crosses (*WI*, 219).

In 637 Omar invaded Syria, leaving behind a trail of devastation that included the brutal murders of numerous Christians, Jews, and Samaritans (*WI*, 219). After a series of battles in various places during the next several years, the next conquered prize was the city of Alexandria, captured in 640. That same year, Omar "expelled the Jews from the Hijaz and the Christians from Najran, denouncing a treaty which Muhammad had negotiated with them and according to which they had been assured the right to live on the land forever."[7] Then, in 641, Omar's Muslim forces took Egypt, and in 642, Persia (modern Iran) came under his domination. In 643 Muslim Arabs launched westward along the shores of northern Africa, where they ransacked and took over the distant port of Tripoli to establish a foothold and from where the Muslim Moors would later invade Spain in 711.

In 646 a Persian intruder stabbed Omar in the back while he was praying in a Medina mosque. He died soon after and was buried next to Muhammad and Abu Bekr. Now the caliphate went to Uthman, a son-in-law of Muhammad. Uthman expanded his ambitions by setting his sights on Europe, and so in 649 he conquered the island of Cyprus. In 653 the island of Rhodes fell into Uthman's hands. Even though he was able to destroy the Byzantine navy along with capturing Cyprus and Rhodes, he fell out of favor.

His final undoing was aggravated by his decision to reduce Aisha's pension. She was Muhammad's widow, and she thought she deserved more than the other widows of the prophet because she was his favorite wife. Disgruntled Muslims, who may have had the support of Aisha, demanded Uthman abdicate. He refused and asked for Aisha's intervention, but she declined. Soon they murdered him at age 80 as he sat in his palace with the Koran on his lap.[8] As a side note, it is interesting to note that Uthman was also the man who compiled and edited the Koran, transcribing it from various palm fronds and other fragments.[9]

The fourth caliph to assume office was Ali, who was both a cousin and son-in-law of Muhammad. Of the three caliphs whom he succeeded, his military efforts were the least noteworthy in terms of forcing conquered cities and countries to bow to Islam and make it their religion. In 661, Ali, like his two immediate predecessors, was also murdered. His demise was brought about when a poisoned sword was plunged into him in front of the mosque door in Kufa.[10]

Assassinating Omar in a mosque, killing Uthman while he held the Koran on his lap, and murdering Ali in front of the mosque door were acceptable ways for Muslims to advance their cause.[11] To Muhammad, the end justified the means. Thus, the assassinations of the three caliphs are not surprising to anyone familiar with Muhammad's ethics. If Muhammad could use the sword, why could others not do so, too? As two former American Muslims have noted, if one wants to understand the violent acts of so many members of Islam, in the past and now, one need only look to its founder.[12]

Growth and Geographical Expansion of Islam in Southwestern Europe

It has long been debated whether it was Islamic religious zeal or the Arabian love of war from the tribal era, or a combination of the two, that propelled the Muslim Arabs to conquer one foreign place after another. Regardless, in 710 Tarifa ibn Malik, a Muslim Berber from Morocco, crossed the Straits of Gibraltar from northwestern Africa with "four hundred soldiers, three hundred infantry and a hundred horsemen,"[13] landing on the shores of Spain. Even though Tarifa's brief excursion was purportedly a reconnaissance venture, he nevertheless raided the Spaniards and then returned safely with booty that included women of rare beauty.[14] The next year (711) the Moors, as Spaniards called them, launched a second invasion. This one was led by Tariq ibn Ziyad. He and his army landed at ancient Calpe, "the limestone mass they called *jabal-tariq* (Tariq's rock), origin of the name Gibraltar."[15] That same year the Moors conquered Toledo, the city that once hosted 18 Christian church councils from 400–702. With the fall of Toledo, "Tariq gave orders that a group of prisoners be cut to pieces and their flesh boiled in cauldrons. The rest of the captured Goths were released and told to spread the word of Moorish methods. The tactic worked and token resistance melted away."[16]

After conquering Toledo, the Muslim Moors lost no time in wielding their scimitars to gain more territories as well as more followers for Islam. Their zeal to conquer, in part, was also motivated by the lure of the rich treasuries of churches and monasteries in Western Europe. Thus, by 718, they had captured most of the Iberian Peninsula. Later, they even crossed the Pyrenees into France and achieved some success there, too. But in 732 their greed for more territorial possessions came to an abrupt end when "they encountered and were defeated by the Frankish leader Charles Martel in the celebrated battle of Tours and Poitiers."[17]   Had Martel's men not been equipped with superior fighting equipment (lances and saddles with stirrups that enabled the knights to drive home their lances with the full force of their galloping horses without being thrown from their mounts),[18] the Muslims would likely have won this battle. The Muslim Moors, who had come within a mere hundred miles of Paris, suffered a loss so pronounced and devastating that they gave up trying to acquire more territories in western Europe.

The defeat of the Muslims in France by Martel (a.k.a. Charles the Hammer) in 732 did not, however, affect their presence in Spain. They continued in power and discriminated against Christians and Jews, especially with the appearance of the Almoravids in the latter part of the 11th century, and later the Almohads who followed them some 50 years later. One of the ways in which the Muslims in Spain discriminated against Jews and Christians was under the Islamic institution of dhimmitude (discussed in greater detail below), which basically confined them to the status of second-class citizens, or worse. "A Christian who claimed Jesus was divine was automatically executed. ... The ringing of church bells was also forbidden [and] non-Muslims had to stand aside if a Muslim passed them in the street" (*JW*, 107). Muslims were forbidden to greet *dhimmi*s (a. k. a. *zimmi*s) with the common Muslim greeting: "Peace be with you."

The "Golden Age" of Islam

Muslims and some historians sometimes speak of the "Golden Age" of Islam. It is commonly seen as having had its presence primarily in Moorish Spain. To some extent, this assessment has some validity, especially when Muslim Spain is compared to other Islamic countries in the Levant. Frequently, education is cited as one of the hallmarks of this golden age. But upon closer examination, some scholars have found that, even in the realm of education, there was no true golden age of Islam. Hence, Richard Fletcher has critically asked: "Learning? Outside of the tiny circles of the princely courts, not a great deal of it is to be seen."[19] Regarding other aspects of life, Fletcher has argued: "Moorish Spain was not a tolerant and enlightened society even in its most cultivated epoch."[20] Bat Ye'or says when the Muslims conquered Spain "almost all of the churches were destroyed."[21]

The golden age of Islam (900-1100) was also not so golden for 6,000 Jews when they were massacred by Muslims in the city of Fez in 1033.[22] Three decades later, 3,000 Jews were slaughtered, this time in Granada in 1066 (*DE*, 89). And it was by the power of the sword that Christians were deported to Morocco in 1126 by the Muslim Almoravids (*WI*, 236). Then, in 1148, the Jews suffered again, this time as the Muslims expelled many of them from Spain unless they converted to Islam. Interestingly, as Rodney Stark has noted, this expulsion of the Jews is almost never mentioned in history textbooks. On the other hand, textbooks almost never fail to report the edict issued by Queen Isabella and King Ferdinand in 1492, which gave the Jews, except those willing to accept Christianity, three months to leave Spain.[23] Why the expulsions by Muslims are not mentioned raises the question of whether historians have an anti-Christian bias and thus judge Christian leaders more harshly than they judge Muslims.

Growth and Geographical Expansion of Islam in Southeastern Europe

Although Spain's *La Reconquista* (regaining the country for Christianity) theoretically began in 718—with numerous military skirmishes and battles fought periodically for almost eight centuries—it did not achieve its goal until the forces of Queen Isabella and King Ferdinand captured Granada on January 2, 1492. As the city's capture became imminent, a fleeing sultan looked back from one of the rocky heights and gave a huge sigh, symbolizing what has often been referred to as the "last sigh of the Moor" on the Iberian Peninsula.

Although after 1492 southwestern Europe was no longer under the Muslim scimitar, with its accompanying yoke of tyranny and oppression, not all was well for the rest of Europe. Southeastern Europe had already been experiencing the power of the Muslim sword from the attacks of the Ottoman Turks since the mid-14th century.[24] A noteworthy incursion occurred in 1317, when the Muslims attacked the Byzantine city of Bursa (southwestern Turkey) and took control of it in 1326. In 1353 the Muslim Turks, led by their leader Sultan Orkhan I, captured the European peninsula of Gallipoli. He did so largely with the Janissary corps, the elite fighting force he himself had founded.[25]

The Janissary Corps

Around 1329, less than 50 years after the Crusades had ended in 1291 at Acre, Orkhan I, who ruled from 1326–1359 as head of the Ottomans, created his famous Janissary corps, an elite military unit. Initially, it acquired its men by capturing Christian boys in the Balkan jihads, "but, as this source proved inadequate, there was a switch to *devshirme* from the late 14th century onwards."[26] Under this system, Christian boys were forcibly recruited and taken from their homes to be trained as military slaves. Every fourth year, about one-fifth of the Christian boys between the ages of 14 and 18 (some reports say between 8 and 18), were forcefully conscripted, and all were compelled to become Muslims. The Ottomans trained these boys to fight for Islam.[27]

During the recruitment period, if a Christian father of a teenage boy did not appear before a Muslim official with his son, he was severely punished. Quadrennial recruitment eventually became a yearly event. Ibn Warraq, a former

Muslim, says the number of boys taken each year varied: "Some scholars place it as high as 12,000 a year, others at 8,000, but there was probably an average of at least 1,000 a year."[28] One source describes the Janissary Corps this way: "They were well-drilled and moved in compact masses, which for many ages no foe proved competent to sunder and disperse. So thorough was the physical and moral discipline to which the Janissaries were subjected, that it was almost unknown for any to turn back from this group and return to Christianity."[29] Throughout the Ottoman Empire, they had the reputation of being the "most feared soldiers in the world" (*JW*, 217). Peter F. Sugar has stated that the *devshirme* system was "the best known form of forced conversion. ... "[30]

Conquering Thrace

In 1359, Murad I, son of Orkhan I, succeeded his father to become head of the Ottomans. He advanced farther into European territory than his father, but for the first time the Turks encountered military opposition from the West. Serbians and Hungarians had joined forces to stop the Muslim intrusions into southeastern Europe. On September 26, 1371, in the middle of the night at Cenomen on the Marizza River, Murad's Muslims, led by him in person, suddenly attacked. Murad, who was so cruel that he gouged out his own son's eyes,[31] stopped at nothing in order to achieve his jihad objectives. So, when his men entered the Serbian camp, they started swinging their scimitars, brutally slashing the bodies of the Serbian soldiers, cutting off their arms and heads. Thousands were slain, and when it was over, Murad returned triumphantly to Adrianople (now Edirne), the Ottoman capital.[32] Before the Turks took their jihad to Serbia, they had captured Adrianople in 1361 and made it the Ottoman Empire's capital until they later conquered Constantinople in 1453.

The Battle of Kosovo

Next on the warmongering agenda of the Ottomans was the Battle of Kosovo, which took place in June 1389 on the Field of the Blackbirds. Although Murad's men were outnumbered, the story is told that they were nevertheless encouraged to fight by being given verses from the Koran: " 'Oh Prophet, fight the unbelievers and hypocrites.' " and " 'Verily, a large host is often beaten by one smaller.' "[33] When the fighting began, the Serbian (Western) forces, led by King Lazar, should have won, for they outnumbered the Ottomans. But the Serbs were not as united as they needed to be; their feudal lords had engaged in too many squabbles over the years.[34] When the battle was over, the Ottoman forces had defeated the Serbs and thereby forcefully brought Islam deep into the hills and vales of southeastern Europe, extending all the way to the Danube. Although there have been some periods of peace since the Muslims entered and captured a good portion of the Balkans 600 years ago, the area is still sometimes called "the most miserable corner of Europe."[35] The conflict and bloodshed that transpired recently in the 1990's between the Christian Serbs and Muslims in Kosovo and Bosnia make this expression painfully true.

The Muslim Craving for Constantinople

History books have ignored the craving Muslims had for Constantinople, a craving that existed for virtually 800 years before they finally captured it in 1453. One wonders whether historians fear it might reflect negatively upon Muslims if they reported the many attempts the followers of Muhammad made over a span of eight centuries to capture the city Constantine the Great made the capital and the glory of the eastern Roman Empire in A.D. 330.

The first attempt to capture Constantinople occurred in 668 (some historians say 670 and others say 672), when

Muawiya, a Muslim from Damascus, undertook this objective barely 40 years after Muhammad had died in 632. In this first Islamic attempt to conquer Constantinople, Muawiya and his troops failed miserably. The Byzantines of the city repelled the Muslims with a burning chemical known as "Greek fire," a lethal weapon whose chemical composition remains unknown today.[36] Finally, after nearly seven years, Muawiya saw that he and his jihad-directed troops would not be able to conquer the city. He and his remaining troops retreated, but great loses were still incurred because there were not enough ships left to take the soldiers back to Syria. They had to make their way by foot, and many perished on the long trek in the winter.

In 678 Muawiya consented to sign a peace treaty with the Byzantine emperor. The treaty required the Muslims to pay large sums of gold, along with 50 choice Arabian horses and, unfortunately, some slaves. In 717, for the second time, the Saracens (Muslims) under the military leadership of Moslemah, brother of the ruling caliph, tried to capture Constantinople, the citadel of Eastern Christianity. Again, the Byzantine Christians, this time under the leadership of Leo III, did what they had done so successfully some 40 years earlier. They employed their Greek fire again to repel the invaders, and once more it worked in defeating the Muslims.

Given the second defeat of the Muslims at Constantinople, the words of one historian, Ferdinand Schevill, are noteworthy. He wrote: "For, had the forces the forces of Islam broken down the Greek barrier and made their way up the Danube, they would in all probability have brought the whole occident under their yoke. Nay, the probability becomes almost a certainty when we extend our vision to take in the whole Mediterranean world, and observe that the Arabs were at the same time—in 711 to be exact—crossing from Africa to the famous southwestern promontory of Europe, known ever since after the name of their leader as Gibraltar (*Gebel-al-Tarik*, Hill of Tarik)."[37]

Schevill concludes: "Never in its history was Europe exposed to a graver danger from Asiatic foes."[38] More accurately, he could have said "Muslim foes."

In 1453 the Muslim Turks, now led by Mahomet II, launched yet another jihad against Constantinople. This beleaguered city had been besieged 29 times since its founding, when it was called Byzas in 658 B.C. and later Byzantium by the Christians. Seven of the 29 attacks came from the Muslims between 668 and 798, says one historian (*JW*, 250). After months of fighting, the Christians tried valiantly to defend their city, but to no avail. It fell to the Muslim Turks, who ignored their own heavy losses by bringing in more troops, many of them being the elite and fearful Janissaries.

Before the siege was over, a divine liturgy was held in the famous St. Sophia church, built 900 years earlier. Christian men, women, and children prayed, sang, and embraced one another, imploring God's mercy before the final hour. As Paul Fregosi poignantly notes, the participants in St. Sophia knew the next day not only would bring the downfall of their city, but it would also bring defilement to the most majestic cathedral in Christendom once the Muslims took control of it. They also knew that on the following day they would experience "rape, sodomy, slavery, or death, or all four [as they] took part in what has been described as a "liturgy of death" (*JW*, 256).

Fregosi gives a graphic account of what transpired the next day, May 29, 1453,—the day that Constantinople fell. He says several thousand Christians sought refuge in St. Sophia before Mahomet II (the Ottoman caliph and sultan) gave his troops license to wield their scimitars. They then massacred 4,000 refugees, raped women, and slaughtered them as well. Then Mahomet ordered a *muessin* to mount the cathedral's pulpit to give the church formally to Allah. In addition, 50,000 inhabitants were taken away as slaves. The corpse of the Emperor Constantine XI was brought to Mahomet, who ordered it decapitated in keeping with the treatment given to all Greek corpses killed in battle by the Turks.[39] Constantine's head was later embalmed and sent to various cities of the Ottoman Empire to be put on display (*JW*, 256–57). Mahomet continued in this manner after his victory, decapitating leading nobles and noteworthy citizens of Constantinople.

On to Vienna

In the Ottoman march westward, farther into Europe, the Muslims under the leadership of Suleiman I fought and gained control of Hungary after defeating the army of King Louis II on the Plains of Mohucs in August 1526. After this victory, he took back with him to Constantinople (now Istanbul) thousands of Hungarian men, women, and children to be sold as slaves in various cities of the Ottoman Empire (*JW*, 283). Three years later, Suleiman returned to the West with a massive army, this time in pursuit of Vienna. Although the Viennese were greatly outnumbered, they successfully defeated Suleiman's Turkish forces.

After the Ottoman forces were defeated in Vienna in 1529, many Viennese citizens and Christians in other parts of Central Europe thought the Muslim terror in Europe was over. For 150 years, this indeed appeared to be the case. But in 1683 the Muslims returned, determined to capture the city. Knowing the dire consequences that would befall them as Christians, the Viennese appealed for assistance from their neighbors, the Germans and the Poles. Their appeal was heeded, which resulted in putting together combined forces of Germans, Poles, and native Austrians. These defenders fought bravely and in the process overwhelmed the Turks and defeated them. One historian says it was not just a defeat, but a rout. Before Suleiman left Vienna to return to Istanbul, in true Islamic fashion, he freely used the sword to massacre all his captives, many of them being kidnapped peasants and their families (*JW*, 286). Similar to Tariq in Spain, some centuries earlier, Suleiman obeyed the wishes of the Koran, which tells all Muslims what they must do to non-Muslim captives—namely, "seize them and kill them wherever you find them, and take not from among them a friend or a helper" (Sura 4:89).

After the defeat of the Turks in 1683, the Treaty of Karlowitz was signed 16 years later on January 26, 1699. It called for the Turks to evacuate Transylvania and Hungary. Venice retained Morea in Greece, Poland regained Podolia, and only Belgrade remained in Ottoman hands. The treaty put territories under Western (Christian) control that had long been in Muslim hands.[40]

The Massacre of Armenian Christians

The Muslim invasions and battles fought to advance the presence of Islam discussed thus far are not the only ones that occurred. Space does not permit discussing the other blood-stained events that were initiated by the Ottoman Muslims for several centuries. But this chapter would be incomplete if it were not to provide a brief discussion about the frequent massacres of Armenian Christians. The Turks engaged in these massacres off-and-on for hundreds of years, but especially in the 1890's and intermittently into the 1920's.

Although it is virtually ignored in historical discussions of the Crusades, one of the major factors that prompted the first Crusade in 1096 was the massacring of Armenians by the Muslim Seljukid Turks (*ID*, 117). Some 900 years later, in the mid-1890's the Kurds and Turks took to the sword again and massacred between 50,000 and 75,000 helpless and harmless Armenians in Anatolia.[41] In 1909, some 30,000 Armenian Christians were slaughtered at Adana. In 1915, the Turks annihilated thousands more in the Harput region of Turkey (*DE*,

442). That same year, the Muslim Turks arrested and soon executed hundreds of Armenians in Istanbul. Also, that same year, in the province of Sivas, only 10,000 Armenians escaped with their lives out of 160,000.[42] The *Christian Science Monitor* described these 1915 massacres as the worst in history.[43] By the end of 1916, the anti-Armenian measures exercised by the Turks "were virtually complete."[44] Thus, of the almost 1.9 million Armenians in the Ottoman Empire before World War I, about one million were killed (half of them women and children); some 250,000 escaped to Russia; and about 200,000 were forcibly Islamized.[45]

But the anti-Armenian atrocities were not over yet. In 1922 the Turks burned, sacked, and liquidated another 280,000 Armenian refugees who were not taken aboard a fleet of British, French, and American warships that were anchored in the harbor of Smyrna.[46] Thus, as Bat Ye'or has noted: "The Armenian genocide is a tragic extension of a long history of [Islamic] dhimmitude, marked in the course of conquests and invasions by deportations, enslavement, and massacres." Sadly, whether it was the apathy of the Western media or their desire to not publish news that would reflect negatively on Muslims, these horrid events received only scant notice in the press and were then "followed by periods of silence" (*ID*, 371).

Recent Massacres

On April 6, 2000, some 5,000 Muslims rallied in Jakarta, Indonesia, calling for a jihad against the majority Christian population in the Moluccas Spice Islands. The next month, at least 1,000 Laskar jihad warriors gathered in Moluccas. They came from several countries: Pakistan, Afghanistan, Saudi Arabia, and the Philippines. They attacked the Christian villages, killing over 1,000 innocent people. In another raid, 200 Christians were killed and their bodies mutilated. In June 2000, a Christian church was torched, killing another 100 victims. In July 2000, the Christian university in the city of Ambon was destroyed, and by September several islands had been "cleansed" of all Christians (*ID*, 414, 415). By May 2002, the jihads against Christians in Indonesia had taken the lives of 10,000 Christians in three years. The preponderance of these deaths occurred in the Maluku islands and in Sulaweisi.[47]

Recent massacres have also occurred elsewhere. For instance, on December 31, 1999, militant Muslims protected by the secret police in the village of El-Kosheh in Egypt damaged 25 Christian homes and then killed at least 23 Christians.[48] On October 28, 2001, Muslims attacked a church and gunned down 15 Christians in Bahawalpur, Pakistan.[49] In Sudan, where the Muslim government in Khartoum declared a jihad against mostly Christians, approximately two million have perished as a result of war and genocide since 1985.[50] Recently, *New York Times* writer A. M. Rosenthal expressed the Sudanese tragedy this way: "More southern Sudanese [mostly Christians or animists] have died from guns, bombs, and starvation than all the victims in Bosnia, Kosovo, and Rwanda combined—at least 1.9 million."[51] And not all is well in the state of Kaduna, Nigeria, where militant Muslims in February 2000 "attacked the Christians. Hundreds died in the clash, and news reports cited dozens of bodies left lying in the streets."[52]

The Koran's Violent Prescriptions

The brutal killings and massacres noted above are not an anomaly in Islam. As already noted, they follow the examples of Muhammad, and they are mandated by the Koran as well in its prescriptions for killing "infidels," for example: "Fight those who do not believe in Allah … " (Sura 9:29) and "O you who believe fight those of the unbelievers who are near to you and let them find in you hardness … " (Sura 9:123). Numerous other jihad verses could be cited. (see Appendix A).

56

As the two Caner brothers, former Muslims who are now Christians, have recently stated, "War is not a sidebar of history for Islam; it is the main vehicle for religious expansion."[53] Both the Koran and Islamic history show their remark to be painfully true. In this regard it is well to remember that the sword of steel—the scimitar—is a principal symbol of Islam, as opposed to the Christian cross, a symbol of God's love.

Indirect Methods of Forced Conversions

Superficially viewed, Islam's use of the sword in conquering various countries and regions, as presented thus far, might only be seen as achieving political and military objectives, divorced from converting non-Muslims to Islam. Such a conclusion would be erroneous. Once in control of a given area, Muslim authorities often engaged in converting people to Islam through indirect methods. For instance, when the Ottoman Turks invaded the Balkans, they made it attractive for the Bosnians to convert to Islam; if they embraced Islam, "they were allowed to retain their lands and possessions."[54]

Although the Koran does not advocate forced conversions to Islam, given the nature of Islam' jihad, it is not difficult to understand the numerous indirect methods of coerced conversions Muslims employed to convert those whom they conquered. It should be also remembered that the religious goal of gaining more Muslims by converting the *kuffar* (infidels) is never absent in loyal Muslim circles. Muslims do not distinguish between religion and politics. Thus, when Muslims engage in military combat, they are also engaged in religious combat, fighting for the soul and the numerical expansion of Islam.

Nevertheless, one finds statements by Muslim and non-Muslim apologists saying that Islam does not seek to convert non-Muslims. Talking about the Muslim past, one writer asserts: "They [Berbers and Turks, both Muslims] sincerely respected the tenets of the [Islamic] faith and became tolerant of other religions."[55] Another pro-Muslim writer, Henri Pirenne, trying to contrast Islam with Christianity, writes: "There was no propaganda, nor was any such pressure applied as was exerted by the Christians after the triumph of the church."[56]

These pro-Islamic comments in regard to conversion are contradicted by a plethora of reliable historical facts. Apologists for Islam ignore these facts. Instead, they argue that all conversions to Islam occurred as a result of "the exemplary conduct of the Muslims, combined with the vigor of their Message. ... "[57] Ezzati even argues it is not scholarly to assert "that Islam was imposed at the point of the sword."[58]

To be sure, when Muslims conquered given regions or countries, there were always some people who, either not having very firm religious convictions or being opportunistically minded, voluntarily joined Islam. But to argue that forced conversions, especially by indirect methods of forced conversion, did not happen is absolutely false as the evidence below in the discussion of *jizyah* and dhimmitude clearly demonstrates. In addition, Cyril Glasse's *The Concise Encyclopedia of Islam* (1989), contradicts those who argue that forced conversions never occurred, for it says only that Christians and Jews were not to be forcibly converted. It states: "The *Ahl al-Kitab* ["People of the Book," that is, Christians and Jews] could not be forcibly converted, as could pagans or unbelievers."[59]

The Jizyah

In claiming that Islam is a tolerant religion, many Muslims and some non-Muslim apologists for Islam often cite Sura 2:256 from the Koran: "There is no compulsion in religion." But those who point to this passage fail to mention that the Koran also requires a special tax or levy—the *jizyah*—

to be imposed on all non-Muslims: "Fight those who do not believe in Allah . . . until they *pay the tax* [emphasis added] in acknowledgement of superiority and they are in a state of subjection" (Sura 9:29). A non-Muslim can, of course, usually avoid paying this tax by converting to Islam; in the course of history, many have done so for this very reason. Thus, the *jizyah* is another subtle but clever way of indirectly forcing non-Muslims to convert to Islam.

Dhimmitude

Official Muslim propaganda states the *dhimmi* status provides protection for those who are not Muslims—primarily Christians and Jews—to live in Islamic societies. *Al-dhimma* in Arabic means "the protected people." The origins of dhimmitude go back to Muhammad himself, who in 628 demanded the Jews in Khaybar give him one-half of what they produced, even though he reserved the right to drive them out whenever he wished. "On these conditions," says Bat Ye'or, "he granted them his *dhimma*, that is to say, his protection for their lives and safety" (*ID*, 37).

Dhimmitude is a highly discriminatory institution. It drastically curtails the human rights and freedom of every non-Muslim. For instance, *dhimmis* commonly may not: (1) have Muslims as servants; (2) build or repair a place of worship; (3) dress like Muslims; (4) give their children Islamic names; (5) wear signet rings on their fingers; (6) ride on horses with saddles; (7) deter someone from becoming a Muslim; (8) possess firearms; (9) mourn their dead publicly; (10) prevent Muslim travelers from staying in their homes; (11) defend themselves when attacked by a Muslim, and if they do, they will have their hand(s) cut off or even suffer death; (12) give evidence in a court of law; (13) marry Muslim women, though Muslim men may marry *dhimmi* women; (14) drink or sell liquor openly; (15) build houses in Muslim neighborhoods; (16)

59

bury their dead near a Muslim graveyard; (17) have their cemeteries look like Muslim graveyards; (18) display a Christian cross; (19) read or pray aloud at home or in churches; or (20) speak to Muslims unless spoken to first.[60] Finally, a *dhimmi*, says Bernard Lewis, is "strictly forbidden ... to try to convert a Muslim to his religion, and if he by any mischance succeeds, the penalty for apostasy is death."[61]

Clearly, dhimmitude serves as another indirect mechanism to get many non-Muslims to convert. Writing about Muslim-occupied Spain of the Middle Ages, even W. Montgomery Watt, who is quite gentle in his comments regarding dhimmitude, admits that as a result of it, "a steady trickle of conversions occurred from Christianity to Islam."[62]

By becoming Muslims, *dhimmis* were able usually able shed to their old socio-religious status. Usually, they were no longer *dhimmis* and no longer subjected to the numerous discriminatory and demeaning practices. Many pro-Muslim writers and non-Muslim apologists for Islam ignore the powerful effects this institution had on non-Muslims when they argue that Islam did not force or coerce non-Muslims to convert to Islam.

There is a close relationship between the *dhimmi* status and the practice of *jizyah*. In fact, *jizyah* is a vital component of dhimmitude. Recently, this was clearly evident when in the Christian village of El-Kosheh, Egypt, the police chief threatened Christians, saying he would burn down their village as Nero burned ancient Rome. He withdrew his threat after he collected 50 pounds from each Christian in the village as "protection money."[63]

This Egyptian example shows that the *dhimmi* status still exists today, even though Muslims say it is a thing of the past. A recent report from the *Pakistan Christian Post* (October 29, 2003) provides further evidence that the *dhimmi* rule is still operative. It said that "the same discrimination faces Christians today as it did centuries ago, especially in countries like Iran that have reimposed Shari'ah [in 1979]." The *Post* continued: "For many Christians it is a de facto reality of living in a Muslim country that they are thought of and treated as second-class citizens. In virtually every Muslim majority context around the world Christians face social discrimination on a daily basis. They are faced with prejudice and social exclusion."[64]

Dhimmis (usually Christians and Jews) in many regions were also compelled to wear a "distinguishing mark or garb to indicate their faith."[65] Historians are not certain whether this sort of practice was a Muslim invention or not. Some historians have suggested that Hitler's idea to tag Jews with a yellow Star of David during Germany's Nazi era was borrowed from the practice of Caliph al-Mutawakkil in Baghdad, who in the ninth century forced Jews to wear a yellow badge to indicate their *dhimmi* status.[66]

Finally, Muslims sometimes boast of the *dhimmi* protection they accorded non-Muslims. But this protection begs an important question: From whom and from what are *dhimmis* protected? This question is rarely asked. The answer clearly indicts Islam, because the protection they receive is from zealous Muslims desirous of harming or killing them.

Other Forced Conversions

The *devshirme* system employed by the Turks in the 14th century, discussed above, is a clear example of forced conversions to Islam being carried out in Muslim-occupied lands. During the system's approximate 300 years of existence, it forcefully converted some hundreds of thousands young Christian men that provided slave soldiers for the Sultan's armies. This, however, was not the only method of forced conversions.

One scholar writes that, in the Middle Ages, there were occasions when "non-Muslims were subject to physical assaults by the masses, to official persecution, and to forced conversions."[67] This same scholar states: "Such pressures were particularly apparent in Egypt, where a strong Christian community survived into the late Middle Ages."[68] Also in Egypt, under Caliph el Hakim (996-1021), Muslims destroyed 3,000 Coptic churches and forced large numbers of Christians to convert to Islam.[69] We further find, as Bat Ye'or has shown, that in Antioch, about 1058, Greeks and Armenians were converted to Islam by sheer force as torture was employed to "persuade" them to do so. In 1159, Jews and Christians in Tunis were given the choice of death or conversion to Islam. Some, however, did not capitulate (*DE*, 89).

Muslims also forced conversions in India. Murray T. Titus documents that, after the Muslim warriors in India had subjugated a given territory, as in Sind, they either forcibly converted the natives to Islam or killed their wives and children.[70] Also in India, many Rajput landowners in the Campore district were compelled to embrace Islam during the 16th century of the Mugal era.[71] Even though not all conversions to Islam in India occurred as a result of force, "the fact remains that the use of force in some form or other has always been recognized by Muslim rulers of India, and by the orthodox lawyers of Islam, as being a proper and lawful method of propagating the faith of the Prophet."[72]

Kenneth Scott Latourette, a renowned historian, says that in the ninth century the conquering Muslims "in Crete compelled part of the Christian populace to accept Islam. ... "[73] Latourette has also shown that in 1670 several thousand Christian children in Crete were taken from their parents, circumcised, and reared as Moslems."[74] This bears resemblance to the actions of the Islamic Almohads in Spain. Doubting the sincerity of voluntary conversions to Islam on the part of the

Jews, they at times took Jewish children without parental permission and put them under the supervision of Muslim educators (*ID*, 88).

In the 16th century forced conversions of Jews to Islam occurred from 1558 to 1589 in Libya. Earlier, Jews were also compelled to convert in Tabriz in 1291 and in 1338 and in Baghdad in 1333 and 1344. Finally, "In Persia [Iran] waves of forced conversions from the sixteenth to the beginning of the twentieth century decimated Christian and particularly Jewish communities" (*ID*, 88).

Forced Conversions in Recent Years

In regard to forced conversions occurring today, Bat Ye'or chronicles a cruel account that occurred on Bacan Island, Indonesia, in which 1,150 Christian men and boys in November 2000 were "forcibly circumcised (as a sign of conversion to Islam)." She continues: "Elsewhere a whole village was captured and told they would be released if they gave up their village elders and church leaders. The elders and leaders surrendered themselves and were beheaded. The rest of the villagers, both men and women, were forcibly circumcised. Any who refused were killed. (*ID*, 415).

Also in November 2000 reports surfaced saying that 700 Christians on the island of Seram in Indonesia were warned they would be killed unless they converted to Islam. Many acquiesced. Later the news accounts reported that another 5,000 Christians on this island were forced to convert. In addition, many Christian women were forced to marry Muslim men (*ID*, 415). In such instances, children born of a Muslim man and a non-Muslim woman are always Muslims, without exception. Documented reports such as these have appeared regularly in the past decade within the pages of the monthly Christian newsletter *The Voice of the Martyrs*. In December 2000, President Abdurrahman Wahid of Indonesia, speaking at a mosque in Jakarta, verified and condemned forced conversions to Islam. And he added, "This is not right."[75]

Forced conversions in recent years have not been confined to Indonesia. In 1995 reports from Sudan revealed that militant Muslims used food, medicine, and clothes to entice displaced southerners in northern Sudan to convert to Islam. One report stated that those who rejected these enticements to become Muslims were refused shelter, food, and rest, and that "non Muslims are forcibly converted to Islam and have their identity changed by being given Arabic names."[76] A report in the *New York Times* in 1999 stated countless individuals in Islamic Sudan are "branded, flogged, raped, tortured into renouncing their religion. ... "[77] Still another report reveals that abducted slaves in Sudan are forced to say Muslim prayers, and that captured girls are forced to "undergo female circumcision."[78]

Coerced conversions have also been occurring in Bangladesh. One report states that "forced conversions to Islam have been endemic" in this country. This report also said that Prime Minister Khaleda Zia has used government resources at her disposal "to intimidate, terrorize, and torture people into either leaving the country or submitting to convert. ... Today, forced conversion to Islam has become a corrosive fodder to the fundamentalists. ... "[79]

While it is theoretically true that the Koran states "there is no compulsion in religion," yet as Bat Ye'or has correctly observed, "At no time in history has it been respected. The *jihad,* or rather the alternative, forced on the Peoples of the Book—namely, payment of tribute and submission to Islamic law or the massacre and enslavement of survivors—is, in its very terms, a contravention of the principle of religious freedom" (*DE*, 88).

Conclusion

While some conversions to Islam occurred voluntarily, others were often the result of indirect or direct methods prompted by the presence of its sword. The former produced results when conquered individuals desired to avoid becoming *dhimmis* or paying the *jizyah* tax, or worse, becoming slaves. Countless other conversions, however, were the result of direct force of the scimitar, Islam's prominent symbol, in clear view. By using the sword to bring about conversions, Muslims were following the words of Muhammad, who said: " 'I therefore, the last of the prophets am sent with the sword.' "[80] In fact, forced conversions to Islam are as old as Islam itself. They began with Muhammad. For instance, when he fought the Banu Qurayza (a Jewish tribe), one of his lieutenants suggested that if the tribe would believe Muhammad and convert to his religion, their lives would be saved.[81]

Many, in spite of well-established facts in history, deny that Islam advanced geographically by use of the sword, or that its adherents frequently forced many to convert to Islam through the same power. One can only speculate why apologists, especially those who are non-Muslims, close their eyes to these corroborated facts. Perhaps they do so because they dislike Christianity—despite the many freedoms and rights it has given them in the West.[82]

3

WOMEN: VEILED OR UNVEILED?

What would be the status of women in the Western world today had Jesus Christ never entered the human arena?[1] One way to answer this question is to look at the status of women in most present-day Islamic countries, where women still are denied many freedoms, rights, and privileges available to men. When women appear in public, they must usually be veiled or wear head scarves. In Saudi Arabia, for instance, women are even barred from driving an automobile. In the summer of 1999, news reports revealed that women in Iran are forbidden to wear lipstick, and if they do, they can be arrested and jailed.[2]

In addition, whether in Saudi Arabia, Iran, or most other Islamic countries, the low status of a Muslim woman is present in other ways, one of them being that the Koran tells a husband he may beat and sexually desert his wives. "[A]dmonish them, and leave them alone in the sleeping-places and beat them; then if they obey you, do not seek a way against them, surely Allah is High, Great" (Sura 4:34). This command is the exact opposite of what the New Testament says regarding a Christian husband's relationship with his wife. St. Paul told husbands in Ephesus, "Husbands, love your wives, just as Christ loved the church and gave himself up for her" (Ephesians 5:25). And to the Colossian Christians he wrote, "Husbands love your wives, and do not be harsh with them" (Colossians 3:19).

The high and honorable marriage ethic set forth in Ephesians, which stems from Christ's view of women, cannot be found in the pagan literature of the Greco-Romans or in the cultures of Islamic societies. The civil and humane behavior that is expected between a Christian husband and wife today reflects a sea-change effect Christ bequeathed to the life and well-being of women. A renowned historian of ancient Rome corroborates this by saying that "the conversion of the Roman world to Christianity [brought] a great change in woman's status."[3] Another has added: "The birth of Jesus was the turning point in the history of woman."[4]

To understand more fully how Christ's teachings improved the status of women in much of the world, we need to take a brief look at the abjectly low status women had in the cultures of his day, and how many of these the practices of that time are still alive and well in many Islamic societies today. We go first to ancient Greece.

The Low Status of Greek Women

Before and during the time of Christ, a respectable Athenian woman was not permitted to leave her house unless she was accompanied by her husband or a trustworthy male escort.[5] When her husband had male guests present in his home, she had to retire to her woman's quarter (*gynaeceum*).[6] The Greek wife had virtually no freedom. Even in Sparta, where women had somewhat more freedom than in Athens, men kept their wives "under lock and key," according to Plutarch, the early second-century Greek biographer and essayist (*Lycurgus* 15:8). The average Athenian woman had the status of a slave.[7] And according to Euripides' tragedy *Medea*, a wife could not divorce her husband, whereas he could divorce her anytime and for any reason. So, it is not surprising to hear Medea lament in Euripides' play: "Surely, of all creatures that have life and wit, we women are of all unhappiest" (*Medea* 231–32).

And, of course, she had to be veiled. Thus, the epic writer Homer (about 900 B.C.) in *The Odyssey* depicts Penelope, the wife of Odysseus, wearing a veil as she appeared before her male suitors. Once the Greek bride was married, she always wore a veil, similar to the wife wearing a wedding ring in Western society today, says one scholar.[8] In the Greek culture, as in many others of that era, the face of a wife was only to be seen by her husband. As a veiled woman, she was also required to be silent in public. For instance, in Homer's *The Odyssey* Telemachus rebukes his mother, Penelope, for speaking in the presence of men. Dogmatically, he tells her "speech shall be for men" (*Odyssey* 1:350).

The Athenian woman was also deemed inferior to man and less trustworthy. Greek poets portrayed woman as personifying evil. The poet Euripides (480–406 B.C.) has Hippolytus, one of his characters, ask: "Why hast thou given a home beneath the sun, Zeus, unto woman, specious curse to man?" (*Hippolytus* 616–17). In another example, Aeschylus (525–456 B.C.) has a chorus declare: "Evil of mind are they [women], and guileful of purpose, with impure hearts" (*Suppliant Maidens* 748–49). And, of course, the Greek myth of Pandora's jar blamed women for bringing evil into the world.

The Low Status of Roman Women

Although Roman women had a bit more freedom than their Greek counterparts, pre-Christian Roman culture also assigned them a low status. Similar to the Greek wife, a married Roman woman was not allowed to be present with her husband's guests at a meal.[9] Also similar to the Greek culture, a Roman man could divorce his wife, but she could not divorce him. Cato notes that a wife even lacked the right to tell her husband's slave what to do (*Aulus Gellius Noctium Gellius* 17:6). *Lex Voconia,* a law decreed in 169 B.C., prohibited a woman under *manus* (absolute rule of her husband) from inheriting property. This law was still in effect in the early fifth century after Christ's birth. A wife was under the strict rule of her husband, and she could not appear on a public stage or speak in public. If she did, she was labeled *infamia*.[10] The situation was not much better if she left her husband's home, even for a religious festival: "Women's journeys from the house for religious purposes were regarded by the elegists and satirists with grave suspicion."[11]

Like the Greeks, the Romans also saw women as evil. This cultural view was reflected by Roman writers. The satirist Juvenal said: "There is nothing a woman will not permit herself to do" (*Satires* 6:457). Seneca, a first-century philosopher, said human anger was the trait of a woman (*De Ira* 1:190). And a respectable wife, was required to wear a *ricinium* (a type of veil).[12]

The Low Status of Hebrew Women

There were many parallels in the life of a Hebrew woman to her counterpart among the Greeks and Romans. This was particularly true during the rabbinic Oral Law era (ca. 400 B.C. to ca. A.D. 300). Similar to Greco-Roman woman, she was barred from public speaking. The Oral Law taught that "out of respect of the congregation, the woman should not read [out loud] in the Law [Torah]" (*Megillah* 23a). Another rabbinic teaching proclaimed that it was "shameful" to hear a woman's voice in public among men (*Berakhoth* 24a).

While the Old Testament does not shed much light in regard to a Hebrew woman wearing a veil, when we come to the rabbinic era, we do find some details. For one, the veil had to cover the woman's entire face. The rabbis also indicate that the veil was worn for chastity purposes. One reference states: "It is a godless man who sees his wife go out with her head uncovered" (*Kethuboth* 2). Another rabbinic teaching said: "Why does a man go about bareheaded while a woman goes out with her head covered? She is like the one who has done wrong and is ashamed of people; therefore she goes out with her head covered" (*Genesis Bereshith* 17:18). The rabbis also enjoined men: "Do not converse much with women, as they will ultimately lead you to unchastity" (Nedarim 20a). Here, similar to Greek culture, the perceived evil nature of woman is evident once again.

The Low Status of Assyrian Women

From all indications, the life of Assyrian woman around the time of Jesus Christ was quite similar to that of Greco-Roman and Hebrew woman. The husband considered her to be his private property, and by veiling her face he could keep her facial appearance private as well. Assyrian prostitutes were considered public property for all men to see and use, and so they were forbidden to wear a veil.[13] Two notable scholars of Near Eastern history have shown that in ancient Assyria a man's ears were pierced with a cord passed through them and tied behind his head if he failed to report having seen a veiled prostitute.[14] So strong was the prohibition of prostitutes to wear a veil. Given this cultural norm, a prostitute caught wearing a veil was flogged, her clothes confiscated, and pitch poured on her head.[15] Thus, the veil served the function of distinguishing which women were married—and hence private property—as opposed to prostitutes, who were unmarried and public property.

Jesus Accords Women Freedom and Dignity

The extremely low status that Greek, Roman, Hebrew, and Assyrian woman held for centuries was radically altered by the appearance of Jesus Christ. His actions and teachings raised the status of woman to new heights, often to the consternation and dismay of his friends as well as his enemies. By word and deed he went against the ancient, taken-for-granted beliefs and practices that defined woman as socially, intellectually, morally, and spiritually inferior as well as evil.

True to his own words, Jesus once said: "I have come that [you] may have life, and have it abundantly" (John 10:10).

If any group of human beings was in need of a more abundant life—more respectful and humane—it was the woman of his day.

His Encounter with the Samaritan Woman

The humane and respectful way Jesus treated and responded to the Samaritan woman (recorded in John 4:5–29) may not appear unusual to readers in today's Western culture. Yet what Jesus did was highly unusual, even radical. He ignored the Jewish anti-Samaritan prejudices along with the prevailing view that saw women as inferior beings.

Meeting a Samaritan woman at Jacob's Well, Jesus asked her for a drink. Shocked, she asked him: "You are a Jew and I am a Samaritan woman. How can you ask me for a drink?" (John 4:9). His speaking to her, a woman, was part of her shock. She might merely have asked: "How is it that you, a Jew, ask a drink of me, a Samaritan?" But instead she said: "a Samaritan woman." To speak to a Samaritan was bad enough, but Jesus also ignored the extant rabbinic norm that a self-respecting man did not speak to a woman in public. The rabbinic Oral Law was quite explicit: "He who talks with a woman [in public] brings evil upon himself" (*Aboth* 1:5). Another rabbinic teaching prominent in Jesus' day taught: "One is not so much as to greet a woman" (*Berakhoth* 43b).

The account of the Samaritan woman reveals that Jesus' disciples, as faithful Jews, "were surprised to find him talking with a woman" (John 4:27, NIV). They were not surprised he talked to a Samaritan, but that, as the text says, she was a woman.

He Taught Martha

On one occasion Jesus told Martha, "I am the resurrection and the life. Whoever believes in me, though he die, yet shall he live, and everyone who lives and believes in me shall never die. Do you believe this?" (John 11:25–26). These words, which contain the heart of the Christian gospel, are recorded only once in the four Gospels. And to whom were they spoken? To a woman! To teach a woman was bad enough, according to rabbinic law, but Jesus did more than that. He called for a verbal response from Martha. Once more, he went against the socio-religious custom of his time by talking to a woman and having her respond publicly to him, a man.

He First Appeared to Women after His Resurrection

That Jesus accorded women rights and honor equal to men is clearly evident from the two previous examples. But by first appearing to several women at his open tomb on Easter Sunday morning, he gave women an honor and privilege he had not extended to his disciples. He told several women: "Do not be afraid; go tell my brethren to go to Galilee, and there they will see me" (Matthew 28:10).

Why did Jesus not tell Peter and John, who also had come to the tomb, to tell the other disciples what had happened? Why did he want the women to tell the men? He often came to the defense and assistance of the despised and neglected. Women were indeed socially and religiously neglected. His action here brings to mind the words he spoke on another occasion: "There are those who are last who will be first, and first who be will be last" (Luke 13:30 NIV).

He Allowed Women to Follow Him

All three of the Synoptic Gospels note that women followed Jesus, a highly usual phenomenon in first-century Jewish culture. It would have been equally unusual in the Arabian culture of Muhammad, the founder of Islam. Luke mentions by name some women who went with him (Luke 8:1–3). This behavior may not seem unusual today, but in Jesus' day it was highly unusual. Scholars note that in the prevailing culture of Jesus' time only prostitutes and women of low repute would follow a man in public without a male escort.[16] So welcome was Christ's message to women that they defied conventional social norms in order to follow him, and he uttered no words of reproof. On another occasion, a woman with an issue of blood came up from behind him to touch the hem of his garment so she would be healed of her physical infirmity (Mark 5:25–34). Jesus' response? He healed her and told her to go in peace.

Lest modern readers conclude that Jesus started a woman's movement, it needs to be said that he did not. He came to change the hearts and minds of people, not to implement a social or political movement. Yet by treating women with respect and honor equal to men, he not only broke with the anti-female culture of his era, but he set a standard for his followers to emulate.

The Apostolic Church Welcomed Women

The acceptance Jesus accorded women was not lost on the early apostolic church. Following Christ's precedent, the early Christians ignored the confining, restrictive cultural norms to which women were subjected in their society. Soon after Christ's physical resurrection, his followers regularly assembled on the first day of the week (Sunday) to renew their joy of this unique miracle. They commonly gathered in synagogues or in private homes, known as house churches. In the latter, women were often very prominent, not just passive participants, but also as leaders. St. Paul notes that Apphia "our sister" was a leader in a house church in the city of Colossae (Philemon 2). And Paul states Priscilla was one of his "fellow workers" in his promotion of the gospel of Jesus Christ (Romans 16:3). In Romans 16:1–2 Paul refers to Phoebe as a *diakonos* (deacon), a position designated by a male term that she held in the church at

Cenchreae. He also referred to her as a *prostatis*, a leading officer.

In his letter to the Christians in Philippi, Paul says that two women, Euodia and Syntyche, "labored side by side with me in the gospel together with Clement and the rest of my fellow workers" (Philippians 4:2–3). By calling these two women fellow laborers, one scholar says "Paul esteemed women as his peers. They helped gather and lead members in the church; they prayed and prophesied in public assemblies."[17] He followed the examples set by Christ by honoring women as his co-workers. That is apparently why he told the Galatian Christians: "There is neither Jew nor Greek, slave nor free, male nor female, for you are all one in Christ Jesus" (Galatians 3:28).

Christianity's Appeal to Women

As already noted, neither Christ nor his apostles promoted or organized a woman's movement. Yet Christ's message of repentance and salvation proclaimed by his apostles had revolutionary effects on the lives of women. The early Christians not only included women in the life of the church, but they also gave them freedom and dignity unknown to women at that time.

The acceptance women received in Christian circles was not an end in itself. It moved them to become active evangelists and missionaries, as we saw with Phoebe, Euodia, Syntyche, and others. The work and zeal of faithful Christian women was a powerful force in the early church's spiritual and numerical growth and expansion. As every church historian knows, women commonly were more active in the early church than men. St. Chrysostom (late fourth century) said: "The women of those days [early church] were more spirited than men." The historian W. E. H. Lecky credits women "in the great conversion of the Roman empire," and he adds, "In the ages of persecution female figures occupy many of the foremost places and ranks of martyrdom."[18]   Leopold Zscharnack says: "Christendom dare not forget that it was primarily the female sex that for the greater part brought about its rapid growth. It was the evangelistic zeal of women in the early years of the church, and later, which won the weak and the mighty."[19] They exercised the sword of the spirit to promote the growth of the church.

Some Anomalies

With the end of the apostolic church era (after A.D. 150), some of the church's leaders, many of whom had either come from a pagan background or who had been deeply steeped in the pagan literature of the time, reverted to some former practices of the pagan Greco-Romans. They often contradicted the spirit and actions of Christ, his disciples, and the pristine church with regard to women in the church. As the German sociologist Max Weber observed in his analysis of early Christianity, women were slowly excluded from the leadership roles as the church routinized its activities.[20] He might have added that it was also the influence of the anti-female values and beliefs of the Greco-Roman and other cultures that later resulted in women being excluded in some aspects of the life and structure of the church. The ancient prejudices against women that Jesus and his early followers rejected began to enter the church in the latter part of the second century.[21] By the fourth and fifth centuries the anti-woman views of the ancient Greeks, Romans, Assyrians, and Judaizers (Christians who believed they had to follow Jewish laws and customs) were even more widely incorporated into the church's theology and practice by some prominent church fathers. Many of them had studied and unwittingly absorbed some of the teachings of the Greco-Roman poets and philosophers as well as rabbinic thought, all of which espoused numerous negative views regarding women.

Thus, Clement of Alexandria (d. 215) believed and taught that every woman should blush because she was a woman (*Instructor* 3:11). The Latin Christian lawyer Tertullian (d. ca. 220) said: "You [Eve] are the devil's gateway. ... You destroyed so easily God's image, man. On account of your desert, that is death, even the Son of God had to die" (*On Apparel of Women* 1:1). Cyril of Jerusalem (d. 368), a bishop, argued that women were to pray in church by only moving their lips. Specifically, he wrote: "Let her pray, and her lips move, but let not her voice be heard" (*Proatecheis* 14). St. Augustine (d. 430) expressed beliefs that a woman's image of God was inferior to that of the man's (*On the Trinity* 12:10). Similarly, Thomas Aquinas (13th century) thought the image of God was different in woman than in man (*Summa Theologiae* 1a, 93:5).

Similar statements could be cited from other leaders in the church. Their negative statements were uttered occasionally for more than a thousand years, extending well beyond the Protestant Reformation era. All too many clergy and theologians had apparently forgotten how differently Jesus and the apostles viewed women. These critics of women often talked and acted more like the pagan Greco-Romans, the rabbis, and the Arabs of the Middle East than like St. Paul or Christ himself.

Christ's Pro-Woman Posture Prevails

Although after the apostolic era Christian women within the organized church were for centuries often viewed and treated contrary to the way Christ and his apostles related to them, they still experienced more freedom than their pagan counterparts did in the Greco-Roman and Jewish cultures, both before and during the time of Christ. In a number of ways, the church always treated woman as man's equal. For instance, before becoming a member of the church, she received the same catechetical instruction as did a man, she received the same rite of baptism, she participated equally with men in receiving the Lord's Supper, and she prayed and sang with men in the same divine services.

A New Family Standard

The new ethic Christ introduced in his interactions with women had significant side effects with regard to family life. Cognizant that Christ treated women equal to men, St. Paul commanded the husband to love his wife as Christ loved the church (Ephesians 5:25). He also said: "Fathers do not provoke your children to anger, but bring them up in the discipline and instruction of the Lord" (Ephesians 6:4). Such directives were in direct conflict with the Roman institution of *patria potestas*, which gave the father absolute power over his family, even the power of life and death.

Did Christian men, as husbands and fathers, heed Paul's directions? There is no evidence to suggest they ignored what he commanded them. In fact, it seems they followed his admonitions so well that this new family ethic eventually undermined the Roman *patria potestas* and its unjust patriarchal by-products. Thus, after the legalization of Christianity in A.D. 313, the teachings and examples of Christ with regard to women moved Emperor Valentinian I (a Christian) in the year 374 to annul the 1,000-year-old law of *patria potestas*.[22] The pagan husband now had lost the power of life and death over his family. A magnanimous change, indeed!

With the abolition of *patria potestas*, the accompanying cultural mores of *manus* and *coemptio* became extinct, too. As noted earlier, *manus* placed the married woman under her husband's absolute rule; and *coemptio* gave the Roman father the right to sell his daughter to her husband-to-be. With the repeal of *patria potestas*, the validity of marriage without the consent of the father began to be recognized.[23] Soon this

77

practice was widely accepted with the support of Christian leaders and theologians.

Not only did the mores of *manus* and *coemptio* become extinct, but "women were [also] granted substantially the same rights as men in control of their property, and they were no longer compelled to be subject to tutors."[24] They also received the right of guardianship over their children, who previously were the sole possession of men.[25] The Christian ethic gave women freedom and dignity previously unknown.

Bridal Freedom

Whether in Arabia, Greece, or Rome, men in the ancient world frequently married child brides, often as young as 10 or 12 years of age. The men were considerably older than their brides, often in their 20's or older. Plutarch (d. 120) in his *Parallel Lives of Illustrious Greeks and Romans* shows that Roman fathers gave their daughters into marriage at age 12 or younger.

Research reveals that now in the Christian era women married later than their pagan counterparts.[26] They not only used their freedom to marry later, but they also, by no longer being under *patria potestas,* had a choice as to whom they married. This new marital freedom under Christianity in time grew and spread. Thus, a woman in the Western world today is no longer compelled to marry someone she does not want; nor can she legally be married as a child bride. But lest we forget, in some countries where Christianity has little or no presence, child brides are still legal today, as they currently are in some Islamic countries. The Koran (Sura 65:4) states that before a man may obtain a divorce he must wait for three menstruations to occur. The same time period is required for a wife who has not yet menstruated. The latter clearly refers to a child bride.

Reuters News Agency reported in January 1999 that in the Maasi tribe in Kenya, Africa, a father may give his 12- or

13-year-old daughter in marriage to a man who is often old enough to be her grandfather.[27] Although it is theoretically illegal in Bangladesh, where daughters are seen as a financial burden, young girls in their early teens are frequently given in marriage to much older men. The law that formally bans child marriages is regularly circumvented by parents falsifying their daughter's age.[28] In Mauritania, Africa, largely a Muslim country, it is common to find brides as young as 10 or 11 years of age.[29] And Iran's Ayatollah Kohmeini at age 28 married a 10-year-old girl, who became pregnant at age 11.[30] This is not unusual when one remembers that Muhammad, the founder of Islam, married Aisha when she was six years old and consummated the marriage when she was nine (*Sahih Al-Bukhari* 62:60).

Removal of the Veil

When Christianity came on the scene, the veiling of women was widespread in many cultures. Alfred Jeremias, in his 1931-study *Der Schleier von Sumer Bis Heute* (*The Veil from Sumer to Today*), has shown that women at the time of Christ were veiled by the Sumerians, Assyrians, Babylonians, Egyptians, Greeks, Hebrews, Arabs, Chinese, and Romans. In some instances a man would divorce his wife if she left his house unveiled. The Roman divorce of Sulpicius Gallus is one such case.[31]

As already noted, the freedom Christ and the apostles made available to women, ironically, was not always fully accepted or adopted by everyone in the church. Just as some of the church's leaders tried to keep women silent in public settings, there were also some who wanted them to remain veiled, retaining ancient cultural customs. Clement of Alex-andria (d. 215) argued that when a woman attended church with her face veiled, it would protect her "from being gazed at. And she will never fall ... nor will she invite another to fall into sin by covering her face" (*Instructor* 8:11). Tertullian, a contemporary of Clement, chided women who came to church unveiled: "Why do you denude [unveil] before God [in church] what you cover before men? Will you be more modest in public than in church?" (*On Prayer* 22). St. John Chrysostom in his *Homilies on I Corinthians* (fourth century) even contended that women were to be veiled on a continual basis. And St. Augustine (early fifth century) linked the veiling of women to their lacking the image of God: "Have women not this renewal of the mind which is the image of God? Who would say this? But in the sex of their body they do not signify this; therefore they are bidden to be veiled" (*Of the Works of Monks* 32). The pagan culture sometimes led these men to forget Christ's liberating view of women.

Some of the church fathers were not alone in commanding women to wear a veil. At least two synods did so, too. One was an Irish synod in the mid-fifth century, led by St. Patrick. It announced in its fourth canon that the wife of a priest "must be veiled when she goes out of doors."[32] The other was the Synod of Auxerre in 585 in France. In its 42nd canon it demanded that women attending communion be veiled.[33] And as late as 866 Pope Nickolaus I declared ex cathedra: "The women must be veiled in church services."[34]

Pope Nickolaus' declaration appears to be the last formal announcement regarding the veiling of women in the church. Apparently, this practice disappeared by the end of the first millennium. How consistent and widespread veiling was in the church for its first thousand years is difficult to say. St. Paul did urge women in the Corinthian church to cover their heads (I Corinthians 11:5–16). But did he mean that women also were to cover their faces? It appears he did not. Yet many of the church's leaders who said women should be veiled apparently did so on the basis of this Pauline reference. But they failed to note that Paul, in his first letter to Timothy, in which he tells

80

women to dress in modest apparel and not to braid their hair, makes no mention that they needed to be veiled (I Timothy 2:8–9). He does not even tell them to cover their heads.

Evidently, it was the lack of specific references by the New Testament writers, plus the example set by Christ, that increasingly prompted women in congregations during the second millennium to no longer veil themselves. Thus, by the time of the Protestant Reformation in the 16th century, veiling was no longer an issue as it is no longer an issue in the Orthodox Church today. Today it is virtually a universal practice within Christian churches, that women are no longer veiled. In time, the freedom and dignity that Christ gave women became a cultural standard, notably distinguishing of the Orthodox East and the Roman Catholic and Protestant West from Islamic countries, where most women continue to be veiled.

Polygyny Nullified

Although Greek and Roman men had their mistresses, their culture did not permit polygynous marriages. However, among other ancient societies, especially in the Middle East, polygynous marriages were common. Numerous such marriages are found in the Old Testament. Biblical heroes such as Abraham, Jacob, Elkanah, David, Solomon, and others had multiple wives. In referring to the time of Christ and before, Josephus, the Jewish historian, said: "It is the ancient practice of us [Jews] to have many wives at the same time" (*Jewish Antiquities* 17:1, 2, 15).

Thus, polygynous marriages still occurred at the time of Jesus. Yet he never lent any support to them. Whenever he spoke about marriage or used a marriage illustration, it was always in the context of monogamy. For instance, in speaking about the nature of marriage, he said: "The two [not three or four] will become one flesh" (Matthew 19:5). Jesus Christ's view of marriage as a monogamous institution complemented his high regard for women in that polygyny invariably demeans women. This is also recognized today by some liberal Muslims who want more freedom for Muslim women. For instance, Qasim Amin, an Egyptian Muslim, says: "Polygamy implies an intense contempt for women, because no woman wants to share her husband with another woman, just as no man will accept the love of another man for his wife. This monopoly over love is natural for both men and women."[35]

Additional Christian support for monogamous marriages is found in St. Paul's words that said a bishop (overseer) in the church was to be "the husband of one wife" (I Timothy 3:2). Whenever marriage or married life is mentioned in the New Testament, monogamy is the only form of marriage assumed. Thus, as Christianity spread and gained ascendancy, monogamy became the norm in all countries where the church became prominent.

The freedom and dignity women enjoy in much of today's world is largely the result of the valiant efforts of Christians who, little by little, have made life in a fallen world more humane. A prominent example can be seen in the abolishment of the practice of *suttee* (or *sati*) in India, which was accomplished by the British in 1829. This practice, which had existed for at least a thousand years in India, involved burning a widow on the funeral pyre of her deceased husband. It is also known to have existed in pre-Christian Scandinavia, among the Chinese, the Finns, and the Maori in New Zealand, and by some American Indians before European colonization.[36] A similar example of the positive in-fluence of Christianity on the lives of women is found in China, where Christian missionaries encountered the long-established practice of foot binding, which, in effect, crippled girls at a young age and for the rest of their lives. Lin Yutang has shown that Christian missionaries were highly influential in helping to bring about the abolishment of this practice in 1912.[37]

The West's Deference to Women

It is fitting at this point in the discussion to cite Bernard Lewis, a renowned American scholar of Islam. Speaking about the presence of Muslim Turks in Vienna, Austria, in the 16th and 17th centuries, he writes: "One feature of Christian society never failed to startle Muslim visitors—the public deference shown to women."[38] This deference was largely the result of Christianity's influence. Unlike the anti-female cultures of his own day, Christ did not see women as inferior or evil or as sex objects. Thus, the deference women continue to receive in the West, as opposed to the subservient role of Muslim women in either the East or the West, cannot be divorced from the influence of Jesus Christ. As one observer noted, "The birth of Jesus Christ was the turning point in the history of woman."[39] Another said, "Whatever else our Lord did, he immeasurably exalted womanhood."[40]

Women in Islam: Back to Yesterday

While the cultures found in ancient Greece, Rome, Assyria and the Rabbinic era were not completely alike, their women were treated in remarkably similar ways. A look at many Islamic countries today in the 21st century shows that many such practices are still very much a part of women's lives.

Let Her Be Veiled

Around the world, the use of a veil by Muslim women varies. In certain regions, such as in the West or secular Turkey, some Muslim women do not wear a full-facial veil or even a headscarf. On the other hand, in some Muslim countries women still wear a black *chador*, which covers the arms, hair, and face. And in other regions, such as Afghanistan under the power of the Taliban, women until recently even were required to wear the *burqa*, which covered a woman's body entirely with no bare skin visible.

As we have seen, the practice of veiling women can be found in ancient Greco-Roman society, in Assyria, and is detailed in the rabbinic Oral Law. Thus, the present-day veiling of Muslim women did not originate with Muhammad and his followers, for it was practiced long before Muhammad founded Islam. He merely continued it. In the Koran, Muhammad states:

> And say to the believing women that they cast down their looks and guard their private parts and do not display their ornaments except what appears thereof, and let them wear their head-covering over their bosoms, and not display their ornaments except to their husbands or their fathers, or the fathers of their husbands, or their sons, or the sons of their husbands, or their brother, or their brothers' sons, or their sisters' sons, or male servants not having need (of women), or the children who have not attained knowledge of what is hidden of women, and let them not strike their feet so that what they hide of their ornaments may be known, and turn to Allah all of you, O believers! So that you may be successful (Sura 24:31).

Another verse in the Koran reads: "O Prophet! say to your wives and your daughters and the women of the believers that they let down upon their over-garments, this will be more proper, that they may be known, and that they will not be given trouble; Allah is ever Forgiving, Merciful"(Sura 33:59). This passage indicates that the *hijab* (the veil) does not necessarily mean covering the face, but it does mean covering the trunk, limbs, and hair.[41] This latter requirement is supported by one of the four Islamic jurisprudence schools—the Hanifites. The other three schools stipulate that a woman's face is to be covered.

Neither Sura 24:31 nor Sura 33:59 give detailed specifics of what is the correct veil of a woman, that is, whether her head and face must be entirely covered or if a partial covering such as a headscarf is enough. This is apparently what Qasim Amin has in mind when he states that many Muslims have "exaggerated its use, and dressed it up in religious raiment, just as other harmful customs have become firmly established in the name of religion, but of which religion is innocent."[42]

The full veiling of Islamic women, as required in some Muslim regions, is not only stifling in hot summer weather, but it often produces harmful physical effects. Jan Goodwin, a critic of such veiling, says: "There is a high incidence of osteomalacia, a softening of the bones, in Muslim countries where women are completely veiled."[43] This medical condition is the result of the body not receiving sufficient sunshine, resulting in a deficiency of vitamin D, which is necessary for healthy bones.

The Veil's Rationale

There are primarily three reasons why Muslims veil women. The first two under discussion here are mentioned by Fatima Mernissi, a Muslim sociologist in Morocco. She says the veil came into use in Medina, during Muhammad's time, so non-slave women would not be sexually accosted by men, a concern not extended to slave women.[44] Thus, the woman's veil "reintroduced the [Arabic] idea that the street was under the control of the *sufaha*, those who did not restrain their desires and who needed a tribal chieftain to keep them under control."[45] In short, as Islamic purists argue, the veil protects good women from sexual assaults.

If women need to be protected from the *sufaha*, it shows that Islam believes primarily in external controls, whereas Christianity, says Gene Edward Veith, believes that the hearts of men can be converted, effecting internal controls that restrain men from making sexual advances. Internal control means it is not necessary "to swathe women in yards of cloth so it is impossible to see the woman's body."[46] Veith adds: "This is why, historically, Christianity is associated with political freedom. Those who govern themselves morally do not need a strong central governmental power to maintain social order. Conversely, Islam, for all its high moral teachings, enforces them with coercive external control."[47]

The proper covering of a woman's body has on occasion become an end-in-itself, overruling the health and safety of women or girls. For instance, in March 2002 a fire broke out in a girls' intermediate school in Mecca, Saudi Arabia. It took the lives of 14 girls when they were forced back into the burning building by the *mutawiyin* (religious police) because the girls, according to Islamic standards, were improperly dressed. The religious police even attacked the adults who tried to rescue the girls.[48] This was an extreme situation, indeed, yet one that was consistent with orthodox Islamic doctrine.

Another reason for the veiling of women stems from the Islamic belief that women have to be controlled because they are too powerful. Veiling them is a necessary way of curbing their power. In the words of Fatima Mernissi, who opposes the veiling of women, it is not that woman is seen as inferior, but that she is "a powerful and dangerous being." In addition, she states: "Men and women were and still are socialized to perceive each other as enemies." Thus all sexual institutions, of which veiling is an example, "can be perceived as a strategy for containing her power." [49] Mernissi argues that this Islamic ideology goes back to Abu Hamid al-Ghazali (1058–1111), the conservative Muslim philosopher, who had a great impact on Islamic thought and theology. He argued that women must be controlled to prevent men "from being distracted from their social and religious duties."[50]

Mernissi further maintains that, in Islamic theology, woman is "the embodiment of destruction, the symbol of disorder. She is *fitna* [chaos or disorder], the polarization of the uncontrollable, a living representative of the dangers of sexuality and its rampant disruptive potential."[51] The discipline or control exercised by veiling women becomes especially effective when women accept and internalize the practice to the extent that they do not view it as coercive or misogynistic.

A third reason why Muslims veil women is that the veil has become the symbol of Islamization. As Nilufer Göle says, "the question of veiling is not an auxiliary issue for Islamist movements but, on the contrary, highlights the centrality of the gender issue to Islamist self-definition and implied Western criticism."[52] Thus, it is "women who serve as the emblem of politicized Islam."[53] If the latter is true, does it mean the veiling of women is an ingenious method of the male-oriented culture of Islam using women to further male objectives? If Mernissi's above argument is correct that men perceive women as too powerful, then this question is not impertinent.

Until traditional Islamic countries take seriously the words of Ataturk Kemal, the man who greatly reformed Turkey in the 1920's, the status of most Muslim women will not improve. Ataturk said: "In some places I have seen women who put a piece of cloth or a towel or something like over their heads to hide their faces, and who hide their backs or muddle themselves on the ground when a man passes by. What are the meaning and sense of this behaviour? Gentlemen, can the mothers and daughters of a civilized nation adopt this strange manner, this barbarous posture? It is a spectacle that makes the nation an object of ridicule. It must be remedied at once."[54]

Let Her be Silent

Earlier we saw that the ancient Greeks, Romans, and Jews forbade women to speak in public outside the home, a

87

social norm that Jesus and the early Christians ignored. This norm is still kept alive by Muslims in many contexts. For instance, the Shariah manual of the Sunni Muslims, known as *Reliance of the Traveller,* states: "It is better for women to pray at home than at a mosque. ... It is offensive for an attractive or young woman to come to the mosque to pray" (f12.4). This manual also says it is unlawful for a menstruating women to "recite any part of the Koran, even part of a single verse ... " (e10.7e). And Muslims of the fundamentalist persuasion do not even permit a woman to laugh.[55]

Although it is occasionally violated in some places, it should be noted that Islamic doctrine does not allow a casual conversation to take place in public between a man and a woman alone, when the man is not her husband. Thus, a non-Muslim man is wise not to speak to a Muslim woman without her husband's presence.[56] This, of course, prompts a couple of questions: Who, in the minds of Muslim men, is the one that cannot be trusted in this kind of situation? Is it the man? Or is it the woman, who purportedly is seen as dangerous and needs to be controlled?

Woman as Unequal

According to the Koran, men are superior to women in that they "are a degree above them"(Sura 2:228). This Koranic teaching shows itself in a number of ways in the lives of Muslim women.

Aside from a woman being obligated to wear a veil, or at least a headscarf, while a man has no such obligation, she may not marry more than one man at a time, though a man, according to the Koran (Sura 4:3), may marry up to four women. A Muslim wife, even in modern Europe, can only divorce her husband by having his permission to go a judge, but the husband can divorce his wife without a judge, and he is not required to discuss it with her.[57] He needs only to tell his wife

88

"I divorce you" three times; no reason needs to be given. (Some Muslims do require the husband to wait for three menstrual cycles to make sure the wife is not pregnant before the divorce actually goes into effect.)

In a mosque men are in front, then the boys, and finally the women. This stems from Muhammad himself having "enforced a rule that no man should stand shoulder to shoulder with a woman in a mosque, not even her husband or father."[58] Thus, according to the Shariah (*Reliance of the Traveller*, f12.32), a wife may not pray beside her husband in the mosque, but behind him. This practice is reminiscent of the ancient Jewish custom that existed during the rabbinic era of Judaism, when women in a synagogue were separated by a divider (*michetza*), which placed them behind men.[59] Already at Muhammad's funeral procession in 632, the men went first, followed by the women.[60]

Muslim women are also not permitted to visit graves, not even those of their relatives. Khaled Abou El Fadl says women are barred from visiting graves because they are considered "intellectually meek and emotionally weak; if they visit the graves they are prone to commit reprehensible acts such as screaming, wailing, and beating their chests in grief."[61]

The Athenian wife in ancient Greece, as noted above, could not leave her home without being accompanied by her husband or an approved male escort. The Koran, even today, dictates a similar practice: "It is not lawful for a wife to leave her house except by permission of her husband, though she may do so without permission when there is a pressing necessity" (*Reliance of the Traveller,* m10.12:2). And the Koran also tells women: "And stay in your houses, and do not display your finery like the displaying of the ignorance of yore … " (Sura 33:33). A man is at liberty to leave his house whenever he desires, but his wife, in her state of inequality, only has an extremely limited right to do so.

The Islamic woman also does not have equality with a man in a court of law. The Koran in Sura 2:282 states that one man's testimony is equal to that of two women. One Muslim apologist defends this doctrine by saying "the testimony of women in court is less than that of men, because their life of the home does not force them to objectify themselves as the world forces men to do."[62] In the case of a capital punishment trial, only male testimonies are permitted.[63] It is also noteworthy that a woman in Islam is only worth half a man in terms of receiving family inheritance.[64]

In January 2004, *The Wall Street Journal* reported that in Saudi Arabia, at the Jeddah Economic Forum, a female banker in public spoke "before a sea of white-robed men." The article called this "a female first in Saudi Arabia." In her speech this woman said: " 'If we want Saudi Arabia to progress, we have no choice but to embrace change.' " By change she meant that Saudi Arabia needed to give women freedom and rights they now lack. Her speech was reluctantly tolerated by the men at the forum. One of them said: " 'I don't think women should ask for equality. But they should ask for justice.' "[65] Given that women in Western societies are equal before the law, a by-product of Christianity's influence, one wonders how Muslim women could have justice without equality before the law?

Woman as "Evil"

As we saw earlier, women among the ancient Greeks, Romans, and Jews were seen as evil. It is also true in the Islamic world, which from its beginning in the seventh century has seen women as evil. This perception is plainly stated in the Hadith, which says the majority of hell's inhabitants are women. The Hadith quotes Muhammad saying: "I stood at the gate of the Fire and saw that the majority of those who entered it were women" (*Sahih Al-Bukhari* 62:88). This belief has also

90

recently been stated by Saudi Arabia's Council for Scientific Research and Legal Opinions (CRLO) in its following *fatwa*: "The Prophet said to a group of women, 'O women, give charity, for you are the majority of the people of Hell-fire.' "[66] It is the CRLO that also bars women from driving automobiles in Saudi Arabia.

This view of women as evil, according to Khaled Abou El Fadl, goes back to Muhammad, who reportedly said: "A woman comes in the image of a devil, and leaves in the image of the devil."[67] The perceived evil nature of woman is also implied when the Koran tells every Muslim husband, as already noted, that he may have to beat his wife physically.

The philosopher Abu Hamid al-Ghazali (1058-1111), in one of his aphorisms, said: "A sage wished (that) his short wife (might have been) tall. People asked him, 'Why did not you marry a wife of full stature?' 'A woman is an evil thing,' he answered, 'and the less (there is) of an evil thing the better.' "[68] He also declared: "A teacher was teaching girls how to write. A sage passed by and said, 'This teacher is teaching wickedness to the wicked.' "[69]

Women as Sex Objects

The Koran states: "Your wives are a tilth [field] for you, so go into your tilth when you like ... " (Sura 2:223). To a Muslim man, his wife (or wives) is there to satisfy his sexual needs. Note the words "when you like." Her sexual needs are not taken into account (*WI*, 302). One Muslim jurist says marriage for a Muslim man is "the contract by which he acquires the reproductive organ of a woman, with the express purpose of enjoying it" (*WI*, 302). As Ibn Warraq, a former Muslim, has noted, "The converse, of course, is not the case; the reproductive organ of the husband is not exclusively reserved for one woman" (*WI*, 302). Truly, as the Muslim woman Fatna

A. Sabbah (pseudonym) says, women, "according to the tenets of Muslim orthodoxy, are exclusively sexual beings."[70]

In *The Revival of the Religious Science*, al-Ghazali says: "She [the wife] should be clean and ready to satisfy her husband's sexual needs at any moment" (cited in *WI*, 300). In this regard, it is reported that Muhammad once said: "The woman should never refuse her husband even on the saddle of a horse"(*WI*, 304). Moreover, Muhammad reportedly said: "When a husband calls his wife to his bed and she refuses to come, the angels curse her until morning."[71] In light of this Islamic perception of the wife, Jan Goodwin has noted that, "For Muslim women, marriage begins a life of sex on demand—his demand, that is."[72] Goodwin points out that this perception follows from Sura 2:223 in the Koran, cited above.

Muslim Girls and Clitoridectomy

In recent years, much has been written about clitoridectomy (a. k. a. female genital mutilation, or FGM), a practice that is common among Muslims in many African countries, including Egypt. One report revealed that, in Egypt in the 1990's, some 6,000 girls underwent FGM every day. It is important to note, from the outset, that clitoridectomy is not a universal practice among Muslims. To some degree, with the large influx of African-Muslim immigrants to Europe, it is now also practiced there, though clandestinely, because France, England, Germany, and Sweden have outlawed it. It has been also occurring illegally among African-Muslim immigrants in the United States, where many American states, similar to European countries, have outlawed this barbaric practice.

Clitoridectomy (often but erroneously called female circumcision) is an age-old cultural practice. One recent source indicates that it is performed in 26 African countries. Depending on the country and region, between 5 and 99 percent of the girls are subjected to this rite.[73] Minimally, clitoridectomy involves the removal of a young girl's clitoris. Frequently, however, there is also the procedure of infibulation, which includes removing the inner and outer labia. Sometimes "almost all of the girl's genitalia are cut away and the remaining flesh from the outer labia is sewn together. The girl's legs are then bound from ankle to waist for several weeks while the scar tissue closes up the vagina almost completely."[74] One physician says that even in its mildest form this procedure "is anatomically equivalent to amputation of the penis."[75] Those performing the clitoridectomy commonly force a young girl to submit by tying her down. Often it is done by one of the parents using a razor blade.[76] Sometimes, especially in America, Muslim immigrant mothers want their daughters to have the operation because they believe it will make them less desirous of having sex in their teenage years.

Although clitoridectomy is not mentioned in the Koran, it is referred to in the Shariah as being "obligatory" (*Reliance of the Traveller*, e4.3). The Hanbali school of jurisprudence (one of four) does not make it obligatory. However, another Islamic jurisprudence authority—the Hanifite school—encourages it out of courtesy to husbands.

Clitoridectomy "has become a common practice in Muslim countries, not only in Africa but also in Indonesia."[77] The practice predates Islam, apparently by several millennia.[78] Thus, similar to the veiling of women, it is a rite borrowed from ancient pagan societies in the Middle East.

The age at which it is performed varies from region to region. In some instances it is performed during infancy, but most often it is done before girls reach the age of puberty. It is a procedure that causes a number of health problems, such as hemorrhaging, urine retention, ulceration of the genital area, infections, and severe pain. Later, many develop cysts and abscesses, others experience damage to the urethra, pain during sexual intercourse is common, and difficulties in childbirth also occur.

One scholarly article recently reported: "Approximately 100 to 130 million girls and women have been crippled by this procedure. Daily in Africa and some Asian countries another 6,000 are forced to undergo this 'rite of passage' increasing the number of mutilated women by two million yearly."[79] Even though not all Muslim girls undergo this gruesomely painful rite, at least "one in five Muslim girls lives in a community where some form of clitoridectomy is sanctioned and religiously justified by local Islamic leaders."[80]

It may seem strange to Westerners, but clitoridectomy among Muslims is most strongly supported by the mothers of young girls. The fact that mothers are behind this cruel practice is an indication of the power of culture that permeates people's minds (in this case, the minds of mothers) to such an extent that it overshadows the horrible and gruesome physical consequences: great pain and sometimes even death. A similar example of this dynamic is seen in the practice of *suttee* (widow burning) in India by Hindu women, who were the strongest supporters of this practice when the British outlawed it in 1829. In fact, when a young widow was burned, contrary to existing laws, on her husband's funeral pyre in Deolora, India, in 1987, the action was supported not by men, but by a throng of cheering women.[81]

Clitoridectomy, of course, has some support from Muslim men, too. One man, for instance, sympathizes with the defenders of clitoridectomy by saying "a campaign to eradicate female circumcision will carry with it a largely hidden agenda to change people's lives according to a particularly Western model of development." He continues, saying that, "Muslims will quickly suspect that 'female circumcision' is not what is really at stake: what is at stake is Islam itself, the presence of a

Christian as a campaign leader suggesting yet another missionary assault on Islam."[82]

Supporters of clitoridectomy, of course, ignore the numerous physical and mental consequences of the practice. In addition to the above brief reference to the physical problems, one study reports that as a result of infibulation (a common procedure in clitoridectomies) babies are frequently "born dead or brain damaged, and there is a 20 percent maternal mortality rate."[83] Also often ignored is the following assessment: "Following the terrifying, brutal, and destructive assault on their genitals and the terrible physical sequelae, girls become docile and submissive. Their source of pleasure has been eradicated, their spirit broken. They cannot trust and have a sense of safety since it was their mothers who were part of the attack on their physical integrity. In time however, to survive, defensive mechanisms evolve."[84] The words "their spirit broken" and "cannot trust ... their mothers" go a long way in explaining why countless Muslim women have conformed to the inferior status they have as women in Islam. Thus, many Muslim women will say they like wearing a veil or headscarf and a long dress with long sleeves, and that they even choose this type of attire without any coercion. This is not unlike the troubling accounts of certain American slaves who, during the Civil War, liked being slaves and did not really want to be free.

Polygynous Marriages[85]

Polygyny is never a plank in the platform of freedom for any group of women who seek more freedom and dignity. One does not have to read volumes in pro-women literature to see that polygyny is rejected by women who love freedom and dignity. Yet, not only does the Koran permit polygyny (a man have up to four wives), but most Islamic countries today also permit polygynous marriages; Turkey and Tunisia do not. In

1985, Egypt passed a law that allows a Muslim man to marry up to four wives, a law consistent with the Koran.

Polygynous marriages in Muslim countries are not isolated phenomena. For instance, in 1995, Egypt recorded 1,200 marriages with four wives; 9,000 with three wives; and 12,000 with two wives.[86] It is also interesting to note that the Koran assumes polygynous marriages, for in Sura 4:34 it tells a husband he may beat (scourge) his disobedient wives—not his only wife.

G. H. Jensen has said that one major disadvantage of Islam is that it "puts one half of the human race, women, into subordinated position to the male half—no amount of apologetics about respect for women, protection of their rights, and so forth, can get around this basic and unjust discrimination. It is firmly embedded in Islamic practice because it is there in the Koran, as are the canonical punishments."[87] Thus, even in what today is called secular Turkey, where women were given a great deal of freedom by Ataturk in the 1920's, "in small towns and villages in the interior of the country women are rarely seen on the streets without being covered by a black *chador*. ... "[88] Oddly enough, even after veiling was abolished, some pictures in the 1920's show Ataturk's wife wearing the black *chador*.

Islamic Apologists

In spite of the evidence outlined above, one often hears and reads statements made by Muslim and non-Muslim apologists that Muslim women have freedom, dignity, and rights similar to non-Islamic women in the West. One apologist writes: "That Islam has ameliorated the lot of women in Arabia is hardly to be doubted."[89] This statement, however, is at odds with the observations of Joseph Schacht, a renowned scholar of Islam, who says the position of women actually became worse after Muhammad. As an example, he cites Muhammad's

96

approval of polygyny: "It led to a definite deterioration in the position of married women in society, compared with that which they had enjoyed in Pre-Islamic Arabia."[90] Ibn Warraq cites Hind bint Otha, the wife of Abu Sufyan, the head of an aristocratic Meccan family, who "reproached Muhammad for having imposed obligations on women that he had not imposed on men"(*WI*, 292–93).

Another apologist, Ahmed Rashid, gives the impression that it is not Islam that has repressed women but rather groups like the Taliban in Afghanistan. Thus, he says "the Taliban have tried to rewrite Afghan history in order to justify their repression of women. ... "[91] Still another defender, Paul Findley, a non-Muslim American and a former member of the U.S. House of Representatives, says: "Islam may be the single most liberating influence on the status of women in recorded history, greater than Christianity and Judaism."[92]

It is puzzling how these and similar statements can be made, when they are clearly contradicted by the Koran, the Hadith, the Shariah, and by a Muslim woman's attire. Moreover, are the apologists not concerned about Islamic women having obviously fewer rights than men? We need only point out that a man has the right to have up to four wives (so stated in the Koran), while the woman has no such right. Furthermore, a Muslim man, according to Sura 24:32, may also have concubines.

Given the inferior position of Muslim women, it is astounding that many Muslim women are strong defenders of their inferior social, cultural, and religious status. For instance Rana Kabbani, a Muslim woman living in London says: "I am always pained by Western misconceptions about the lives of Muslim women."[93] Quite similar are the sentiments of Naheed Mustafa, a Canadian-born Muslim woman. In trying to defend the Muslim requirement of having women wear a veil, she says: "Wearing the *hijab* has given me freedom from constant attention to my physical self."[94] Here again, one also sees the power of culture as it has socialized and conditioned Muslim women to accept and internalize values and practices that are clearly against their personal well-being. In short, the fact that some Muslim women say Islam's restrictive norms on their deportment and freedom are noble and good for them is no proof that they are right. Rather, it demonstrates they have been co-opted by their Islamic culture, which is detrimental to their own interests and well-being.

Conclusion

When one considers the status of women in the West, where Christianity has left its salutary and indelible mark by giving them freedom, rights, and dignity that they had never attained anywhere else in the world before Christ made his appearance, the words of St. Paul in Galatians 3:28 have the ring of authenticity: "There is neither male nor female, for you are all one in Christ Jesus." Similarly significant are these other words that Paul spoke to husbands and wives: "Be subject to one another out of reverence for Christ" (Ephesians 5:21).

By comparison, when we recall that in Islamic circles men apparently perceive women as too powerful—even as enemies, according to Mernissi—it is difficult to see how Muslim women in traditional Islamic countries will ever achieve freedom, rights, and dignity equal to men. This task looks even more formidable if Mernissi's following assessment is true: "What is feared is the growth of the involvement between a man and a woman into an all-encompassing love, satisfying the sexual, emotional and intellectual needs of both partners. Such an involvement constitutes a direct threat to the man's allegiance to Allah, which should be the unconditional investment of all the man's energies, thoughts, and feeling in his God."[95]

In order to overcome this fear, they would do well to take the advice of St. Paul: "husbands should love their wives as their own bodies. He who loves his wife loves himself" (Ephesians 5:28). Given that the Koran to some degree honors the Bible, even though some Muslim authorities say it has been corrupted, Muslim men should be able to take Paul's advice to heart. Until they do, the status of the Muslim woman will not improve.

Today, radical feminists in the West, many of whom detest Christianity, do not seem to recognize that, had it not been for the precedent set by Jesus Christ, women would likely have no more freedom in the West than Islamic women have in the Middle East. Indeed, freedom has its ironies. It allows its beneficiaries to deny and despise the source of their freedom— in this instance, Jesus Christ's highly commendable influence in the lives of women.

4

SLAVERY

"No longer as a slave but more than a slave, as a beloved brother" (Philemon 16)

Slavery was indigenous to African and Arabian countries before it made its way to Europe.[1] It grew rapidly once it arrived in Europe; by the time of Christ, slaves made up an estimated 75 percent of the population in ancient Greece and well over half of the Roman population. Across the Atlantic, slavery was also widely practiced by many American Indian tribes long before Columbus set foot on the shores of the New World. Wherever it existed, kings, priests, and philosophers, with few exceptions, approved of it. The influential Greek philosopher Aristotle saw it as natural, expedient, and just (*Politics* 1.1255).[2]

It is not commonly known that the tragedy of slavery flourished in a number of countries for more than a hundred years after it was outlawed in the British Empire in 1833 and in the United States in 1865. Ethiopia had slavery until 1942; Saudi Arabia, until 1962; Peru, until 1964; and India, until 1976. Moreover, it still exists to this day in the Islamic countries of Mauritania, Senegal, Sudan, the latter being Africa's largest country. Slavery in these countries, as the present chapter shows, is closely associated with the Islamic religion.

The presence of slavery in these African countries today is not widely known, largely because most major media outlets apparently have not deemed it worthy of coverage. The little coverage this topic does receive is mostly found in minor news outlets. The major mass media news services have also not reported that a Christian organization—Christian Solidarity

International (CSI)—currently buys slaves (primarily black Christians) in Sudan in order to set them free. In some instances this org-anization pays 50,000 Sudanese pounds per slave.[3] In December 1999 the "Christian Solidarity International 'redeemed' 5,514 slaves during an eight-day visit by its representatives to Sudan .... These redemptions brought to more than twenty thousand the number of slaves freed by CSI since it commenced its purchase program in 1995."[4] Nor is it widely known that in the past several years approximately two million Sudanese Christians, mostly black slaves, under Muslim rule have been executed because they were Christians.[5]

Early Christian Opposition to Slavery

When St. Paul in the first century told Philemon that he was no longer to treat the runaway slave, Onesimus, as a slave but as a brother, he uttered a revolutionary statement, one that was contrary to the values and beliefs of all societies of that era. Paul in effect told Philemon that, as a Christian, he was no longer to practice slavery. Similarly, he told the Galatian Christians that from a Christian perspective there was "neither slave nor free ... for you are all one in Christ Jesus" (Galatians 3:28). To the Christians in Corinth he declared: "For by one Spirit we were all baptized into one body—Jews or Greeks, slaves or free ... " (I Corinthians 12:13). And to the Colossian Christians he wrote: "Here there is not Greek and Jew, circumcised and uncircumcised, barbarian, Scythian, slave, free man, but Christ is all in all" (Colossians 3:11). With these four references St. Paul laid the foundation for the abolition of slavery. There is nothing equivalent to these references in either the Koran or in the Hadith.

Even though some who professed to be Christians did not heed Paul's statements, numerous other actions and statements incompatible with the ethic of slavery soon surfaced in the early church. Here are a few examples: Christians interacted with slaves as they did with freemen, slaves communed with Christians at the same altar, and they were catechized and treated as non-slaves. These practices contrasted sharply with the contempt the Romans had for slaves (*HE*, 77). Slaves fared no better among the Greeks, whose philosopher Aristotle argued that "a slave is a living tool, just as a tool is an inanimate slave. Therefore, there can be no friendship with a slave as slave" (*Nichomachean Ethics* 8:11)

In many instances, Christians freed slaves. During the second and third centuries, according to Robin Lane Fox, the early Christians "were most numerous in the setting of urban households where freeing [of slaves] was most frequent." He further notes "the freeing of slaves was performed in the presence of the bishop."[6] How many were freed during the early years of Christianity will never be known, but that they were numerous is illustrated by the historian W. E. H Lecky, who says: "St. Melania was said to have emancipated 8,000 slaves; St. Ovidius, a rich martyr of Gaul, 5,000; Chromatius, a Roman prefect under Diocletian, 1,400; Hermes, a prefect under Emperor Trajan, 1,200. [And] many of the Christian clergy at Hippo under the rule of St. Augustine, as well as great numbers of private individuals, freed their slaves as an act of piety"(*HE*, 2:69). It is also known that Constantine the Great in 315, only two years after he issued the Edict of Milan, imposed the death penalty on those who stole children to bring them up as slaves.[7]

Freeing slaves took not only Christian conviction, but courage as well. Edicts issued by Roman emperors did not favor liberating slaves. In time, an emperor (Justinian, 527–565) arose who was sympathetic to what many of his fellow Christians had been doing for a long time. He abolished all laws that prevented freeing slaves. This change, together with the numerous slaves who had already been freed and who still were being liberated, was consistent with what some of the leading theologians had been saying. Early in the fourth century, Lactantius (the "Christian Cicero," as he has been called) in his *Divine Institutes* said that in God's eyes there were no slaves. St. Augustine (354–430) saw slavery as the product of sin and as contrary to God's divine plan (*The City of God* 19:15). St. Chrysostom, in the fourth century, preached that when Christ came he annulled slavery. He proclaimed that "in Christ Jesus there is no slave. ... Therefore it is not necessary to have a slave. ... Buy them, and after you have taught them some skill by which they can maintain themselves, set them free" (*Homily 40 on I Corinthians* 10).

These words and actions, as well as others, had continuing salutary effects. Slavery was also condemned in the fifth century by St. Patrick in Ireland. For several centuries bishops and councils recommended the redemption of slaves, and for five centuries the Trinitarian monks redeemed Christian slaves from Moorish servitude in Muslim-occupied Spain.[8] By the 12th century slaves in Europe were rare, and by the 14th century slavery was almost unknown on the Continent in counties where Christianity had a significant presence (*HE*, 2:71). W. E. H. Lecky, a historian whose writings at times are quite critical of Christianity, says: "In the thirteenth century there were no slaves to emancipate in France" (*HE*, 2:74).

The honor, acceptance, and freedom that Christianity extended to slaves resulted in "multitudes" of them embracing Christianity, according to Lecky. Herbert Workman, historian of the early church, has shown that the early Christians truly saw slaves as their brothers. He says no grave of a dead slave in the Christian catacombs was ever inscribed with the name "slave."[9] Some slaves even became priests in the church—in the third century Callixtus, once a slave, became not only a priest but also the bishop of Rome. In fact, the Roman Catholic Church lists him as one of its early popes. Some slaves were honored as martyrs. For instance, in the first half of the sixth century Emperor Justinian built and dedicated the grandest example of Byzantine church architecture in Ravenna, Italy—the Church of San Vitale—in memory of a martyred slave of the fourth century (*HE*, 2:69).

Some Erring Christians Condoned Slavery

Although slavery in Europe had virtually come to an end by the 14th century, it is important to remember that, in spite of St. Paul's words to Philemon and the Galatian Christians, many Christians for more than a thousand years owned slaves. This included even some prominent church leaders such as Polycarp, a second-century bishop of Smyrna, and Athenagoras, a second-century Christian philosopher. Others, such as Clement of Alexandria and Origen, both third-century church fathers, spoke approvingly of slavery. Similarly, in the 13th century St. Bonaventure saw slavery as a divine institution, and in 1548 Pope Paul III granted to all men, and to the clergy, the right to keep slaves.

The erring Christians who supported slavery and often owned slaves reveal at least three important truths: (1) as sinful beings, they were either ignorant of Paul's words or knowingly ignored them; (2) they let the prevailing culture of pagan societies influence their behavior; and (3) they ignored Christ's words that said his followers were to be in the world but not of it.

British Revival of Slavery

Although slavery had virtually come to an end in much of Europe, including England, by the 14th century, it was revived by the British in the 17th century, especially in England's colonies. A London church council decision of 1102, which had outlawed slavery and slave trade, was ignored.[10] Slaves were transported from Africa to the colonies in the British West Indies as well as to the American colonies and to Canada. The Portuguese and the Spaniards also went to Africa to get slaves and then shipped them to their colonies in Brazil, Central America, and parts of South America.

The revival of slavery was especially lamentable, because this time it was implemented by countries whose proponents of slavery commonly identified themselves as Christians, whereas during the African and Greco-Roman eras, slavery was the product of pagan societies. However, some serious-minded, devout Christians saw the revival of slavery as a gross violation of basic Christian beliefs and values, and before long some courageous individuals came to the forefront of the battle against slavery.

Abolition of Slavery in the British Empire

One of the courageous Christians who fought against slavery was William Wilberforce (1759–1833), a member of England's House of Commons. He declared: "The Christian's motto should be, 'Watch always, for you know not what hour the Son of Man will come. ... Help me, O Jesus, and by Thy Spirit cleanse me from my pollutions; give me a deeper abhorrence of sin; let me press forward.' "[11] Being a gifted orator, he delivered many powerful speeches during his twenty-some years in Parliament against Britain sending slaves to the West Indies. One biographer has said Wilberforce's speeches were most effective when he "appealed to the Christian consciences of Englishmen."[12] In 1823, two years before he had to relinquish his seat in the House of Commons because of ill health, he presented a petition to the House to abolish slavery, a petition that a close associate of his, Thomas Fowell Buxton, moved "as a resolution declaring slavery repugnant to Christianity and the Constitution."[13] A few days before Wilberforce died on July 26, 1833, he received word that Parliament had passed the Abolition Act. This act resulted in England freeing 700,000 slaves in the West Indies colonies.[14]

It is difficult to find a better example than Wilberforce to show the powerful effect the teachings and spirit of Christ have had in fighting the cultural sin of slavery. No proponent for the abolition of slavery ever accomplished more. Largely as a result of his indefatigable efforts, slavery came to a complete end in the British Empire's possessions by 1840, making it the first country to outlaw slavery.

Slavery and Its Abolition in America

After slavery came to an end in the British Empire, it continued unabatedly to the north and south of the West Indies, most notably in the United States, Brazil, and Mexico. In the United States it had become a deeply entrenched institution, especially in the Southern states, despite the fact that only about 25 percent of Southerners owned slaves.[15]

Given that this "peculiar institution," as it was often called, was so firmly embedded in the South, it had many ardent defenders. Unfortunately, many of them called themselves Christians. Virtually every American church denomination had pro-slavery advocates. In support of their position, they cited man's innate sinfulness, historical precedent, black people's perceived inferiority, and economic necessity. A common argument in favor of slavery was to cite its presence in the Old Testament among the Hebrews. Here they engaged in faulty exegesis, giving descriptive passages in the Bible prescriptive meaning.

In every state, Christian clergy could be found who argued slavery was compatible with biblical Christianity. The abolitionist movement, however, had a considerably higher percentage of Christian clergy than did the pro-slavery defenders. Two-thirds of the abolitionists in the mid-1830's were Christian clergymen.[16] This made for a powerful phalanx of vociferously active clergy abolitionists.

The Impact of Christian Clergy on Abolition in America

Elijah Lovejoy, who was accosted and killed by a group of rioting pro-slavery radicals in his printing office in Alton, Illinois, in November 1837, is often cited as the first martyr of the American abolitionist movement. He was a Presbyterian clergy-man. Two years before he was murdered, he wrote in his newspaper: "I shall come out, openly, fearlessly, and as I hope, in such a manner as becomes a servant of Jesus Christ, when defending His cause."[17]

Abolitionists had a strong connection with clergy through Lane Theological Seminary in Cincinnati, Ohio. This school was founded in the early 1830's by New York evangelicals as an outpost of revivalism in the Midwest to train clergy who would urge Christians to holier and more sanctified lives.[18] It also had ties to Ohio and New York antislavery societies and funding through Arthur and Lewis Tappan, two strong abolitionists and wealthy businessmen from Boston[19] The Tappan brothers strengthened the school's abolitionist core by bringing in Theodore Weld, a convert of revivalist Charles Finney and a zealous abolitionist and fervent evangelical preacher. Weld and others soon made the seminary "a citadel of Yankee abolitionism."

Weld and 40 students (some of whom were already ministers) severed their ties with Lane after they adopted the more radical idea of "immediatism"—meaning that slavery had to end immediately—and, thus, put themselves at odds with school trustees. They soon relocated at the new and fledgling Oberlin College. Charles Finney was another prominent figure who joined the Oberlin College faculty in 1836 to teach theology and later became the college's first president. He used his charismatic talents to convert people not just to Christianity, but also to abolitionism. The college opened its classes to blacks, hired abolitionist instructors, and sheltered black fugitives. In 1839 Weld also joined the Oberlin College faculty.

He authored a best-selling antislavery book—*Slavery As It Is.* This book became one of the resources that Harriet Beecher Stowe used in writing her famous novel in 1852: *Uncle Tom's Cabin.*

Another clergyman, Charles T. Torrey, became the father of the Underground Railroad. His leadership in the fugitive slave movement is credited with having helped 100,000 slaves escape northward to freedom. Torrey, whose involvement in abolitionist causes went back to Lovejoy's chronicles, died a martyr's death in a Maryland jail while serving time for having abetted escaped slaves.[20]

Christianity's teachings definitely have to be credited with having moved many Christian clergy—Lovejoy, Finney, Weld, Torrey, Edward Beecher, Henry Beecher, and many others—to their abolitionist beliefs. That is also how Lyman Beecher, father of Harriet Beecher Stowe, saw it. One researcher cites Lyman Beecher as having said that abolitionism was the offspring of the Great Revival that preceded it in the eastern United States.[21]

Abolitionist clergy in the South encountered more difficulties than their Northern soul mates. Antislavery-minded ministers commonly were muzzled verbally, many lost their positions, and some were even imprisoned. In *Clergy Dissent in the Old South, 1830–1865*, David Chesebrough described the difficulties that antislavery clergy experienced in the South. J. D. Paxton was forced to leave his parish in Cumberland, Virginia, for having authored a small book, *Letters on Slavery*, in which "he called slavery a moral evil and declared that Christians were morally obligated to work for its destruction."[22] John Hersey, a Methodist pastor in Virginia, wrote a book titled *Appeal to Christians on the Subject of Slavery.* After this book's third edition (1843) appeared, matters became very intense for him. Soon copies of his book were burned in Richmond, and he was finally compelled to migrate to the

North.[23] Another clergyman, John Fee, founded Berea College in Berea, Kentucky. This college, modeled after Oberlin College, was the only racially integrated school in the South, a phenomenon that did not sit well with pro-slavery advocates. Over the course of several months (1854–55), Fee was attacked by a mob, thrown into the Ohio River, and eventually forced to flee to Cincinnati.[24]

The influence of Christian teachings that moved so many abolitionist clergy did not, of course, remain with them alone. Through their efforts they converted numerous lay people to the abolitionist cause. The fact that there were also clergy, both in the North and especially in the South, who defended slavery does not nullify the argument that Christianity's antislavery spirit achieved its eventual goal— freedom for enslaved black Americans.

The Role of Non-Clergy Christians in Abolition

Although clergy, mostly evangelical, made up two-thirds of the abolitionist movement in America, it is important to remember that many Christian lay people also played vital roles in abolishing American slavery. One of the prominent and influential laymen in the abolitionist movement was William Garrison, a Baptist from Massachusetts. An associate of his called him "ultra orthodox" in his religious beliefs. He founded his own periodical, *The Liberator*, which for years published strong and frequently strident articles promoting abolition. As a Christian, he "often quoted the passage from Christ's parable: 'a house divided against itself cannot stand.' "[25] So strong were his antislavery beliefs that he sometimes chastised Christian denominations for doing too little to end slavery. Often, clergy were the object of his ire. Thus, he once wrote, "The cause [abolition] must be kept in the hands of the laymen, or it will not be maintained."[26]

Garrison once burned a copy of the 1850 Fugitive Slave Act, as well as a copy of the United States Constitution. Hence, many saw him as a radical even though he always advocated Christian nonresistance. Whatever the accusations were against him, his contributions to American abolitionism were immense, as summarized by Abraham Lincoln: "The logic and moral power of Garrison and the antislavery people of the country and the army have done it all."[27]

A couple additional outstanding laymen in the abolitionist cause deserve mention in this brief discussion. One is Joshua Giddings, a convert of Theodore Weld. When the United States Congress passed the Fugitive Slave Act of 1850, he said: "We cannot be Christians and obey it."[28] Another abolitionist is Julia Ward Howe. Although a Unitarian, her early Christian influence is apparent in some of the lyrics in her "Battle Hymn of the Republic" (1862), an antislavery song that stirred the minds and emotions of countless Americans. And finally, we must remember the prominent non-clergy role of Abraham Lincoln, as president of the United States, especially his Proclamation of 1863, which officially granted black slaves freedom.

Harriet Beecher Stowe's Christian Impact

Most Americans have heard about *Uncle Tom's Cabin* (1852), even though most may not have read it. They know the book depicts the misery of America's onetime enslavement of the Negro. But most have never heard about the Christian motivation that moved Harriet Beecher Stowe to write this stirring, antislavery novel.

The book abounds with allusions to biblical references, and throughout its emotionally moving pages the author reveals the deep spiritual tensions and conflicts, induced by Christian values, that existed among the slave owners. In noting these tensions and conflicts, Stowe shows, of course, how slavery violated the teachings of Christ, teachings she personally had internalized from her Christian upbringing, her father being a Christian clergyman. On one occasion, a sea captain who met her said that he was pleased to shake the hand that wrote *Uncle Tom's Cabin.* She responded that she did not write the book. "God wrote it," she said. "I merely did his dictation."[29] *Uncle Tom's Cabin* con-tributed greatly to the shattering of American slavery. Her book also "took the sting of fanaticism out of abolitionism, and its popularity gave incalculable weight to the idea of emancipation as a moral and historical inevitability."[30]

The First Antislavery Proclamation

In most antislavery discussions in American history books and articles a highly significant event is commonly and unfortunately overlooked. This event happened more than century before the American abolitionist movement arose, when an unknown German immigrant issued America's first formal proclamation against slavery in 1688. He was Franz Daniel Pastorius, a Mennonite, who spoke several languages and had studied law in Germany. William Penn met him in Germany and persuaded him and a number of other Germans to migrate to the colony of Pennsylvania. Upon arriving in America, Pastorius purchased 5,000 acres of land and founded Germantown, Pennsylvania.

When Pastorius came to Pennsylvania in 1683, he soon encountered slavery, which in those days was not unusual even in the North. Negro slavery was repugnant to him and his fellow German settlers, most of whom were Mennonites from the Rhine River area in Germany. In 1688 Pastorius approached his Quaker friends in the Germantown area with a formally written protest against slavery, which he and several other German immigrants had signed. Along with some other arguments, it invoked the Golden Rule: "There is a saying that we shall doe [sic] to all men, like as we will be done ourselves,

111

making no difference of what generation, Descent or Colour they are, and those who steal or rob men, and those who buy or purchase them, are they not all alike?"[31]

The Quakers were indifferent to his proposal, which shocked him and his fellow Germans. How could these pious people harmonize slavery with their religious beliefs?[32] In spite of trying several more times to get the Quakers to approve the proclamation, Pastorius and his co-signers did not succeed. But his efforts were not entirely lost, for in 1705 the Quakers did at least take a stand against the trading of slaves.

There is no doubt that Pastorius' antislavery proclamation was motivated by his Christian convictions. Just before he came to America he had formed close ties with some of the German members of the Pietist movement, which emphasized the Christian's sanctification (living a God-pleasing life) more than his justification. There is good reason to believe that Pietism, an offshoot of Lutheranism, was one way in which Christian values prompted Pastorius to issue America's first proclamation against slavery.

Christianity and the Abolition of Slavery in the West

Although there were many Christians who were involved in the practice of slavery in the Western world, it was the spirit of freedom in Christ that finally brought an end to slavery throughout the British Empire, as noted earlier. In the United States that same spirit produced the abolitionists in the 1830's and 40's In a generation's time, this vibrant movement also brought about the end of slavery in their own country, but contrary to the spirit of Christ, not without bloodshed. Though in Brazil it took another 20 years to end slavery, abolitionists there shared the same Christian convictions that motivated abolitionists elsewhere.[33] When Brazil outlawed slavery in 1888, the entire West had cast off the shackles of slavery. Slaves in the Western world were now free at last.

Today, textbooks typically focus on the ways in which Christians were partakers in the sin of slavery in the West. Yet it is clear that the American abolitionist movement was firmly rooted in the teachings of Christ. Lecky, a 19th-century historian, said it was the influence of Christianity that ended slavery in the Western world (*HE*, 74). Finally, today's well-known sociologist Rodney Stark—not a Christian to my knowledge—supports this assertion in a recent book: "the abolition of New World slavery was initiated and achieved by Christian activists."[34]

Slavery in Islam

The phenomenon of slavery in Islamic societies has been almost completely ignored in many publications. For instance, already back in 1862, H. C. Carey, in his book *The Slave Trade: Domestic and Foreign*, says nothing about Muslims being engaged in the slave trade despite the fact that they were. Similarly, textbooks and essays focusing on slavery have frequently given the impression that slavery has largely been a Western phenomenon practiced mostly by white Europeans and Americans with a Christian background. One reason today's slavery in Africa, which is mostly practiced by Muslims, has been largely been ignored is because, as Rodney Stark says, writers do not wish to risk being accused of minimizing "white guilt" with regard to the West's one-time involvement in slavery.[35]

The following Koranic reference shows that slavery in the Muslim world is as old as Islam itself. Muhammad spoke favorably about slavery in the Koran. Sura 24:32 is but one example: "And marry those among you are single and those who are fit among your male slaves and your female slaves, if they are needy, Allah will make them free from want out of His grace . . ."

In its numerous conquests from the seventh century onward, Islam commonly enslaved countless captives as booty, rewards for the jihad of its followers. The captives became slaves and were used by Muslim leaders. Slaves in excess of what the leaders needed were usually sold or traded to various interested parties. Ibn Warraq says: "Between 652 and 1276, Nubia [under Muslim occupation] was forced to send an annual contingent of slaves to Cairo" (WI, 231). Warraq also shows that "After the conquest of Amorium in 838, there were so many captives that the Caliph al-Mutasim ordered them auctioned in batches of five and ten. At the sack of Thessalonica in 903, 22,000 Christians were divided among Arab chieftains or sold into slavery" (WI, 231).

It is known that a slave market operated in Muslim-occupied Spain in Baena in the ninth century.[36] This is in accordance with what Rodney Stark has noted: "Muslim slave-trading began many centuries before Europeans discovered the New World and carried at least as many Africans into bondage, and probably more, as were shipped across the Atlantic."[37]

The selling and trading of captives as slaves among Muslims started with Muhammad himself. For instance, after he had massacred the Banu Qurayza, he took one-fifth of the booty. The remaining portions he divided among 3,000 soldiers, which included women who were sold as slaves to the highest bidders (*LM*, 320). Regarding the consequences of this massacre for the losers, Sir William Muir says "there were a thousand captive women. ... From his own [one-fifth] share Mahomet made gifts to certain of his friends of some of the fairer of the maidens thus reduced to slavery. The rest of the women and children he sent to Nejd, to be sold in exchange for horses and arms. ... " (*MI*, 150). Even after this event, Muhammad had slaves, some of whom were black male slaves and slave girls (*MI*, 175).

After Muhammad died, the early caliphates (latter half of the seventh century and the entire eighth century) had "slaves [that] came largely from frontier areas where holy war was still being waged," according to Paul E. Lovejoy. Thus, as in the case of the Banu Qurayza, slaves "were often prisoners of war, non-Muslims who had resisted the expansion of Islam." They came mostly from Africa and Western Europe and were used for various activities, commonly physical labor, although some were also used as soldiers. With regard to female slaves, the most attractive ones were enslaved in harems.[38]

From the 14th to the 19th century, the Islamic Ottoman Turks captured and traded slaves, mostly Caucasians, from the territories they had conquered in southeastern Europe. For instance, in Chapter 2 we saw that the Turks enslaved 50,000 Byzantines when they captured Constantinople in 1453; after the Battle of Mohucs in Hungary in 1526, they enslaved hundreds of Hungarian men, women, and children. Later, after some military defeats, their access to white slaves declined, and they turned more and more to Africa for their slaves.[39]

Slavery is assumed and accepted in the Koran and was widely practiced by Muslims from Islam's beginning, as shown by the above citation of Sura 24:32. Verse 33 also speaks of Muslims having "slave girls." Nowhere in the Koran is slavery ever cast in a negative light, and although Muhammad reportedly told Muslims to treat slaves well, as is the case in Sura 4:36, he did not tell them they were under any obligation to free them.[40] Slavery is also assumed and approved in the Hadith, which speaks about "The sale of a slave (for a slave) and an animal for an animal on credit" (*Sahih Al-Bukhari* 34:110). Another section talks about "taxes imposed on the slaves by their masters; and the leniency in imposing taxes on female slaves" (*Sahih Al-Bukhari* 36:17), and still another speaks about "a slave woman who begets a child for her master" (*Sahih Al-Bukhari* 46:8). Clearly, neither the Koran nor the

Hadith has anything negative to say about slavery. As Irshad Manji, the Canadian Muslim critic, rightly points out: "Read it closely and you'll find that the Koran doesn't direct us to release all slaves, just those who their owners decide have the potential to achieve better standing."[41]

Thus, it should not surprise Westerners that slavery still exists today in some African countries where Islam is the predominant religion. In this context it is well to remember the words of Bernard Lewis, an American expert on Islam. He says that to Muslims "to forbid what God permits is almost as great an offense as to permit what God forbids."[42] Specifically, the Koran says: "O you who believe! Do not forbid (yourselves) the good things which Allah has made lawful for you . . ." (Sura 5:87). This Koranic principle helps one understand why it is virtually impossible to see an unequivocal condemnation of slavery, oral or written, by any leading Muslim country or authority.

While it is true that slavery has existed around the globe historically, it is important to note that the Muslim countries that outlawed slavery did so much later than did Western countries. Moreover, as Bernard Lewis has shown, the abolition of slavery in Muslim countries, beginning with the Ottoman Turks, was largely the result of pressure from the British.[43] For instance, Egypt outlawed slavery in the 1880's, largely because the British pressured it to do so. Iran outlawed slavery in 1906; Yemen and Saudi Arabia, in 1962; and Mauritania, not until 1980. One report says: "Muslim countries proved extremely resistant to abolition, many of them had to be dragged into it by the European colonial powers."[44] This helps explain why slavery is still alive and well in some Muslim countries, such as Sudan and Mauritania. It has also recently been reported in Pakistan. [45]

116

Modern Slavery in Sudan

While many Muslim countries theoretically abolished slavery in the 20th century, it is still quite pervasive today in Sudan, Africa. As noted earlier, this fact unfortunately has largely been unreported by the major media networks in the West, including the United States, although recently some reports have come to light. Brian Eads, after visiting Sudan in 1995, published an article in *Readers' Digest,* "Slavery's Shameful Return to Africa." His article said many of the enslaved are from the Dinka tribe, many of whom are Christians. Numerous Nubians are also enslaved. He reports that: "Some are bought by individual owners to serve as field workers, household servants or concubines. Others, confined in camps, work on government farms or are leased to large private landowners. There are [also] frequent and consistent reports that slaves are being exported to Libya and countries on the Persian Gulf." Many slaves, Eads found, were branded as if they were cattle, and those "who try to escape are beaten, mutilated and murdered." He cites an official of the London-based Sudan Human Rights Organization saying: "Taking slaves goes hand in hand with the government's concept of Islamization." [46]

A more recent account in May 2001 of slavery in Sudan, published in Canada's *Maclean's* magazine, stated: "Thousands of people, mostly women and children living on the rolling savanna, have been kidnapped by marauders backed by the [Islamic] government in the north and sold into slavery. Those who do not accept their fate are often butchered, raped, or killed." [47] David Littman, a representative of the World Federalist Movement to the United Nations Office in Geneva, reported in 1996 that the Popular Defense Forces (a Muslim group) in Sudan abducted some 500 women and 150 children who were taken into slavery. [48] The pervasive extent of slavery in Sudan, whose population is 70 percent Sunni Muslims and 5

117

percent Christians, is also evident from the statistics of those who have been freed. For instance, between the years 1995 and 2000, more than 30,000 slaves have been purchased and set free by the organization known as Christian Solidarity International.[49] It pays 50,000 Sudanese pounds ($50 U.S.) per slave.[50]

In 1999, A. M. Rosenthal, a reporter for the *New York Times*, wrote that Americans have largely ignored the enslavement of countless southern Sudanese who are "mostly Christian or animists, and all, you know, are black." Individuals are "captured and sold in Sudan by government soldiers and militias." Rosenthal further declared that the number of slaves "in Sudan can roughly be estimated—tens of thousands. Only owners take precise slave-counts."[51]

Slavery essentially returned to Sudan in 1983 when its Islamic government "amended the country's constitution in favor of Islamic law. This meant the ruling Arab north could attempt to enforce the Muslim *Sharia* code on the entire country."[52] As might be surmised, the Sudan government, in spite of overwhelming evidence, denies that people are enslaved within its borders. Oddly enough, officials of the Nation of Islam in the United States have also denied what is going on in Sudan. This group of American Muslims, headed by Louis Farrakhan, has been so adamant in denying Sudan's slavery that when Mohammed Athie of the International Coalition Against Chattel Slavery asked for time to speak on behalf of the enslaved in Sudan at Louis Farrakhan's "Million Man March" in Washington, D.C., in 1995, his request was ignored.[53]

Modern Slavery in Mauritania

Slavery also flourishes in another African country, Mauritania, which is also predominantly Muslim. As noted above, ostensibly Mauritania banned slavery in 1980, but it never really did come to an end. A report in *Headway*, a

118

conservative black magazine, which recently cited the U.S. State Department's statistics on Human Rights, noted that in 1996 "some 90,000 Mauritanians live under 'conditions of involuntary servitude.' "[54] The presence of slavery in Mauritania has been photographically corroborated by Samuel Cotton in his 1998 book *Silent Terror: A Journey into Contemporary African Slavery.* Cotton, a black American documentary filmmaker and investigative journalist, in his undercover work has interviewed existing and former slaves in Mauritania. His book reveals a white Muslim man giving orders to his slave before he goes "to prepare his ablution for the Muslim prayer."[55] This book also shows pictures of slaves whose bodies have been marred and whose hands have been crippled from torture.[56]

On March 13, 1996, Cotton testified regarding slavery in Mauritania before the House Subcommittee on International Operations and Human Rights in Washington, D.C. He documented that slavery not only existed in Mauritania but also in the neighboring country of Senegal. Slavery in Senegal has been reported by other sources as well.[57]

Of course, government officials and other beneficiaries of slavery deny that slavery exists in Mauritania, a country with a population of approximately 2.5 million. So adamant is the denial that it is now illegal for Mauritanians to say slavery exists in their country. This has prompted an astute news reporter to say that such a law is "a sure sign that it really does [exist]."[58] Moreover, in January 2002, the government of Mauritania banned the opposition party, which demanded slavery be eradicated.[59]

Sounds of Muslim Silence

It is possible for Muslim apologists to say that the Koran does not specifically command slavery; however, the crux of the matter is that the Koran and the Hadith freely permit it.

Furthermore, it is difficult to find any prominent Muslim or credible Muslim publication that has spoken out against or condemned slavery. As reporter Marcus Mabry recently stated, when Muslim leaders from various countries gather at international forums, they never discuss slavery. He further adds: "They feel no remorse for the past, and no responsibility for the present."[60] This lack of remorse is especially regrettable in light of the fact that Muslims have enslaved countless individuals for centuries, since the very earliest days of Islam.

Whether it was the early caliphs who succeeded Muhammad, the Moors in Spain, the Ottoman Turks, or the current Islamic governments in Sudan, Senegal, and Mauritania, together they have enslaved millions of individuals over a period of 1,400 years. In the eighth century, the so-called tolerant Moors enslaved about one-fifth of the Spaniards, forcing them to be "menial domestics, concubines, eunuchs, musicians, and dancers, stewards or agents, soldiers and guards."[61]

The silence regarding the practice of slavery in Islamic countries today is unfortunately shared with many non-Muslims in America and in other Western countries, who know and believe slavery is an abject human evil but are quiet nevertheless. For example, university professors have silenced themselves by not publishing anything about present-day slavery practices in Sudan, Mauritania, or Senegal. As Bernard Lewis has written, "For the central Islamic lands, despite the subject's importance in virtually every area and period, a list of serious scholarly monographs on [Islamic] slavery—in law, in doctrine, or in practice—could be printed on a single page."[62] Lewis further says "the main reason for the lack of scholarly research on Islamic slavery is the extreme sensitivity of the subject [which] makes it difficult, and sometimes professionally hazardous, for a young scholar to turn his attention in this direction."[63]

Given what Professor Lewis says, one must ask why is it seen as professionally hazardous to write scholarly articles or books about Muslim slavery? Would these same reluctant university professors also find it professionally hazardous to write about slavery if it were practiced by countries that identified with Christianity?

Why are so many Westerners—both university professors and non-academics—fearful of saying anything that Muslims do not want them to say, even when Muslim behavior egregiously violates fundamental human rights and values? What is it about Islam that intimidates so many Westerners?

Conclusion

As even the brief evidence in this chapter shows, the abhorrence and the abolition of slavery is one of the great by-products of Christianity's influence on the world at large, especially in the West. Given Christianity's pervasive anti-slavery influence, many non-Muslims, especially those in the West, think that their view of slavery is shared across the globe. This, however, is an erroneous assumption. As recent as 1999 it was reported that a prominent Saudi Muslim cleric, Shaikh Saad Al-Buraik, told Palestinians: "Their [Jewish] women are yours to take, legitimately. God made them yours. Why don't you enslave them?"[64] While some Muslim countries have outlawed slavery, largely as a result of Western pressures, no Muslim country's government or its conservative Islamic imams have ever explicitly condemned it. One cannot find any such condemnations. Nor does the Koran or the Hadith condemn slavery. Here it is also well to remember what Thomas Patrick Hughes noted in *The Dictionary of Islam*: "Slavery is in complete harmony with the spirit of Islam, while it is abhorrent to that of Christianity."[65] Yet many prominent Muslims, for public relations and political reasons, will not admit this undeniable fact of history.

121

If Westerners still find it difficult to understand the Muslim reluctance to abolish slavery, the words of *Newsweek* reporter Marcus Mabry are helpful: "[T]he Islamic world has not experienced the same kind of moral reckoning on slavery that the West has."[66] He could have added that it was the influence of Christianity that moved the West to experience this specific "moral reckoning."

5

CHARITY OR *ZAKAT*?

"As you did not do it to one of the least of these, you did it not do it to me"
(Matthew 25:45)

"I was hungry and you gave me food, I was thirsty and you gave me drink, I was a stranger and you welcomed me, I was sick and you visited me, I was in prison and you came to me" (Matthew 25:35–36). These words of Christ made a lasting impression on the minds of the early Christians, as did the parable of the Good Samaritan (Luke 10:3037), and they diligently sought to emulate this practice of Christian charity. They built steadily upon a tradition that already included the almsgiving practiced by many Hebrews and the Old Testament precedent allowing the poor to glean the fields at harvest time. The present chapter explores the early Christian concept of charity and compares it to the Islamic practice of *zakat*.

Jesus, Healer of Body and Soul[1]

All four of the New Testament Gospels reveal that Jesus had great compassion for the sick. He healed many. Matthew states: "Jesus went throughout Galilee … healing every disease and every infirmity among the people" (Matthew 4:23). For Jesus, healing of the body was never divorced from his concern for people's souls and their spiritual well-being: "For him no healing was complete which did not affect the soul."[2] He healed people holistically.

Jesus expected his disciples, along with preaching and teaching, to heal the sick: "He sent them out to preach the kingdom of God and to heal" (Luke 9:2). When he sent the 70 to enter villages and hamlets, he gave them a similar message

(Luke 10:9). And as the early Christians were dispersed, largely as a result of persecutions, throughout Asia Minor, we find them engaged in healing the sick in addition to preaching and teaching. The New Testament, especially the Acts of the Apostles, cites a number of instances where Peter, Paul, Stephen, Barnabas, Ananias, and other Christians healed people as part of their missionary activities.

Christian Compassion Enters a Pagan Void

The world the early Christians faced in the Greco-Roman era had a colossal void with regard to compassion. Thucydides (ca. 460–400 B.C.), the honored historian of ancient Greece, recounts an example of this during the plague that struck Athens during the Peloponnesian War in 430 B.C. Many sick and dying Athenians were deserted by their loved ones and fellow residents, who feared they too would catch the plague (*Peloponnesian War* 2:51).

Speaking about the Alexandrian plague 700 years later in about A.D. 250, Dionysius, a Christian bishop of the third century, said the pagans "thrust aside anyone who began to be sick, and kept aloof even from their dearest friends, and cast the sufferers out upon the public roads half dead, and left them unburied, and treated them with utter contempt when they died" (*Works of Dionysius, Epistle* 12:5). But the Christians, says Dionysius, cared for the sick and dying, ignoring the danger to themselves: "[V]ery many of our brethren, while in their exceeding love and other kindness did not spare themselves, but kept by each other, and visited the sick without thought of their own peril, and ministered to them assiduously and treated them for their healing in Christ, died from time to time most joyfully … drawing upon themselves their neighbors' diseases, and willingly taking over to their own persons the burden of the sufferings of those around them" (*Works of Dionysius, Epistle* 12:4).

124

The compassion showed by the early Christians, compared to the lack of relative compassion amongst the Greco-Romans, was also corroborated by the Roman emperor Julian the Apostate (ruled 361–363). He lamented the pagan neglect of caring for their own who were sick and ailing, saying: "It is shameful that ours [pagan Romans] should be so destitute of our assistance" (*Epistles of Julian* 49).

Many medical historians in more recent times similarly have noted this reality. Fielding Garrison, a physician and historian, says that before the birth of Christ "the spirit toward sickness and misfortune was not one of compassion;" and he adds, "the credit of ministering to human suffering on an extended scale belongs to Christianity."[3] As 19th-century German historian Gerhard Uhlhorn states: "The idea of humanity was wanting in the old world."[4] This mentality affected even the very youngest and most vulnerable, considering the treatment that the unborn and infants received in Greco-Roman society. Plutarch (ca. A.D. 46–120), a non-Christian Greek writer, mentions the Carthaginians, who he says, "offered up their children, and those who had no children would buy little ones from poor people and cut their throats as if they were so many lambs or young birds; meanwhile the mothers stood by without a tear or moan" (*Moralia* 2:1171D). Seneca (ca. 4 B.C–A.D. 65), a Roman philosopher whose moral philosophy was on a higher plane than that of his culture, said: "We drown children at birth who are weakly and abnormal" (*De Ira* 1:15). History shows that infanticide, abortion, and child abandonment were legal and widely practiced.

It was this compassionless culture that the early Christians entered. Their high degree of compassion was accompanied by a corresponding high regard for human life, prompted by Christ's words: "[A]s you did it not to one of the least of these, you did it not to me" (Matthew 25"45). These words moved them to show compassion for those who were sick and destitute. They saw every human being, regardless of age or condition, as God's handiwork, worthy of their compassion. The historian Ferdinand Schenck has noted: "The intrinsic worth of each individual man and woman as a child of God and an immortal soul was introduced by Christianity."[5]

Reciprocity of Christian Compassion and Charity

The early Christians practiced *caritas*, as opposed to *liberalitis*; the latter was common among the pagan Romans, the former was not. *Caritas* meant giving to relieve the recipient's economic or physical distress without expecting anything in return; whereas *liberalitis* meant giving to please the recipient, who would later bestow a favor in return to the giver.

For centuries the Romans practiced *liberalitis*, not *caritas*.[6] Only in extremely rare instances did some of the Romans give without expecting something in return to any indigent individual(s). It was usually the most honorable— those who really did not need help—who received "all or most of the charity dispensed."[7]

The charity (*caritas*) of Christians also differed with regard to the motive for giving. Rome's pagan religions provided no motive for charity. In pagan religious practices, people were mere spectators at temple sacrifices, where they passively watched priests perform. Some observers gave coins to some god or goddess. Christians, on the other hand, were active participants in their divine services in which they heard God's gracious, redemptive act of love in Jesus Christ, which in turn motivated them to help and give to those in need.[8] Their giving reflected the Apostle Paul's words: "Each of you should look not only to your own interests, but also to the interests of others" (Philippians 2:4, NIV).

Thus, Cyril, the fourth-century bishop of Jerusalem, "sold treasures and ornaments of the church for the relief of a

126

starving people, [and] Ethelwold, bishop of Winchester [10th century] sold all of the gold and silver vessels of his cathedral to relieve the poor who were starving during a famine."[9] Christopher Dawson says: "Every church had its *matriculum*, or list of persons in receipt of relief, and enormous sums were spent in every kind of charitable work."[10]

Finally, Christian charity, so closely tied to compassion, was completely voluntary. According to the Roman culture of the era, such behavior defied common sense; it was seen as a sign of weakness and viewed with suspicion. There was nothing to be gained by expending time and energy, especially if done voluntarily, on people who would not contribute to Roman valor and strengthen the state.

The prevalence of Stoic philosophy also made it disrespectful to associate with the weak, the poor, or the downtrodden. To Christians, however, the individual, regardless of social or economic status, was valuable because he or she possessed a soul redeemed by Jesus Christ. Thus, the differences between Christian and Roman charity were profound, for the Roman acts of relief and assistance were few and isolated state-supported efforts, "dictated much more by policy than by benevolence;" furthermore, the Roman "habit of selling young children, the innumerable expositions, the readiness of the poor to enroll themselves as gladiators, and the frequent famines, show how large was the measure of unrelieved distress" (*HE*, 2:78). La Bleterie, a historian of ancient societies, says before Christianity arrived there were some pagans who did engage in some isolated humanitarian acts. Such acts, however, were not motivated by pagan cultural or religious values, but were exceptions on the part of some individuals. As he expressed it: "Pagans had a morality, but Paganism had none." In a similar vein, Lecky said: "The active, habitual, and detailed charity of private persons, which is such a

127

conspicuous feature in all Christian societies, was scarcely known in antiquity" (*HE*, 2:79).

The Tradition of Christian Hospitals

During the first three centuries of Christianity's existence, Christians were subjected to frequent and severe persecutions. They had to use all their resources to keep from being extinguished. The most they were able to do was to care for the sick where they found them, in many instances by taking them into their own homes. After the Edict of Milan in 313, however, when Christianity attained legal status, Christians were able to direct more attention and energy toward providing care for the sick and dying in a formal manner. Hence, the first ecumenical council of the Christian church at Nicaea in 325 directed bishops to establish hospices in every city that had a cathedral.[11] These hospices, known as *xenodochia*[12] (*xenos* = stranger + *dechesthai* = to receive) were an effort to heed Christ's command to care for the physically sick and the early apostolic admonition that Christians be hospitable to strangers and travelers.[13] When they followed these commands, Christians accomplished something that was unprecedented in their time.

Given the pervasive fear the Greco-Romans had about caring for the sick and dying, it is not surprising that there were no hospitals, at least not charity hospitals for the general public. Charity hospitals, where the common populace and the indigent public could come to be nursed to recuperate from their physical ailments, did not come into being until Christians introduced them in the fourth century.[14] Moreover, it needs to be understood that even if the Romans had some type of hospitals that preceded Christian hospitals, none of them ever became institutionalized. The latter is the result of Christianity's exclusive influence on the world at large.

The first hospital was built by St. Basil in Caesarea in Cappadocia about A.D. 369. It was one of "a large number of buildings, with houses for physicians and nurses, workshops, and industrial schools."[15]   Some historians believe that this hospital was not a *xenodochium* but rather a *nosocomium* (*nosus* =sick + *komeo* = take care of) that ministered exclusively to the sick.[16] The rehabilitation unit and workshops gave those with no occupational skills opportunity to learn a trade while recuperating.   These units reveal additional humanitarian awareness, and it would be difficult to argue that this awareness had nothing to do with the spirit of Christ being alive in St. Basil.

Another hospital appeared in 375 in Edesa, also in the East like Caesarea.   Then Fabiola, a wealthy widow and an associate of St. Jerome, built the first hospital in the West, a *nosocomium* in the city of Rome in about 390.   According to Jerome, Fabiola donated all of her considerable wealth to construct this hospital, to which she brought the sick from off the streets in Rome (*Letter to Occeanus* 5).   In 398, Fabiola, together with Pammachius, founded another hospital, this one in Ostia, about 50 miles southwest of Rome.[17]

The building of Christian hospitals continued.   St. Chrysostom (d. 407), the patriarch of the Eastern church, had hospitals built in Constantinople in the late fourth and early fifth centuries, and St. Augustine (354–430), bishop of Hippo in northern Africa, was instrumental in adding hospitals in the West.   By the sixth century, hospitals also had become a common component of monasteries.[18] Hence, by the middle of the sixth century in most of Christendom—in both the East and the West—"hospitals were securely established."[19]   By A.D. 750, the growth of Christian hospitals, either as separate units or attached to monasteries, had spread from the East and Continental Europe to England.   Also, about this time, the city of Milan in Italy established a hospital that specialized in caring for foundlings.[20]   In the early ninth century, Charlemagne, emperor of the Holy Roman Empire and a strong defender of the sick and poor, constructed numerous hospitals. And by the mid-1500's there were 37,000 Benedictine monasteries alone that cared for the sick.[21]

It is important to note that these Christian hospitals were the world's first voluntary charitable institutions. There is "no certain evidence," says one scholar, "of any medical institution supported by voluntary contributions ... till we come to Christian days."[22]   And it is these hospitals that revolutionized the treatment of the sick and the dying. The Christian origin and influence on hospitals is still very much evident in the Western world in that many hospitals are named for Christian saints or various Christian denominations.

Christian Hospitals and Islam

Surely the Arabic Muslims in the Middle East saw and knew the noble and humanitarian functions that Christian hospitals provided. This undoubtedly motivated them to follow the Christian precedent of building hospitals. There is even some evidence that a physician, Ibn Bakhtishu (d. ca. 771) of the Nestorian Christian sect[23] was summoned by Caliph al-Mansur to build a hospital for Muslims in Baghdad around the mid-700's (*DE*, 233). But Cyril Glasse, author of *The Concise Encyclopedia of Islam* (1989), thinks the founding of hospitals among Muslims in Baghdad did not occur until around 900.[24] It has occasionally been asserted that Arabic Muslims were the first people to build hospitals "as we know them today."[25] Clearly, this is false because the Christian hospitals built in the fourth century were already in existence for 200 years before the birth of Muhammad in 570.

Christian Hospitals during the Crusades

Although the Crusades have been harshly criticized, and rightfully so in some respects, Christians engaged in some commendable activities during those almost 200 years. One of their more noble acts was the construction of hospitals in Palestine and other Middle East areas. Howard Haggard, who is quite critical of some Christian decisions in the context of medicine, nevertheless notes that the Christians gave a major boost to hospital construction during the Crusades.[26]

It was during the Crusades that the military hospital orders became prominent, one of them being the Knights of the Order of Hospitallers of St. John of Jerusalem. This order came into being before the Crusades (about 30 years before), primarily to provide protection for pilgrims on their routes to Jerusalem.[27] Its real claim to fame, however, came from providing hospital services to all during the Crusades— Christians and Muslims alike.[28] In their concern for serving the sick and the wounded, the Hospitallers also recruited women to nurse the wounded and the sick.[29] The Hospitallers (a. k a. Knights of Malta) was the first organization to provide organized medical care on the battlefield.[30]

Later, another military order, the Hospitallers of St. Lazarus, came into being in the Middle East in the 1100's. Initially, its members devoted themselves primarily to nursing leprosy patients. This order soon spread to Europe, where it founded many more hospitals and treated people with diseases other than leprosy.[31] It operated and maintained general hospitals and admitted the insane as well. This order built a hospital with 2,000 beds in Jerusalem in the 12th century, during the Crusades. They later established a Christian insane asylum in 1409 in Valencia, Spain, (*HE*, 81) when the country was still largely under Muslim occupation.

Charitable Christian Institutions During and After the Middle Ages

Christians also established a number of other charitable institutions soon after the Roman emperors Constantine and Licinius legalized Christianity in the year 313. Thus, early in the fourth century, orphans, of which there were many, were provided food and shelter in *orphanotrophia* (orphan + *trophos* = nourisher). Tiny infants or newborn foundlings were cared for in *brephotrophia* (*brephos* = child). Both institutions mark the beginning of orphanages that later became common, especially in the West.

Also in the fourth century, Christians operated asylums for the blind, and in 630 a *typholocomium* (*typholos* = blind + *komeo* = take care of) was built in Jerusalem.[32] In the latter part of the 13th century, Louis IX, who after returning from an unhappy experience in the Crusades between 1254 and 1260, built an asylum for the blind in Paris.[33]

Although life expectancy in the Middle Ages was only about 32 years, some people nevertheless did become septuagenarians and even octogenarians. Thus, in the early part of the sixth century, during the life of Emperor Justinian (483–565) in the East, churches began operating homes for the aged called *gerontocomia* (*geras* = aged + *komeo* = take care of).

The Muslim Concept of *Zakat*

The Muslim word for charity is the Arabic *zakat*. It is one of the Islam's five pillars. Muslim charity, however, differs significantly from Christian charity (*caritas*). First, as noted earlier, Christian charity among the early Christians meant giving to and helping those in need, and nothing was expected in return. Such giving was (and still is) done out of love in response to God's love in Jesus Christ. It is a gospel-oriented response. But for Muslims, *zakat* is a law-oriented response. They are "required [emphasis added] to give of what God blessed them with."[34] Furthermore, "In the *Sharia* the word *zakat* refers to the determined share of wealth prescribed [emphasis added] by Allah to be distributed among the categories of those entitled to receive it."[35] This statement does not even hint at love having anything to do with *zakat,* but rather that Allah prescribes a portion of the giver's wealth to be designated as *zakat.*[36]

Second, because Christian charity is gospel-motivated, it is done voluntarily with no compulsion or law-oriented stipulations. If giving is not done voluntarily, it is no longer Christian charity. *Zakat,* on the other hand, is an involuntary act, done out of sheer compulsion. Muslims must give, rather than ought to give. Thus, *zakat* in Islamic countries is commonly imposed by the government. Moreover, "The state also has the right to penalize anyone who refuses to pay *zakat.*"[37]

Third, Christian charity is received as a privilege, not as a right. In Islamic theology, the recipient has a right to *zakat.* One Islamic source states: "*Zakat* is the right of the poor in the wealth of the rich, a right decided by the true Owner of wealth—Allah."[38]

Society may call it charity when giving to the needy is compulsory, forced, or dictated, but such giving is no longer compatible with Christian charity. It is also not an indicator of Christian compassion. Instead, it is social or state welfare, which does indeed help the needy and indigent, but is a socialistic act. Such a socialistic act, in the context of helping economically deprived individuals, is often called "Christian socialism," a term coined by F. D. Maurice in 1848.[39] Christian socialism, however, is an oxymoron, for it is not compatible with Christian charity or compassion. This incompatibility is well expressed by the Russian writer Fyodor Dostoyevsky in *The Brothers Karamazov*: "The socialist who is a Christian is more to be dreaded than a socialist who is an atheist."[40]

Briefly put, much of Western society, where genuine Christian charity (*caritas*) was first practiced by the early Christians, no longer has a Christian understanding of what charity really is. Thus, today, whenever a needy person or cause receives some financial assistance—even when that assistance is dispensed by some governmental entity that acquired the money by compulsory taxation—it is seen as charity. But it is not charity as the early Christians conceived and practiced it.

The logic and the method of Islamic *zakat,* which specifies and demands that a percentage be given to those in need, is also a form of socialism—namely, Islamic socialism. Given that Islam, unlike Christianity, does not define *zakat* as an act of voluntary love or compassion, there is no problem in having it function or operate as a socialistic deed. It is only inappropriate to call it charity when the act is compulsory and still seen as consistent with Christian values or motivation.

American Charity

Christian charity to the poor did not end with the early church or in the Middle Ages. Churches continued to aid the poor over the centuries, even to the present day. In the United States, for example, most Christian denominations still collect funds to give clothing, food, and medical relief to the poor, in and beyond their country's boundaries. As is well known, the worldwide work done by the Salvation Army in alleviating the plight of the poor is commendatory and significant. This Christian organization, founded by William Booth, a devout Christian, in London in 1865, still practices genuine Christian charity.

The earliest examples of American charity, as Marvin Olasky has shown, occurred among the Pilgrim colonists, governed by William Bradford, in Plymouth, Massachusetts. When deadly sicknesses attacked the group, Bradford said the people willingly toiled to aid the stricken with food, clean clothes, and wood, often risking their own health.[41]   Later, Congregational, Presbyterian, Anglican, and Methodist sermons urged church members to help the poor and the sick, reminding them that without compassion their faith was dead.[42]

With these early American precedents, it is not surprising that astute foreign observers have noticed that the United States, virtually from its beginning, has been a shining example of a charity-minded nation. Fifty years after the nation formally came into being in 1789, Alexis de Tocqueville visited the United States from France and observed: "If an accident happens on the highway, everybody hastens to help the sufferer; if some great and sudden calamity befalls a family, the purses of a thousand strangers are at once willingly opened and small but numerous donations pour in to relieve their distress."[43]

A hundred years after Tocqueville's visit to the United States, Gunnar Myrdal, another foreign observer, in the 1940's remarked: "No country has so many cheerful givers as America."[44]   He attributed this cheerful giving, or "Christian neighborliness," as he called it, to the "influence from the churches."[45]

Americans continue to be cheerful givers. For example, the amount they gave to the poor and needy in 1991 amounted to 650 dollars per American household.[46]   And in 1998 American church members contributed more than 424 billion, amounting to 407 dollars per church member.[47]

In the 1890's, Amos Warner found that much of America's giving was the product of the nation's churches. He said that the church, as a voluntary association, was "the most powerful agent in inducing people to give."[48] This still seems to be true. For instance, in 1994 religious donations in the United States totaled 59 billion dollars. This amounted to 45 percent of all voluntary giving by individuals and organizations.[49] In North America, but mostly in the United

States, there are currently 750 Protestant mission agencies that receive and dispense 42 billion dollars annually.[50] Complementing this action, there are at least 500 rescue missions in the United States that are supported through charitable giving.[51] Americans; Orthodox, Roman Catholic and Protestant also give liberally for the construction of new church buildings and other religious buildings. In 1998 they spent over six billion dollars in church-related construction.[52]

This spirit of Christian charity in the United States has taken root outside the various churches as well. For instance, the United Way, which traces its history back to 1887 when it was founded by a group of Christian leaders, is a shining example of Christ's abiding influence. In 1998-1999 the United Way raised $3.58 billion[53] to be distributed to various charitable organizations. Further examples can be seen in the abundant service organizations in America, such as the Rotary Club, Kiwanis Club, Lions Club, and Optimist Club. These clubs, which draw members from the professional and business classes, exist to provide humanitarian services to their local communities, the nation, and often internationally, too.

The International Red Cross and the Red Crescent

There are, of course, numerous charity organizations on the international scene, but this chapter shall focus only on one—the International Red Cross, an organization known by all. The Red Cross organization was founded by Jean Henri Dunant, who grew up in a wealthy banking family in Geneva, Switzerland.

In 1859 Dunant witnessed the suffering of wounded soldiers at the Battle of Solferino in Italy's struggle for unification. "Never shall I be able to forget," said he, "the eyes of these victims who wished to kiss my hand."[54] Five years later, in 1863–64, Dunant and four associates, together with 24 delegates from 16 nations, formed the International Committee

136

of the Red Cross.[55]   This was part of the first Geneva Convention that set policies in regard to what is permissible or prohibited military behavior in the conduct of war on battlefields.

Although Dunant was at times critical of the organized church, he did not allow his criticisms to mitigate his desire to heed Christ's words in regard to caring for the sick and ailing, especially soldiers. Nor did he let his financial setbacks derail him, for life was not always kind to him. He lost his banking fortune, was expelled for many years from his country, lost his good name, and lived as a virtual vagrant for many years in Paris. But God did not forsake him. A decade or so before he died, his native country Switzerland allowed him to return with honor and dignity, and in 1901 he received the first Nobel Peace Prize ever bestowed. What seemed to matter most to him was his faith in Jesus Christ. This is apparent from the words he spoke on his deathbed: "I am a disciple of Christ as in the first century, and nothing more."[56]

Dunant's Christian faith moved him to establish an organization that would console and bind up the wounds of battle-scarred soldiers. His faith apparently also led him to choose the Christian cross, the symbol of Christ's suffering and redemption, as the new organization's emblem. This symbol is recognized today by Christians and non-Christians alike as a symbol of mercy and love on or off the battlefield. "The significance of the symbol chosen (although it is essentially the Swiss flag in reverse)," say Kennedy and Newcombe, "should not be lost by anyone."[57]

In the United States, Clara Barton is often credited with being one of the founders of the American Red Cross. Barton valiantly nursed soldiers in the American War Between the States. She was known to say: "Follow the cannon." She risked her life on many occasions. At the Battle of Antietam a soldier was killed in her arms.   In keeping with her Christian compassion, she visited prisoners from the Union Army at the notorious Confederate prison at Andersonville.[58]

In 1877, the Muslim country of Turkey adopted the concept that gave rise to the Red Cross organization, but as it did, it changed the Christian symbol to the Red Crescent. But, ironically, by changing the Red Cross symbol to the Red Crescent, as D. James Kennedy and Jerry Newcombe say, "Muslims inadvertently recognized the driving force behind one of the greatest humanitarian movements in history—Jesus Christ."[59]

Indeed, there is more to this change of symbols than meets the eye. First, the Red Crescent, except for its color, is derived from the moon's crescent and harkens back to pre-Islamic pagan moon cults. The crescent, regardless of its color, has never had any historical symbolism with regard to charity and compassion. The cross, however, from the time of Christ's crucifixion, has always symbolized the compassionate suffering of Jesus Christ, which is what prompted Dunant to adopt it as the official symbol of the organization he helped found.

Second, the change to the Red Crescent reveals the dislike Muslims have for Christianity and its symbols. Staunch Muslims do not tolerate Christianity or any of its symbols. For instance, during the Gulf War in 1991, the Saudi Arabian government would not permit Red Cross vehicles on Saudi soil to display their official symbol.[60] It is well known that it is illegal for a Christian to wear even a cross or crucifix necklace in Saudi Arabia. Reports reveal that even the mathematical plus sign is a problem for the Saudi Muslims.[61]

Third, Muslims say they oppose the emblem of the Red Cross because it reminds them of the Crusades of the Middle Ages, when individual Crusaders wore a red cross on a white background on the shoulder. Since most Muslims have an ex-aggerated hatred of the Crusades, not knowing or willing to recognize that the Crusades were largely a Western response to several centuries of Muslim invasions and conquests of Christian countries or territories (discussed at length in the next chapter) they despise anything that resembles the Christian cross.

Fourth, another reason for changing the Red Cross to the Red Crescent is because the Koran, as already noted earlier, denies the historicity of Christ's crucifixion. Thus, if Muslims were to tolerate the symbol of the cross in their midst, much less accept what it signifies, in their minds they would be denying the infallibility of the Koran.

Islamic *Zakat* and Jihad

In recent years, it has been reported that a number of Islamic *zakat* organizations, both in and out of the United States, have been engaged in collecting and dispersing money to support jihad (terrorist) activities such as Hamas, Islamic Jihad, Hezbollah, and the al-Qaeda. In October 2001, the United States Treasury Department froze assets of numerous Muslims and Islamic organizations believed to have been specifically linked to the al-Qaeda terrorists. The Wafa Humanitarian Organization and the Al Rashid Trust were reported as suspect of "furnishing to al-Qaeda or other Islamic terrorist organizations."[62] The Al Rashid Trust, which says it aids widows and orphans of Islamic martyrs, according to one news report, was believed to have given money to suicide bombers. In fact, the Al Rashid Trust recently had one of its clerks in a Pakistan office boast: "We have 800,000 [individuals] signed up with us to fight the jihad against Americans." [63]

The Islamic American Relief Agency in Columbia, Missouri, has reportedly given money to groups in Africa "that employed people with suspected ties to terrorist groups, including Osama bin Laden's al-Qaeda network."[64] Some of the *zakat* organizations operate under aliases and out of offices in Saudi Arabia, Pakistan, Jordan, Kuwait, and the United Arab

Emirates. The Wafa Humanitarian Organization has reportedly used at least four aliases in order to disguise its deviant efforts.[65]

Acting under the authority of "Executive Order 13224, Blocking Terrorist Property," President Bush on December 4, 2001, froze the assets of The Holy Land Foundation for Relief and Development, Beit Al-Mal Holdings, and Al-Aqsa Islamic Bank. This action was taken because all three organizations had links to Hamas, a militant offshoot of the Muslim Brotherhood, an organization founded in 1928 in Egypt. Hamas is a well-known Islamic terrorist group that has admitted responsibility for suicide bombing attacks in Israel and, at the time of the president's Executive Order, had killed two Americans. The Holy Land Foundation for Relief and Development, headquartered in Richardson, Texas, raises millions of dollars annually through its *zakat* committees and other charitable organizations that are part of Hamas, which is dedicated to total destruction of Israel. Beit Al-Mal Holdings and Al-Aqsa Islamic Bank also had Hamas connections.[66]

Organizations that purportedly exist to provide alms and charity, but also channel money to terrorist groups may seem highly incongruous to most Westerners who have been influenced by the Christian ethic. But according to Islamic doctrine, such use of *zakat* money is not incongruous, for to do so is consistent with its philosophy of jihad. This was recently corroborated by Rabid Haddad, a Muslim leader in Ann Arbor, Michigan. He was charged with helping fund terrorism, and upon being questioned in court concerning his activities, he replied that jihad can mean doing good or fighting for what Muslims see as good, "'and that doing charity work was an example of that.'"[67]

Conclusion

There is a great divide between Christian charity (*caritas*) and Islamic *zakat*. Christian charity is a voluntary act of love to help the poor and indigent, prompted by what God has done for mankind in Christ's redemptive act on the cross and the open tomb on Easter Day. Islamic *zakat,* on the other hand, is not a voluntary act of love for the poor and indigent, but rather an act that helps the poor and indigent as a result of being compelled to pay a fixed percentage of one's annual income. As was noted earlier, giving and helping the needy when it is done on a non-voluntary basis, as done with Islamic *zakat* as well as with governmental welfare, is not charity, but the welfare of socialism.

There is also the unfortunate fact that *zakat* at times is used by Muslims to further violent jihad activities. Given the ethics of Islam's founder Muhammad and the Koran, *zakat* monies may be (and often are) directed to conduct war-like activities to advance religious and political goals, goals that are totally foreign to the values espoused by Jesus Christ and his followers who fashioned early Christianity.

Finally, historically, Christian charity, in order to be genuine charity, had to be voluntary giving that went to any and all in need, not just to Christians. However, Muslim *zakat* is not only based on compulsory giving, but its contributions go only to Muslims. Non-Muslims are not eligible for *zakat*.[68]

6

THE CRUSADES AND THE REST OF THE STORY

"Facts are stubborn things" (John Adams)

The verb "crusade," as Thomas F. Madden, a historian of the Crusades, has rightly noted, is a modern, not a medieval, word.[1] The same is true with the noun "Crusades." The latter is commonly used to refer to the European military expeditions in the Middle Ages that were launched in November of 1095 with a sermon by Pope Urban II at the Council of Clermont (France) and ended in 1291 with the fall of Acre. Both verb and noun are derived from the Latin *crucesignati*—"people known by the sign of the cross."[2]

For some time, the word "crusade" has been a highly negative term—both in the West and in the Middle East. The negative connotation of this word is currently being reinforced by many Muslims and by some of their defenders. They accuse the United States and Britain of being modern "Crusaders" in their response to the Islamist terrorist attacks on September 11, 2001. There is a certain twisted logic in renewing the negative tone of the word Crusades by applying it to the Americans and the British fighting terrorism, for it was not they who destroyed the lives of nearly 3,000 people on that tragic day. It was the militant Muslims.

Even before the events of September 11, many in the West have for some time had primarily a pejorative understanding of the medieval Crusades. They believe the Crusaders were evil because they fought the "peace-loving" Muslims in Palestine and neighboring areas in the Middle Ages. This has a lot to do with the fact that there is much about the

Crusades of the Middle Ages that has not been told in history books and articles.

When one compares what is written in encyclopedias about the Crusades vis-à-vis the Muslim jihads, it is amazing to see the difference in terms of space given to these two topics. The 15th edition of *The Encyclopedia Britannica*, published in 2000, has 13 pages on the Crusades and nothing on jihad. *The Encyclopedia Americana*, published in 2003, has five pages on the Crusades and 22 lines on jihad on a split-column page. As Madden has said, "the crusades are quite possibly the most misunderstood event in European history."[3] In short, Westerners have not heard "the rest of the story," to use an expression common to Paul Harvey.

Muslim Holy Wars Preceding the Crusades

Chapter 2 mentioned of some of the many conquests and foreign wars (jihads) that the Arab Muslims engaged in immediately following Muhammad's death in 632. These Islamic jihads, it will be recalled, included invading Palestine in 633, Yarmouk in 636, Syria in 337, Jerusalem in 638, Egypt in 641, Persia in 642, the northern part of Africa in 643, and Spain in 711. Then another invasion took place, but it failed to gain a foothold in France in the Battle of Poitiers/Tours in 732.

Even after 732 the Islamic aggressions continued, spreading to other parts of Europe. Sicily was invaded in 827 and eventually conquered in 902. In 846 the Muslims entered the city of Rome, where they plundered the churches of St. Peter and St. Paul. In addition, there were intermittent attacks against Christians in Spain during the 10th and 11th centuries. And in the Levant, the Battle of Manzikert occurred in 1071 with the Muslims defeating the Byzantine Christians. In 1091 Muslims drove the Christian priests out of Jerusalem.

This brief list does not include many other jihads, for example, as noted earlier, the seven failed attempts to capture

Constantinople, the citadel of Eastern Christianity, between 668 and 798.[4] These attacks and invasions were Islamic jihads ("holy wars"), and all they occurred long before the Crusades were ever launched in 1095.

The numerous Islamic attacks and conquests inflicted on Christians, first in the Middle East and then in Europe, virtually over a period of 500 years, were more than enough reason, humanly speaking, for the Christians to launch the Crusades as a defensive measure in 1095. Unfortunately, these numerous attacks that preceded the Crusades are not mentioned in school textbooks; neither are they noted in books that specifically deal with the history of the Crusades. Instead, there are numerous historians who try to lay the entire fault of the Crusades on the conscience of Christians. One such historian is Kenneth Cragg, who in his book *The Arab Christian: A History of the Middle East* (1992) tries to put Christians on a guilt-trip regarding the Crusades by saying: "The image of them [the Crusades] is one that no century since has been able to exorcise." Comments like this one (and there many others in a similar vein) fail to note, as Serge Trifkovic has rightly pointed out, that "the Crusades were a military response of Christian Europe to over three centuries of Muslim aggression against Christian lands, the systemic mistreatment of the indigenous Christian population of those lands, and harassment of Christian pilgrims."[5]

Other Factors that Prompted the Crusades

All too many historians also fail to mention that when Emperor Alexius in the East asked Pope Urban II in the West to help him recruit soldiers for the Byzantine army, the objective of the Crusades was to roll back the Turkish (Muslim) conquest of Asia Minor,[6] as well as to keep Christianity from being completely destroyed. Historian Kenneth Scott Latourette corroborates this fact: "As originally conceived ... Pope Urban

II declared the objective to be the rescue of the holy places in Palestine [and] the defence [sic] of the Christians of the East against the Moslems, and rolling back the tide of Mohammedan conquest."[7]

In support of these observations, Bernard Lewis, a modern authority on Islam, says the Crusades took place in large measure to recover lost lands of Christendom in the East.[8] Similarly, Roland Armour, in *Islam, Christianity, and the West: a Troubled History* (2003), notes that one of the major reasons for the Crusades was to restore the Holy Land to Christians.[9] Evidently the Muslims at that time understood this, too, which helps explain why they for a long time did not see the Crusades in the same way that they do today. In this context, W. Montgomery Watt, a British authority on Muslims, says: "For the Muslims in general the Crusades were little more than a frontier incident—a continuation of the kind of fighting that had been going on in Syria and Palestine for the last half century."[10] Similarly, Bernard Lewis also states that the Crusades, which for sometime in Western history books have been portrayed as an example of Western imperialism, were initially not seen in that light, neither by Christians nor by Muslims.[11] Lewis notes that Arabic historiography of the Crusade era does not even use the terms "Crusades" or "Crusaders." Instead, says Lewis, Arab historians used "Franks," sometimes "infidels," and only rarely "the Christians."[12] Another scholar of the Crusades says "it was not until the mid-nineteenth century that Arabs even coined the term *Hurub al-Salibiyya* to refer to the Wars of the Crusades."[13] Unfortunately, this longstanding view and different view of the Crusades has become lost, and few, if any, in the West know of it.

Another factor behind the Crusades that receives little attention today is that they sought to provide protection for the many Christian pilgrims who trekked to the Holy Land from Europe and Asia Minor. The city of Jerusalem, for instance, which had once belonged to the Byzantine Christians, had become as important to Christians as Mecca is to Muslims.

Given this historically verifiable context for the Crusades, it is not an exaggeration to call them a *defensive war*, as Thomas Madden does.[14] Being a defensive war, they therefore cannot be called a venture in imperialism, as is often done. Here the words of British historian Paul Johnson come to mind: "The Crusades, far from being an outrageous prototype of Western imperialism, as taught in most schools, were a mere episode in a struggle that has lasted 1,400 years, and were one of the few occasions when Christians took the offensive to regain 'occupied territories' of the Holy Land."[15]

What is not commonly known today is that in the Middle Ages Palestine was seen as belonging to the Christians, not the Jews; thus, the Crusaders merely sought to regain it from the Muslims who had taken it from them by military might in the seventh century. It is also important that, nearly 400 years after the Muslim conquests in Palestine, they destroyed the Church of the Holy Sepulcher in Jerusalem in 1009 under Caliph el Hakim.[16] Thus, when the Crusaders arrived in the Levant a hundred years after 1009, they merely tried to regain what once was theirs.

Islam's Jihads after the Crusades

The Muslim jihads (their "crusades") did not end in 1291, when the Christian Crusades essentially ended with the fall of Acre. There is a noticeable blindness in the West today regarding this historical fact. As Paul Fregosi has shown: "History has largely bypassed the Muslim attacks on and invasions of Europe that lasted from the seventh to the twentieth centuries, but has remained transfixed on the Christian Crusades to the Holy Land that lasted only from the eleventh to the thirteenth century. We could say that the historical perspective is greatly out of focus" (*JW*, 24).

Less than 50 years after the Crusades ended, the Ottoman Muslims launched numerous attacks on Christians in southeastern Europe. Chapter 2 has already provided some details of the repeated attacks made by Muslim forces throughout this region. After defeat in their conquest of Vienna in 1683, when Germans and Poles joined forces to help defend this city, other jihads by the Turks increasingly became jihads in retreat. However, jihads did continue elsewhere. This is perhaps most notable in the massacring of Armenian Christians in Turkey and neighboring regions in the 1890's and into the 1920's (see Chapter 2).

In reality, Islamic jihads have been ongoing since Muhammad himself launched his numerous jihads in the seventh century. Despite the West's apparent blindness to the truth, the numerous atrocities and killings of non-Muslims during the last decade or two in Israel, Lebanon, Sudan, Afghanistan, Nigeria, Indonesia and the Balkans in Europe are pertinent examples. And the Islamist terrorist acts that erupted in the United States on September 11, 2001, are also part of militant Islam's ongoing jihads.

Why Not the Rest of the Story?

Why have historians, almost without exception, reported a one-sided story of the Crusades by omitting the fact that the major objective of the Crusades was primarily to regain the territories Christians once possessed in Palestine before the Arab Muslims took them from by force? Why have they not reported that Muslims forcefully occupied the Iberian peninsula for 800 years in contrast to the Crusades, which lasted less than 200 years? Why have historians omitted mentioning the numerous Muslim jihads that took place over several centuries even after the Crusades had ended? Why have history books given the impression that the Crusades were the epitome of evil and unprovoked aggression on Muslims?

Undoubtedly, this one-sided portrayal helps explain why well-intentioned individuals, many who call themselves Christians, are appalled regarding the Crusades. They have never heard the rest of the story.

As Paul Fregosi has shown, the Muslim jihads have effected and engulfed far more countries, and for much longer, than did the Crusades in the Middle East. The Crusades were only eight in number, compared to numerous, ongoing Islamic jihads before and after the Crusades. As already noted, Muslims invaded and occupied Spain for 800 years; Portugal, 600; Greece, 500; Bulgaria, 500; Rumania, 400; Serbia, 400; Sicily, 300; and Hungary, 150. In addition, the Muslims fought in Austria, Italy, Malta, Cyprus, Armenia, Poland, Georgia, Ukraine, and parts of Russia. The Crusaders primarily sought to regain lost territories, whereas the Muslims, even after the Crusades, wanted occupy Europe in order to Islamize it. Thus, Bosnia, Kosovo, and Albania today are largely Islamic. As Fregosi also reports, it took Hungary 200 years to recover from the devastation and ravages the Muslims caused on their soil (*JW*, 23–24).

Finally, "The Muslim occupations of Europe have left a far deeper and more lasting trace of their former influence than any of the European occupations of Islamic North Africa and the Near and Middle East. There are still large Muslim populations in the Balkans, sometimes the majority, as in Albania and Bosnia" (*JW*, 25).

The Crusades and Western Guilt

Given the widespread, pejorative view of the Crusades, it is not surprising that recently many in the West, including Christians, have been seeing the Crusades as the zenith of all historical evils. The negative slant on the Crusades has even prompted some Christians recently to believe they needed to apologize to Muslims for the Crusades. Perhaps these

148

Christians are concerned with what Christ taught, for instance, in The Lord's Prayer: "Forgive us our trespasses, as we forgive those who trespass against us." Recognition for the need of repentance and forgiveness is a definite mark Christianity has left on Western societies, and it may be, at least in part, the reason why many Westerners or Christians have in recent years apologized to Muslims for the Crusades in which their ancestors participated 900 years ago.

These recent apologies contrast sharply with the beliefs and behavior of Muslims, for in Islam's theology there is no recognition of the need to repent and ask for forgiveness. That is not a Muslim doctrine. Unlike the Bible, the Koran does not teach its adherents to repent and ask for forgiveness, even though it says Allah is "the beneficent, the merciful." What a Muslim does in the name of Allah is always in accord with Allah's will, and so there is no need to apologize or to ask for forgiveness. Hence, Muslim or Arab historians, when writing about the Crusades, do not fault Muslims for what their ancestors did in the Crusades, nor does one find any Muslims making apologies.

Recently, some have interpreted the words of Pope John Paul II in March 2000 as an apology to the Islamic world for the Christian involvement in the Crusades, even though he did not specifically mention the Crusades. Responding to this apology by the pope, perceived as referring to the Crusades, Oriana Fallaci chastised him by asking:

> Tell me, Holy Father: Is true that some time ago you asked the Sons of Allah to forgive the Crusaders that Your predecessors fought to take back the Holy Sepulcher? But did the sons of Allah ever ask you to be forgiven for having taken the Holy Sepulcher? Did they ever apologize for having subjected over Seven centuries the super Catholic Iberian Peninsula, the whole of Portugal and three quarters of Spain, so that if Isabella of Castille and

Ferdinand of Aragon had not chased them out in 1490 [sic]
we all would speak Arabic?[17]

Four years before Pope John Paul II made this
generalized apology, a group of Evangelical Christians from the
United States and Western Europe unambiguously apologized
for the Crusades. Under the name "The Reconciliation Walk,"
this group set out on Easter Sunday in 1996 from Cologne,
Germany, one of the places from which the first Crusaders
started their long march in 1096. Members of this group
followed the route the Crusaders took to Istanbul, where they
formally apologized to a Muslim imam. Then on July 15, 1999,
this group's walk reached its terminal point in Jerusalem, where
its members (about 500) apologized to a Jewish rabbi, an
Islamic mufti, and a Greek Orthodox Patriarch. Before arriving
in Jerusalem, the group had traveled through Turkey, Lebanon,
and Syria—all regions where the Crusaders once fought.[18]

A few comments are in order regarding the matter of
Christians making apologies for the Crusades. First, is there a
biblical or Christian requirement to make such apologies for the
Crusades, as the people of the Reconciliation Walk did? It has
been shown that, given the numerous attacks (jihads) Christians
had experienced, the Crusades were a defensive response and
therefore a just war, consistent with St. Augustine's concept of
a just war. According to Jonathon Riley-Smith, a British expert
in the history of the Crusades, this principle "applied to the
crusade no less than to any war. ... "[19] This being true, there is
no need to apologize for the Crusades anymore than there is
need for American or European Christians to apologize for their
involvement fighting the Nazis in World War II. If Christian
soldiers engage in individual acts of evil off the battlefield, or
engage in wrongful actions even on the battlefield (such as
massacring helpless prisoners or civilians), they not only need
to apologize, but also repent and ask God for forgiveness. But

for merely fighting a defensive war Christians have no need to apologize or ask forgiveness, no more so than asking forgiveness for the sins they daily commit as sinful beings in their capacity as farmers, laborers, businessmen, teachers, parents, and so on.

Second, to kill in the name of Jesus Christ is always wrong. But that is not what the Crusades were about. As already noted, their objective was not to kill in Christ's name, but primarily to defend Christian citizens and to regain lost Christian sites. To be sure, many individual Crusaders engaged in sinful, evil acts. Some did so by plundering, raping women, murdering innocent civilians, and enslaving citizens. Many of these evil activities, however, were undoubtedly committed by men who were not Christians, but pseudo Christians.

Third, while Christian descendants of the Crusaders may express compassionate courtesy to others in the event of unfortunate circumstances (e.g., "We are sorry to hear what happened to you."), there is no biblical or Christian doctrine that one must apologize or ask for forgiveness for the sinful deeds done by someone else or by some group, even one's own ancestors. If there is no biblical or Christian requirement to apologize for someone else's sins, what value is there in doing it, other than using it as a mere political ploy? Thus, the apologies and requests for forgiveness that were recently made by well-meaning Christians were primarily political or diplomatic gestures, not biblically required Christian apologies.

Fourth, would Christians of the Reconciliation Walk have taken the time and made the effort to travel to Turkey, Syria, Lebanon, and eventually to Jerusalem to ask for forgiveness had they learned that Muslims invaded and conquered as well as slaughtered thousands of Christians, not only before the Crusades but also for several centuries after the Crusades had ended? Those well-intentioned Christians who asked for forgiveness did not know the rest of the story. Much

151

of the Western world, including countless other devout Christians, do not know the rest of story either.

Unintended Consequences of Crusade Apologies

Sociological research shows that for virtually every intended social action there are usually unintended effects or consequences. Thus, the well-meant apologies and requests for forgiveness recently made by misinformed Christians will have some unintended consequences, and not necessarily favorable ones.

First, militant Muslims, who do not have the concepts of repentance and forgiveness in their theological lexicon, will most likely not consider the apologies as something that they should reciprocate. Rather, they will view them as signs of Western weakness; hence, it is likely that they will feel encouraged to become even more bellicose in their efforts to extend the practices and the boundaries of Islam.

There is no evidence that the militant Muslim posture toward the West, which has been in existence for centuries, has mitigated or diminished recently in the time since the people from the Reconciliation Walk apologized and asked for forgiveness, or since the nonspecific apology Pope John Paul II issued. These efforts did not soften the hearts of Osama bin Laden, al-Qaeda, Hezbollah, Islamic Jihad, Hamas, or other zealous Islamists who follow the Koran's command to fight the infidels. Nor did these efforts have an impact on those Muslims who carried out the attacks on September 11.

Second, apologies by prominent figures may potentially result in the West uncritically accepting the Muslim propaganda that the Crusades were imperialistic efforts to colonize the Middle East. In regard to this matter, much of the Muslim world has learned that this kind of propaganda is successful, so successful that criticism of Muslim tactics have largely been muted in the West for fear of being called modern Crusaders.

As a result, Western political leaders today only speak negatively of "radical Muslims" and even call Islam a "peaceful religion," rather than pointing out the radical statements found in the Koran and the Hadith that inspired the recent terrorist acts by militant Muslims.

Third, apologizing to Muslims helps them ignore the numerous jihads they inflicted on Christians in the West for 400 years before the Crusades had even begun. As Paul Fregosi has remarked, because historians have in effect faulted the West for the Crusades and bypassed the Muslim jihads from the seventh to the 20th century, "Muslims are obsessed with the Christian Crusades, but have forgotten their own, much grander Jihad" (*JW*, 24).

Fourth, many in the West, including historians, tend to believe the Muslim propaganda and thereby give the impression that only Muslims suffered great pain, sorrow, and misery during the Crusades. Thus it is extremely rare to read something similar to the following statement in a history book or article: "Of course, Muslims [were] not the only ones to have suffered at the hands of the crusaders."[20]

Fifth, apologizing creates and confirms a self-righteous attitude on the part of Muslims. In their minds, contrary to the facts, it is only the Christians who are to blame for the Crusades.

Sixth, apologizing strengthens and confirms countless Muslims in their desire to hate the "infidels"—a Koranic term for non-Muslims. Thus, as Madden has said: "It was the West that taught the Middle East [the Muslims] to hate the crusades."[21]

The Crusades and the Role of the Church

The fact that Pope Urban II in November 1095 called for the Crusades, responding to Emperor Alexius' request from Constantinople to protect the Christians in the East, does not absolve him for having acted as head of state, even though the Crusades were a defensive action, as mentioned earlier. The Crusades should have been launched by the appropriate head of state, not the head of the Christian church in the West. St. Paul says, the state (government) indeed "does not bear the sword in vain; he is the servant of God to execute his wrath on the wrongdoer" (Romans 13:4). Muslims had for centuries (from the eighth through the eleventh centuries) been engaged in widespread violent aggression, not only in Spain (711–1095), but also in southeastern Europe and in the Middle East, where they often massacred Christians and Jews and conquered territories largely inhabited by Christians.

Responding to similar situations, St. Augustine (354–430) in the fifth century taught that Christians could rightly fight to defend themselves when attacked because such actions constituted a just war. But nowhere did he say that declaring such a war was the function of the church. Thus, the pope, as head of the Latin church, assumed a role not advocated in the New Testament or by Augustine in his just-war treatise. In a similar vein, even though it was 500 years after the Crusades began, Martin Luther argued it was not the prerogative of the church or its clergy to take up the sword against the menacing Ottoman Muslims, who were threatening to capture Vienna and other parts of the West in 1529. That role, he argued, belonged to the state alone, for war was a secular matter, according to his treatise "On War Against The Turk."[22] Briefly put, the church has only God's command to fight with the sword of the spirit (verbal persuasion on the basis of God's Word), not with the sword or scimitar of steel, as Islam does. If the church violates this command, it no longer functions as the church.

Hence, when Pope John Paul II made his veiled apology in March 2000, he would have been far more in tune with Christian theology had he apologized for Pope Urban II usurping the role of the head of state when he launched the

Crusades in 1095, instead of giving many the impression that he apologized for a war that was defensive and just.

The One-sided Argument of Western Colonialism

One does not have to read a great deal of Muslim writings to soon discover that a common tactic used by many Muslims, and by their apologists, is to accuse the West of colonialist impositions on Islamic nations. As recent as November 29, 2003, *NewsMax.Com* quoted Professor Khaled Abou Al-Fadl, whom President George W. Bush appointed to the Commission on International Religious Freedom, who rehashed this accusation when he said that key figures in the Bush administration "hold beliefs that accompanied colonialism's entrance to the Muslim countries in the 19th century."[23]

To be sure, as Fregosi has noted, "many Muslim countries for more than a century became colonies and protectorates of Britain, France, Spain, Italy, Holland, and Russia" (*JW*, 22). This Western colonialism, however, did not really begin until the 19th century, long after the Muslim Turks had subjected numerous Eastern European countries (Hungary, Greece, Rhodes, Cyprus, and the Balkans) to their Islamic colonialism. Thus, Islamic "Turkey can rightfully be said to have been the first major colonial power, well before Spain, long considered the inaugurator of the colonial race with its occupation of Hispaniola after the discovery of America by Columbus in 1492" (*JW*, 329).

Ironically, it is the Westerners who, in a Christian-like manner, commonly assume all guilt concerning the colonialist accusations Muslims fling at them. While some of the accusations contain some truth, it is, however, even more true that the rest of the story is largely unknown, just as it is unknown in regard to the Crusades. Hence, Westerners, including many Christians, would do well to remember that

155

"Western colonization and conquest of nearby Muslim lands lasted approximately 130 years, from the 1830s to the 1960s. Muslim colonization of nearby European lands, on the other hand, lasted 1,300 years, from the 600s to the mid-1960s," as Fregosi shows. He continues, "Yet, strangely, it is the Muslims, the Arabs and the Moors, to be precise, who are the most bitter about colonialism and the humiliations to which they have been subjected, and it is the Europeans who harbor the shame and guilt. It should be the other way around" (*JW*, 25).

Some Positive Effects of the Crusades

In light of the negative image the Crusades have in today's world, some may see it disingenuous to speak of the Crusades having yielded positive effects. To note briefly some of the positive effects or benefits the Crusades produced is not to ignore St. Paul's advice, namely, that Christians may not do evil so good might come (Romans 3:8). To cite the good that happened as a result of the Crusades is merely to note that God can and often does bring good out of very flawed and even evil human efforts.

Briefly put, the Crusades enhanced commercial trade between the East and the West, benefiting both. The West obtained a number of new products from the Levant. The realm of food items included sesame, carob, rice, lemons, melons, apricots ("Damascus plums"), shallots, spices, cloves, and syrup. In clothing and fashions, Europeans received cottons, damasks from Damascus, muslin (cloth from Mosul, a city in present-day Iraq), and diapers from Byzantium. Household furnishings were improved with rugs, carpets, tapestries, glass mirrors, certain pottery items, and new colors and dyes. In the area of language the West borrowed a number of Arabic words, such as tariff, admiral, amulet, arsenal, alcove, carafe, cotton, caravan, elixir, lute, mattress, sofa, and talisman, to cite only some.[24] And, of course, exporting many of these products greatly improved the economic conditions of Islamic countries of the Middle East.

Conclusion

The Crusades did indeed violate some basic Christian principles and values, both in terms of how they were first launched and by the countless brutal, inhuman acts carried out by many Crusaders, who often went beyond the rules of fighting a just and defensive war. But the Crusades were not an imperialistic or colonial venture. Had the Muslims not attacked, invaded, and conquered numerous lands and sites that Christians possessed for several centuries before the Crusades, there likely would never have been any attempts on the part of the Christians in the West to fight the followers of Muhammad in the Middle East. Nor did the Crusades institutionalize any belief that killing in the name of Jesus is an acceptable practice for Christians. Even when war is fought as a defensive measure, it is still an act stained with sin, as are all human acts since of the fall of man in the Garden of Eden.

7

LIBERTY AND JUSTICE

"People never give up their liberties except under some delusion" (Edmund Burke)

The liberties and justice currently enjoyed in Western societies and some non-Western societies, are increasingly, but erroneously, seen as the products of benevolent, secular governments. There is little or no awareness that the liberties, rights, and justice presently found in free societies, mostly in the West, are to a great degree the result of Christianity's longstanding influence. The architects of civic freedom and justice go back to men like St. Ambrose, Archbishop Stephen Langton, John Locke, Baron de Montesquieu, Thomas Jefferson, and James Madison. All of them drew extensively from the Judeo-Christian perspective regarding humanity's God-given freedoms, which for most of human history had really never been tried, much less institutionalized.[1]

No One Is Above the Law

One of the oldest means of depriving individuals of liberty and justice was for the top ruler (often a king or emperor) of a country to set himself above the law. Functioning above the law meant he was the law, thus curtailing and obliterating the natural rights and freedoms of the country's citizens. The pages of history are filled with examples of such rulers. Here we recall some of the Hebrew kings in the Old Testament, most of the Roman emperors, and the Muslim caliphs or sultans. All deprived people of their freedom, and in the process they often expunged the lives of individuals who opposed—or were perceived as opposed—to their ambitions or policies. Whether the perceived individuals were really a threat

158

to the welfare of the nation was irrelevant. What a ruler wanted is what a ruler got. These kings, emperors, or caliphs were not accountable to anyone for their arbitrary and often bloody acts.

Two or More Witnesses

More than a thousand years before the birth of Christ, Moses commanded the Israelites not to execute anyone for an alleged "crime" without the testimony of at least two witnesses. "A single witness shall not suffice against a person for any crime or for any wrong in connection with any offense that he has committed. Only on the evidence of two witnesses or of three witnesses shall a charge be established" (Deuteronomy 19:15). This biblical requirement became a vital component in the principle that "no man is above the law." Barring false witnesses, it checked arbitrary, capricious acts on the part of rulers or other officials. It told the accuser: "You must have at least two witnesses in order to convict the accused." This meant that the accuser, even a high-ranking official, could not arbitrarily incarcerate or execute the accused; the accuser was subject to the law and could not act as though he were above it.

Requiring at least two witnesses is also mandated in the New Testament for use in ecclesiastical matters. Matthew cites Jesus' instructions regarding an erring Christian. If such a person, upon the urging of a fellow Christian, does not repent, then two or more witnesses are to confront the unrepentant individual, and if he still refuses to repent, then he is to appear before an assembly of Christians. If he continues to persist in his sin, he is then to be excommunicated and treated as a pagan or despised tax collector (Matthew 18:15–17).

Today, the criminal and civil justice systems of Great Britain, the United States, Canada, and many other Western countries employ this Judeo-Christian requirement of having witnesses testify in a court of law where the accused has the right to see his accusers (two or more witnesses) before he can be convicted. In British and American jurisprudence, witnesses are part of what is legally called "due process of law," a concept that first appeared in the 14th century under King Edward III.

St. Ambrose v. the Roman Emperor

It is not commonly known or recognized that Bishop Ambrose was an early architect of liberty and justice. Historical discussions of the growth and development of liberty and justice in the Western world fail to mention his contribution. But he was really the first to apply the principle that no man is above the law, even though it was God's law, "You shall not murder," that was in question.

In A.D. 390 the city of Thessalonica, Greece, experienced a riot that aroused the anger of Theodosius I, a Christian emperor. In response, he overreacted and massacred 7,000 people, most of whom were innocent. Bishop Ambrose, located in Milan, which was also where the emperor resided, did not turn a blind eye to the emperor's vindictive and unjust behavior. He asked him to repent of his massacre. When the emperor refused, the bishop excommunicated him. After about one month of stubborn resistance, Theodosius prostrated himself and repented in the presence of others in Ambrose's cathedral, bringing tears of joy to his fellow Christians.[2]

Ambrose, in effect, told Theodosius: "You are not above the law, even though you are the emperor." It is unfortunate that this confrontation has often been portrayed by historians as a struggle between the church and the state. The facts show otherwise, for Ambrose's letter to the emperor shows that he was seriously concerned about the emperor's spiritual welfare in that he had placed himself above God's moral law.

Today, modern democracies and attorneys take pride in saying that no one is above the law, but they fail to note that this landmark of liberty and justice, now commonly institutionalized in most Western societies, was first

160

implemented by a courageous, uncompromising Christian bishop some 1,600 years ago. In a sense, Ambrose also set the stage for the Magna Carta that followed some 800 years later in England.

The Magna Carta

When the barons forced King John to sign the Magna Carta ("large chart") in 1215 at Runnymede outside of London, they obtained a number of rights they did not have before this historic occasion. Specifically, the charter granted the following: (1) justice could no longer be sold or denied to freemen who were under authority of barons; (2) no taxes could be levied without representation; (3) no one would be imprisoned without a trial; and (4) property could not be taken from the owner without just and fair compensation.[3] These achievements were monumental and history-making. The era of the king being above the law had effectively come to an end in England. Commonly this document is rightly hailed as ushering in British liberty and justice. Some 500 years later it also served as a courageous precedent to the American patriots to establish liberty and justice in America. The early advocates of American independence often referred to the Magna Carta in support of their arguments.

The Magna Carta lifted civilization to a higher plateau, not only in England but eventually in other parts of the Western world, and it had a lot to do with its Christian moorings. The preamble began, "John, by the grace of God ... " and stated that the charter was formulated out of "reverence for God and for the salvation of our soul and those of all our ancestors and heirs, for the honour of God and the exaltation of the Holy Church and the reform of our realm, on the advice of our reverend [church] fathers."[4]

One of the "reverend fathers" involved in the birth of the Magna Carta was Stephen Langton, Archbishop of Canterbury (credited with first dividing the Bible into chapters). Langton's involvement in the Magna Carta, together with the help of his Christian colleagues, did not, however, have the approval of Pope Innocent III, who actually suspended him for two years. The pope's opposition, of course, does not nullify the argument that the Magna Carta bears the marks of Christian influence.[5]

Finally, another Christian influence is worth noting. In 325, at the Council of Nicaea, Christian bishops wrote and adopted the Nicene Creed, a formal code of fundamental beliefs to which all Christians were expected to adhere. This was really the first time in history that a formally written document of religious beliefs had ever been issued. The pagan Greco-Romans had no formal religious creeds or confessions.[6] Although the Magna Carta was a political document, it was also a type of creed in that it showed what its formulators, as Christians (evident in the preamble), believed in regard to liberty and justice. Thus, the architects of the Magna Carta followed a precedent set by the Christian bishops at the Council of Nicaea.

Natural Law and Natural Rights in the West

The concept of natural law has a long history going back at least to the Greco-Roman philosophers several hundred years before the birth of Jesus Christ. Although these philosophers' conceptions of the natural law varied somewhat, there was one essential agreement: Natural law was understood as that process in nature by which human beings, through the use of sound reason, were able to perceive what was morally right and wrong. This natural law was seen as the eternal, unchangeable foundation of all human laws.

When Christianity came on the scene, it added an important element to the Greco-Roman view of natural law. It said natural law was not an entity by itself but part of God's created order in nature through which he made all rational

162

human beings aware of what is right and wrong. St. Paul expressed this position rather cogently when he said: "For when Gentiles [pagans], who do not have the law [Ten Commandments], by nature do what the law requires, they are a law to themselves, even though they do not have the law. They show that what the law requires is written on their hearts, while their conscience also bears witness and their conflicting thoughts accuse or perhaps excuse them" (Romans 2:14-15). With these words, it can be argued, Paul was essentially reinforcing what Moses taught the Israelites more than a thousand years before Christ when he said God's law was "in your heart, so that you can do it" (Deuteronomy 30:14).

Simply put, Paul and Moses said the natural law contains God's Ten Commandments, which, although not communicated in a visible or audible manner, tell human beings in their conscience what is right and wrong behavior. Christian theologians who followed Paul, such as Justin Martyr, St. Augustine, St. Chrysostom, Thomas Aquinas, and Martin Luther, all essentially continued to hold to the Pauline understanding of natural law. Luther maintained the Ten Commandments were the natural law stated more clearly; in response to the question of why one should then teach the Ten Commandments he answered: "Because the natural laws were never so orderly and well written as by Moses."[7]

In the 17th century the concept of natural law was applied to government in the context of people's natural rights. The physician and philosopher John Locke (1632–1703) made this application, especially in his *Two Treatises of Government* (1690). He argued that government existed merely to uphold the natural law and that governmental tyranny violated the natural rights of man. Natural rights were not given to people by kings, emperors, or governments. They belonged to the people by nature.

The American Declaration of Independence

The American Declaration of Independence is an excellent example illustrating the concept of liberty and justice. When Poland was in the process of breaking away from the tyranny of Communism in the 1980's, it was reported that this document served both as an inspiration and as a model for the seekers of liberty and justice in that country.

When Thomas Jefferson in 1776 penned the Declaration of Independence, he leaned heavily on John Locke's concept of natural rights. He even used some of Locke's phraseology, for instance, "but when a long train of abuses," and "consent of the governed."

But does the Declaration reflect a Christian influence? It does in several ways. First, the document clearly reveals its indebtedness to the Christian understanding of the natural law. The words "the Law of Nature and Nature's God" in the Declaration show this to be true. These very words were used and interpreted by the renowned English legal scholar Sir William Blackstone in the context of Christian theology in his *Commentary on the Laws of England* (1765), a work well known to the American colonists. Blackstone's work was required reading at almost all colonial colleges.[8]

Second, the Declaration of Independence specifically states that a government may be deposed when it violates people's "inalienable rights." It asserts: "Whenever any form of government becomes destructive of these ends, it is the right of the people to alter or to abolish it, and to institute new government." This concept reflected "thoroughly medieval Christian notions" that by 1776 had become "American conceptions."[9]

Third, although Jefferson was essentially a deist, he was nevertheless greatly influenced, as was Locke, by Christian thought and values. Forty years after he had scripted the Declaration of Independence, he said of the teachings of Jesus,

"A more beautiful or precious morsel of ethics I have never seen." He even created his own so-called Jefferson Bible, which contained the teachings of Jesus from the four Gospels minus Christ's miracles, to show, as he said, that "I am a real Christian."[10]

Fourth, the Declaration speaks about truths being "self evident." This particular term has Christian roots going back to the theological writings of the eighth century. To the medievalists, "self evident" knowledge, says Gary Amos, "was truth known intuitively, as direct revelation from God, without the need of proofs. This term presumed that man was created in the image of God, and it also presumed certain beliefs about man's rationality which can be traced as far back as St. Augustine in the early fifth century."[11] Amos also shows that St. Paul in the Epistle to the Romans wrote that since creation, even to the pagans, God's "invisible attributes are clearly seen" (Romans 1:20 NKJV), that is, self-evident. In the previous verse (Romans 1:19), Paul says that this truth is "plain to them" (in Greek, *phaneron estin en autos*). Thus, it is quite probable that Paul's biblical concept of "self-evident," knowingly or unknowingly, influenced Jefferson when he declared "We hold these Truths to be self-evident."

Fifth, the last paragraph of the Declaration of Independence uses the term "Supreme Judge," a term used in Locke's *The Second Treatise of Government*, where he refers to Jephthah calling God "the Judge" in Israel's fight against the Ammonites (Judges 11:27).[12] Amos says that if this term for God in the Declaration was taken from Locke's work, "then we have a direct link between the Bible and the Declaration of Independence."[13]

The Constitution of the United States

In documenting Christianity's influence on the American Constitution, heralded as the world's greatest charter of liberty and justice, it is instructive to remember the political theorist whose thinking is commonly cited as having had the greatest influence on the 39 formulators of this document. That man was the French Christian and philosopher Baron de Montesquieu (1689–1755). His imprint on the Constitution is evidenced by the American government's three branches: legislative, executive, and judicial. One historian has said that Montesquieu's book, *The Spirit of Laws* (1766), "[gave] American Constitution writers their holy writ."[14] And as is well known, Montesquieu is called "the godfather of the American Constitution."

The incorporation of Montesquieu's political theory into the American Constitution was largely the work of James Madison, the Constitution's principal architect, often referred to as "the father of the American Constitution." The Federalist Papers show that Madison borrowed extensively from Montesquieu's thinking. His indebtedness to the French philosopher's political theory reveals at least an indirect Christian influence on him. But Madison also reveals some direct Christian influence in his own political thinking. For instance, in defending his argument for the separation of powers, he reflected the Christian teaching of the fallen nature of man when he boldly asserted: "The truth [is] that all men, having power ought to be distrusted, to a certain degree."[15] And in the Federalist Papers (No. 51) he wrote: "If men were angels, no government would be necessary." These words clearly reflect the Christian doctrine of mankind's innate sinfulness. In Madison's thinking, the sinful nature of human beings required three branches of government so that each branch would keep a watchful eye on the other and thereby maintain honesty and integrity.

While many American history books have noted that the three branches of government in the United States are derived from Montesquieu's theory, none to my knowledge have ever noted that the concept of three branches ("three powers," as he called them) was influenced by his knowledge of Christianity. He saw Christian spiritual ideas as vital to a nation's liberty: "It is not enough for religion to establish a doctrine, it must also direct its influence. This the Christian religion performs in the most admirable manner, especially with respect to the doctrines of which we have been speaking. It makes us hope for a state which is the object of our belief; not for a state which we have already experienced or known."[16]   Contrasting governments under Christianity to those under Islam, Confucianism, Hinduism, and Greek paganism, he found those under Christian influence far superior in fostering liberty and justice. "The Christian religion," said he, "is a stranger to despotic power. The mildness so frequently recommended in the Gospel, is incompatible with the despotic rage with which a prince punishes his subjects, and exercises himself in cruelty."[17] Again, "[W]e shall see, that we owe to Christianity, in government, a certain political law; and in war, a certain law of nations; benefits which human nature can never sufficiently acknowledge."[18]   He defended Christianity by chiding a critic who did not "distinguish between the orders for the establishment of Christianity, and Christianity itself."[19]   It was these Christian convictions that led him to say: "There is no liberty if the judiciary power be not separated from the legislative and executive."[20]

To argue that Christian influences underlie the American quest for liberty and justice in the Declaration of Independence and in the Constitution of the United States may seem incredible to many. If so, it is largely because secular historians have given Christianity's influence, as Ellis Sandoz has noted, "short shrift in recent political discussions [in spite of the fact that] it constitutes the deepest basis for ever asserting that there ought to be democracy or self-rule by the people."[21]   The Christian values underlying the Constitution may not be well known to many Americans, and even less so to non-Americans, but they were taken for granted by America's Founding Fathers and their contemporaries. For instance, John Adams, one of the signers of the Declaration of Independence and the second president of the United States, saw the American government as "grounded on reason, morality, and the Christian religion."[22]

Given that the Declaration of Independence and the American Constitution bear the marks of Christian influence is not, however, to say they are Christian documents, like the Nicene Creed, for example. But it is to say that liberty and justice would not have occurred as they did had it not been for the Christian values that prompted and shaped the formation of these documents.

Freedom and Rights of the Individual

Advocates and loyalists of socialism, fascism, communism, and Islamic governments have a strong dislike for freedom of the individual because such freedom hampers and impedes authoritarian/totalitarian leaders from controlling the expressions and movements of its citizens. Without freedom of the individual there is no real freedom, whether it is on the economic, political, or religious level.

When one examines the essence of individual freedom, it soon becomes evident, as in many other areas of human life, that the influence of Christianity looms large. For instance, Jesus strongly emphasized the importance and the significance of the individual person when he proclaimed: "For God so loved the world that he gave his only Son, that whoever believes in him should not perish but have eternal life" (John 3:16). The word "whoever" in this passage makes it clear that no one will get to heaven unless *he* or *she*—as an *individual*—believes in the atoning merits of Jesus Christ. No one can obtain eternal life by merely belonging to a group.

168

The high value that Christianity, from its inception, placed on the individual person was in stark contrast to the Greco-Roman culture in which the individual was always subordinate to the state. Christianity's accent on the individual was a necessary condition for freedom and liberty to surface in the Magna Carta (1215); in England's Petition of Rights (1628) and Bill of Rights (1689); and, of course, in the American Bill of Rights (1791), an integral part of the American Constitution.

Political, economic, and religious freedom can only exist where there is liberty and justice for the individual. Group rights that determine an individual's rights on the basis of belonging to a given ethnic or racial group, as presently advocated by multiculturalists and by affirmative action laws, essentially nullify the rights of the individual. Group rights greatly minimize freedom of the individual in that his or her rights stem from the group; thus, if one does not belong to a given group, one's rights are greatly curtailed or even eliminated.

"Individual rights and group rights," says Balint Vazsonyi, "are mutually exclusive; we cannot have it both ways."[23] Ethnicity, race, sex, or party affiliation today are increasingly determining a person's rights. This is reminiscent of Hitler, who once said: "The individual is nothing. The group [the Nazi Party] is everything." When group rights get the upper hand, gone are the "inalienable rights" given to the individual by his Creator so admirably expressed in the American Declaration of Independence. Indeed, the great documents of liberty and justice cited in the above paragraphs know nothing of group rights, and neither does Christianity.

Individual liberty and justice are most prevalent where Christianity has the greatest impact and presence. This truth, often not known or recognized, needs to be told and retold. All freedom-loving people would do well to recall the words of Malcolm Muggeridge, once an atheist but later a strong defender of Christianity: "We must not forget," said he, "that our human rights are derived from the Christian faith. In Christian terms every single human being, whoever he or she may be, sick or well, clever or foolish, beautiful or ugly, every human being is loved by his Creator, who as the Gospels tell us, counted the hairs of his head."[24] It also worth noting that the Christian foundation for the value of the individual gives no license to selfish individualism. When personal or individual selfishness raises its ugly head, it is a serious abuse of basic Christian values.

Bringing individual freedom into the human arena has had many positive effects in the history of Western societies. For instance, the Austrian economic philosopher F. A. Hayek attributed the growth and advance of science to freedom in Western society, for it led to "the unchaining of individual energies."[25]

While freedom and rights of the individual in the West are synonymous with freedom itself, Islamic societies have a decidedly low view of individual rights. To Muslims, says Kenneth Cragg, "Individualism breeds heresy (the name for it in Islam is 'innovation,' *bida*). ... But communal convergence of mind is likely to be orthodox."[26] Similarly, Ibn Warraq states: "Individualism is not a recognized feature of Islam; instead, the collective will of the Muslim people is constantly emphasized. There is certainly no notion of individual rights, which only developed in the West, especially during the eighteenth century" (*WI*, 183).

The low regard for individual rights and freedom helps explain why Islamic countries have not been on the forefront of democracy. For without these rights democracy cannot take root, much less prosper or flourish.

Equality of Individuals

In recent years there have been a plethora of political discussions regarding equality and inequality, virtually all of them in the secular vein. Once again, as with the many other influences that Christianity has contributed to Western freedoms, the concept of equality has definite Christian roots. But the Christian concept of equality must not be confused with the Marxian concept of equality.

The biblical or Christian understanding of equality focuses solely on the spiritual equality of human beings before God. Moses told the Israelites that spiritually God "is not partial and takes no bribe" (Deuteronomy 10:17). In the New Testament, Peter told Cornelius: "God shows no partiality, but in every nation any one who fears him and does what is right is acceptable to him" (Acts 10:34). Similarly, St. Paul told the Roman Christians that "all have sinned and fall short of the glory of God" (Romans 3:23). Briefly put, all human beings are equal as fallen, sinful creatures. And when sinful individuals place their faith in God's Son, they acquire spiritual equality, as Paul assured the Christians in Galatia: "There is neither Jew nor Greek, there is neither slave nor free, there is neither male nor female; for you are all one in Christ Jesus" (Galatians 3:28).

Early Christianity's concept of spiritual equality showed itself in the fellowship of its members. They treated each other as equals in terms of male-female relationships, mutual support, and fellowship activities. Even slaves had equal access to the church's rites such as baptism, the Lord's Supper, catechetical instruction, and other activities. In time, the notion of equality was extended. Some of the extensions were not always in conformity with Christ's precepts, especially with regard to economic equality. One such example occurred in the 12th century when some Crusaders "decimated the nobles and divided their possessions."[27] They had forgotten Christ's

171

words: "Man, who made me a judge or arbitrator over you?" (Luke 12:14).

Another incident in history that sought equality, this one in the context of politics, was the attempt by the Puritans, most notably the Independents in the British Parliament during England's Civil War (1642–1645). They believed that "all Christians were, as Christians, free and equal and therefore entitled to a voice in the affairs of a Christian state."[28] After the British monarchy was restored in 1660, however, the Puritan doctrine of political equality greatly diminished until it was revived by John Locke in the 1690's. From there it drifted across the Atlantic to America, where Puritans in New England kept the doctrine alive.[29]

The desire for a broader application of equality, especially in the realm of political life, continued to grow in the Western world. Thus, Alexis de Tocqueville argued that by the 19th century there was "greater equality of condition in Christian countries at the present day than there has been at any previous time, in any part of the world."[30]

As many Americans know, the American desire for equality is even enshrined in the Constitution of the United States. For instance, the formulators of the Constitution in 1787 stipulated in Section 9 that "No title of nobility shall be granted by the United States." The formulators also stated that the office of the President had to be "a natural born citizen" of the United States. Apparently the Constitution's designers wanted to avoid all semblance of European-like aristocracy, an old symbol of inequality. And given that most of the formulators came from a Christian background, Christianity's concept of equality undoubtedly played a role in the wording of these two parts in the Constitution.

Tocqueville, the French analyst of American equality, argued that "equality pushed to the furthest extent, may be confounded with freedom."[31] Insightfully, he added: "The taste which men have for liberty and that which they feel for equality are, in fact, two different things."[32] These words indicate that communist nations, which after Tocqueville's time, tried to implement widespread equality—for instance, "economic equality" in Cuba, China, and the former Soviet Union— invariably sacrificed individual freedom. In these communist countries, people lost much of their personal freedoms such as the freedom of speech, privacy rights, and the right to own private property. Such "equality" no longer has any relationship to Christianity's concept of equality. This is one reason why communism can rightfully be called a Christian heresy.

Muhammad's Medina Covenant

Muslims who argue that Islam is superior to the West in regard to freedom sometimes refer to Muhammad's Medina Covenant as the "world's first written constitution." The Medina Covenant (a k a the Medina Constitution) was an agreement—really a peace treaty—Muhammad made in Medina in about 622 with warring tribes of the Medina area shortly after he arrived from Mecca. The bellicose tribes or clans were the Muhajirun (emigrants of Mecca who came with Muhammad), the Ansar (two local clans in Medina), and some Jewish and Arab tribes.[33] According to the ninth century Muslim authority Ibn Ishaq who published *The Life of Muhammad,* these tribes or clans, as a result of the Medina Covenant, became "one community (*umma*) to the exclusion of all men."[34] A few comments are in order regarding the Medina Covenant.

First, even if one grants that this document was a constitution, it was not the first written constitution, as some Muslims refer to it. Two centuries before Muhammad was born, the Syrian Christians in about 375 composed The Apostolic Constitutions. This Christian document set forth

173

ordinances in regard to how Christians and their churches were to govern themselves.

Second, the document has also been hailed as an example of democracy. However, there is no wording in any of the 47 clauses (some versions have 52) that either mentions or implies any democratic processes. In fact, one clause sounds decidedly undemocratic. It states: "Whenever you differ about a matter it must be referred to God and Muhammad." This statement sounds more like a theocracy than a democracy. It stands in stark contrast to the Magna Carta, which specifically denied the king any such right.

Third, compared to the Magna Carta, the Medina Covenant says nothing about basic civil rights. In fact, the Covenant does not even hint at the most significant components of liberty and justice—namely, whether an accused person maybe imprisoned without a trial—nor does it say anything about the accused being judged by his peers. Had concerns like these been part of the Medina Covenant, Muslim laws and jurisprudence might not have become the oppressive instruments they are under the Shariah laws in many Islamic countries.

Liberty and Justice Under Islam's Shariah (Sacred Law)

In 1981, Muslim officials from Islamic countries assembled in Cairo and drafted a Universal Human Rights Declaration (UHRD), a document that ostensibly gives Muslims and non-Muslims liberty and justice. In 1990, the nine-year-old document was slightly revised. The revised version, which consists of 25 articles, has been touted as a great humanitarian achievement. It talks about the right to life, safety from bodily harm, protecting a person's name and honor, women being equal to men, humans being born free, the right to live in security (including one's religion), equality before the law, the right to privacy, and so on. All of this sounds good until one

174

takes a close look and reads some of the qualifying statements. For instance, Article 24 states: "All the rights and freedoms stipulated in this Declaration are subject to the Islamic Shariah." Article 25 reads: "The Islamic Shariah is the only source of reference for the explanation or clarification of any of the articles of this Declaration." Simply stated, all human rights and liberties in the Declaration are subordinated to Shariah, the holy law of Islam. Recently, Irshad Manji, a Canadian Muslim who calls herself a "Refusenik," says the 1990 Cairo document is a "specious human rights charter."[35]

The Nature of Shariah

This Islamic Declaration does not remove any of the chasm-wide divide between Western societies and Muslim countries in regard to liberty and justice. An examination of the role the Shariah plays in Islamic countries makes this quite evident, and thus it must not be forgotten that for all true-believing Muslims the Shariah is unequivocally important, every bit as important as the Koran itself. These laws have a two-fold objective: one, to regulate man's relationship to Allah, and two, to regulate man's relationship to his fellow human beings (society).[36] As one scholar put it, Shariah has "shaped not just Muslims but Muslim civilization."[37] And, more importantly, it must not be forgotten that it continues to do so even now in the 21st century.

The Shariah derives its logic and force from the Koran and the Hadith. In Arabic history, *shariah* once meant "the straight path leading to an oasis" in the desert of Arabia. Now in the context of Islamic religion it means the straight path to a spiritual oasis—living the life Allah wants Muslims to live by observing his holy laws. It denotes total commitment to the Islamic way of life. Shariah laws were devised in the eighth century. They are laws to be kept without equivocation, and they make up the Islamic "system of divine laws that governs worship, ritual, conduct, and legal matters such as commercial contracts, marriage, divorce, and inheritance."[38] When its laws are broken, it also prescribes specific forms of punishment, some of which are detailed below.

Although not all of the 50 member countries of the Organisation of Islamic Conference follow every Shariah law, it needs to be noted that in recent years "A lot of states in the Middle East are taking more elements of sharia into their state laws."[39] Thus, there is no moving away from the Shariah in most Islamic countries.

Shariah Punishments

The punishments for violating the Hadd laws of Shariah are usually severe and physically brutal, often employing the ancient *lex talionis* principle, as stated in the Koran: "And We prescribed to them in it that life is for life, and eye for eye, and nose for nose, and ear for ear, and tooth for tooth ... " (Sura 5:45). Thus, for theft it states: "And (as for) the man who steals and the woman who steals, cut off their hands as a punishment for what they have earned, an exemplary punishment from Allah; and Allah is Mighty, Wise"(Sura 5:38). While it is important to note that not all of the 50 countries of the Organization of Islamic Conference have adopted all of the Hadd laws and their physical punishments,[40] there are many instances of such punishments being carried out.[41] The injustice of such punishments is not hard to see; for example, after a person has his hand(s) cut off it becomes virtually impossible for him to earn a living, and his freedom and rights thus have been greatly curtailed.

Execution by Stoning

The punishment of death by stoning is prescribed for both men and women who commit adultery. What follows is a brief account by an American who recently witnessed the stoning of a 30-year-old woman in Riyadh, Saudi Arabia. The woman was forcefully placed in a hole dug in the ground. Only her head and neck were visible. When the order was given, people started throwing fist-sized stones at her head and face. After about an hour her face became unrecognizable, covered with lacerations and blood, and when her head dropped, the Islamic authorities checked her neck for a pulse beat. She was still alive, but barely. The stone missiles kept coming. Finally, after another couple hours, death came. Then the woman was left for a few more hours in the hole so others could see her fate and thereby be deterred from committing adultery.[42]

As noted in Chapter 1, in order to obtain a conviction for adultery, four eye-witnesses are required. At first blush this may not provoke much thought, but when one thinks about this requirement a bit more, it poses a number of unthinkable aspects. One, how likely is it that four individuals will witness a couple having sexual intercourse? (Here it might be noted that, in the Old Testament, two eye witnesses were required to convict a woman of adultery, but not a single execution for adultery can be found in the Old Testament. Most likely, no adulterous act was ever witnessed by two individuals.) Two, what kind of persons would watch a couple cohabiting in secret? Three, why would anyone consider four such individuals as reputable witnesses?

The stoning of the woman in Riyadh is not the only one that has occurred in some Islamic countries in recent years. Since Khatami became president of Iran in May, 1997, 25 stoning sentences have been carried out in his country, 17 of which were women.[43] Interestingly, Article 104 of Iran's Law of Hodoud specifies that the stones used in an execution may not be so large that the offender would die from being struck by one stone; nor may the stones be mere pebbles.[44]

Stoning sentences also have been reported in Nigeria, Pakistan, and Sudan.[45] Many other Muslim jurisdictions that

177

carry out acts of stoning do not report them. In fact, because this form of punishment provokes strong reactions in the West, officials in these countries deny that such punishments occur. Some officials have said that Western reports of stoning are merely propaganda efforts to make Islam look bad.

In September 2003, the scheduled stoning of a 17-year-old Nigerian woman, Amina Lawal, who gave birth to a baby daughter while she was divorced, attracted international attention. She had been convicted of adultery under the Shariah. In response, at least in part, to the international uproar, a Shariah appeals court on procedural grounds acquitted the woman in late September.[46] But being acquitted only on procedural grounds indicates that the morality of punishment by stoning was not questioned. At least one other Nigerian woman in 2003 was sentenced to death by stoning for adultery.[47]

Also in September 2003, it was reported that a 43-year old man was sentenced to death by stoning by a Shariah court in Bauchi, Nigeria, for the crime of sodomy. He was convicted of sodomizing boys aged 10 and 13. How long it will take for the sentence to be carried out is not known at this point.[48]

Other Punishments.

In May 2002, a Shariah court in Nigeria sentenced a 19-year-old woman, Adama Unusua, to 100 lashes for having had sex with the man to whom she was engaged.[49] In December 2001, an 18-year-old Christian, Abok Alfa Akok, in the West-Sudanese Darfur received the sentence of death by stoning, but in March 2002 the sentence was commuted to 75 lashings.[50] In Iran the punishment for unmarried males or females committing fornication under its Law of Hodoud is 100 lashes.

Amnesty International recently (December 2002) reported that lashing is also the punishment meted out to fornication offenders in Yemen. Its law prescribes 100 lashes for fornicators, and, as in Iran, married adulterers are subject to stoning.[51]

Once a person becomes a Muslim, there is no turning back. Rejecting Islam is a capital crime, according to the Sharia and the Hadith. The latter declares, "according to the statement of Allah's Apostle, 'Whoever changed his Islamic religion, then kill him' " (*Sahih Al-Bukhari* 84:2:57).

Apostasy (*irtidad* in Arabic) has been punished by decapitation and also by hanging. For instance, in 1985, Mahmud Muhammad Taha, who had founded the Republican Brethren to promote his principles of minimizing the Koran as a source of law, was hanged in Khartoum, Sudan, for leaving Islam.[52] Following Iran's 1979 revolution, the crime of apostasy was made a part of its national constitution, and in 1990 we know that Hossein Soodmand, who converted to Christianity, was hanged.[53] In 1992, the Sudanese beheaded Sadiq Abdul-Karim Malalla for blasphemy and apostasy. Although executions for apostasy are less common than for some other Shariah violations, countries such as Yemen, Qatar, Saudi Arabia, and Mauritania, in addition to Sudan, have the death sentence for apostasy in their criminal codes. The *Criminal Code of Mauritania*, Article 306, states: "Every Muslim guilty of the crime of apostasy, whether by word or action, will be invited to repent over a period of three days. If he does not repent within this time limit, he is to be condemned to death as an apostate and his property will be confiscated by the Treasury."[54]

Even in non-Muslim countries, where Muslims are not able to enforce the Shariah, the "crime" of apostasy is not ignored by inveterate Muslims. In December, 2003, Uwe Siemon-Netto, a United Press International religious affairs editor, reported that Muslims who converted to Christianity in Leipzig, Germany, were harassed, spied on, and beaten physically. Siemon-Netto cites a Lutheran pastor in Leipzig saying: "Even now they [the converts to Christianity] are not safe from physical abuse. Some of my congregants have been beaten to a pulp while riding on a Leipzig streetcar."[55] This pastor said that the thugs are apparently part of the Iranian intelligence sent to spy on his parish, presumably because his congregation has 50 converts, and more in prospect.

Even in non-Muslim countries apostate Muslims are not without danger, prompting them in many instances to assume pseudonyms, for example, Ibn Warraq, Fatna A. Sabbah, Bat Ye'or, and Salman Rushdie. Warraq has published three noteworthy books: *Why I Am Not A Muslim* (1995), *The Quest for the Historical Muhammad* (2000), and *Leaving Islam* (2003). Bat Ye'or has also published three scholarly books exposing Islam; they are *The Dhimmi* (1985), *The Decline of Eastern Christianity under Islam* (1996), and *Islam and Dhimmitude* (2002). Sabbah authored *Woman in the Muslim Unconsciousness* (1984), and Rushdie published *Satanic Verses* (1988). For telling the truth about Islam to the world at large, they have taken pseudonyms to avoid being harassed or even assassinated by Islamists who do not tolerate criticisms or apostates.

Another horrible "crime" in the eyes of Muslims is blasphemy, which includes saying something considered to be derogatory about Muhammad or the Koran. For instance, Pakistan's current Penal Code in Section 295-B states: "Whoever willfully defiles, damages or desecrates a copy of the Holy Qur'an or an extract there from or uses it in any derogatory manner or for any unlawful purpose shall be punishable for imprisonment for life." Section 295-C asserts: "In respect of the Holy Prophet: Whoever by words, either spoken or written or by visible representation, or by any imputation, innuendo, or insinuation, directly or indirectly, defiles the sacred name of the Holy Prophet Mohammed shall be punished with death, or imprisonment for life, and shall also be liable to fine."[56] Section 298-B states the misuse of epithets, descriptions and titles reserved for holy personages or places are offenses punished by three years imprisonment and fine.[57]

Dhimmitude and *Jizyah*

Although less prominent than in the past, *dhimmi* laws (discussed in Chapter 2 with a different focus) are still present in some Islamic countries. Some publications, such as Cyril Glasse's *The Concise Encyclopedia of Islam* (1989), state that the institution of dhimmitude no longer exists, but reports from Islamic Pakistan indicate otherwise.

In 1977, Pakistan began imposing the Shariah with its courts and supporting elements. Since then, as Robert Spencer (grandson of *dhimmis*) says, the Islamic hardliners have "enforced the Sharia wherever they could within the country, including the laws of dhimmitude."[58] Patrick Sookhdeo, author of *A People Betrayed: The Impact of Islamization on the Christian Community in Pakistan* (2002), notes some current dhimmitude norms imposed on non-Muslims (mostly Christians) in Pakistan today. Similar to *dhimmis* of the past, non-Muslims are not permitted as witnesses in court against a Muslim defendant. Christians, for instance, find it next to impossible to get permission to build new churches. Non-Muslim parents have great difficulty enrolling their children in government schools and have great difficulty finding jobs that are not the most menial.[59] Many Muslim Pakistanis even see Christians as impure and often prevent them from touching food items or containers.[60]

Dhimmi-like expectations or norms still exist today in some other Islamic countries as well. For instance, in Saudi Arabia, Christians are not only prohibited from having churches, but they also may not read or own a Bible or recite a prayer in their homes.[61] In December 2002, "seven foreigners living in Saudi Arabia were arrested, beaten, and imprisoned for participating in a private Christmas celebration."[62]

On September 26, 2002, a sheikh, Marzouq Salem Al-Ghamdi, in Saudi Arabia stated in a sermon that there is nothing wrong in having non-Muslims pay the *jizyah,* and that if they were to violate stipulated conditions, "they have no protection."[63] This was clearly a reference to dhimmitude. In the Gulf Emirates, Christians may not ring their church bells, but the almost deafening loudspeakers on minarets beckoning Muslims five times per day to pray are everywhere.[64] This prohibition concerning bells goes back to Muhammad himself who called bells the "devil's pipes." Even on the West Bank in Israel, from where the Palestinian Authority operates, one hears the longing for the dhimmitude of the past. Sheikh Ibrahim Madhi recently said: "We welcome, as we did in the past, any Jew who wants to live in the land as a Dhimmi. ... "[65]

Whether Christians are formally classified as *dhimmis* or not, they are nonetheless in many Muslim countries frequently treated as though they were. For instance, the Sunni manual of Shariah declares Christians "are forbidden to build new churches" (*Reliance of the Traveller*, o11.4:7).

No Freedom of Movement

One of the marks of a free society is allowing its people to move about from one geographic area to another or reside where they wish without restrictions. Such freedoms do not exist in most Islamic countries, especially not for those who are not Muslims. Thus, the Shariah states: "They [non-Muslims] are forbidden to reside in the Hijaz, meaning the area and towns around Mecca, Medina, and Yamana, for more than three days (when the caliph allows them to enter there for something Muslims need)."[66] Freedom of movement, even on an occasional or casual basis, is also not allowed for non-Muslims. The Shariah is pointedly explicit: "A non-Muslim may not enter the Meccan Sacred Precinct (*Haram*) under any circumstances, or enter any mosque without permission (nor may Muslims enter churches without permission)."[67]

This lack of freedom in Islamic countries is to Westerners incredible, given the freedom of movement and travel most of them have had for centuries. Once again, as noted in Chapters 3 and 4, which discussed the status of women and the practice of slavery, where does one find the greatest amount of freedom, whether it is the freedom of speech, religion, or movement? History leaves no doubt. Where Christianity has had its greatest and longest presence, there one finds the greatest liberties known to mankind.

Conclusion

Whether it is the concept that no one is above the law, the minimum requirement of two or more witnesses in the trial of an individual, the notion of natural law and natural rights, the belief that all individuals are equal before God, the motivation behind the Magna Carta, the philosophy underlying the American Declaration of Independence and Constitution of the United States, history shows that these major hallmarks of liberty and justice owe their existence to the influence of Christianity. These Western landmarks of freedom often prompt Muslims to react by arguing that Islam has something equally good or even better. Hence, some Muslims point to Muhammad's Medina Covenant of 622 as a document equivalent or superior to the Magna Carta, which of course it is not, as noted above. When Muslims or their apologists make an assertion such as this, we need to remember what William Muir said more than a 100 years ago. He pointed out that in Muslim countries "freedom of thought and private judgment are crushed and annihilated. Toleration is unknown, and the possibility of free and liberal institutions foreclosed" (*LM*, 522).

Many Muslims have an extremely difficult time recognizing and accepting the fact that the West, greatly influenced by Christianity, has been on the forefront of giving people liberty and justice. They also have an equally difficult time granting liberty and freedom to their own citizens that the West has granted its citizens for centuries, and so even when they do formulate documents on freedom and human rights, such as the Universal Human Rights Declaration of 1981 and 1990 (drafted in Egypt), these efforts fall short of genuine liberty and justice found in documents and in practice of Western countries.

Many Muslims are so closely bound to the Koran, the Shariah, and the Hadith that it is essentially impossible to grant freedoms to their fellow citizens, freedoms that are common and taken for granted in most Western countries. For instance, how is it possible to give people freedom of speech when those same people may not, according to Shariah laws, question or make critical comments about given teachings or beliefs of Islam? Another major problem pertains to Muhammad, who Muslims admit was a man and not God, but no one is permitted to say anything uncomplimentary about him. Or what Muslim may, even on scholarly grounds, question the accuracy of Caliph Uthman's compiling the Koran, which he put together (20 years after Muhammad's death) from previous recordings found on oyster shells, shoulder bones of sheep, bits of wood, stone pieces, strips of leather, odd sheets of parchment, and flimsy palm branches?[68] Such a person will be condemned, perhaps even executed for blasphemy in some Islamic countries. Thus, as Serge Trifkovic has observed: "Like all totalitarian ideologies, Islam has an inherent tendency to closing the human mind. The spirit of critical inquiry essential to the growth of knowledge [and freedom] is completely alien to it."[69]

8

SCIENCE

"To know all things is permitted" (Horace)

In his book *Why I Am Not A Muslim* (1995), former Muslim Ibn Warraq notes that "There is a persistent myth that Islam encouraged science" (*WI*, 273). He then notes that some Muslims often cite a couple of passages from the Koran to prove their point, which he says is "nonsense," because these passages do not speak about acquiring or honoring scientific but rather religious knowledge. Warraq further states that orthodox Muslims have "always been suspicious of 'knowledge for its own sake,' and unfettered intellectual inquiry is deemed dangerous to the faith" (*WI*, 273). The following pages in this chapter show that Warraq's argument is not an exaggeration.

In studying the history of science one soon discovers that the word science commonly is not defined. Muslims who say Islam is pro-science do not define it either. The lack of a definition may seem strange, for people today tend to see science as that human pursuit which provides and consists of precise and accurate knowledge derived from empirical research, and so they probably assume there is a definition to that effect. Yet, when historians refer to science among the ancient Greeks, Romans, Chinese, and Muslim Arabs the word has a different meaning than it has today. Most commonly historians have in mind some form of technology, and sometimes their reference is to knowledge derived from natural philosophy by mostly deductive thinking.

The latter meaning of science is similar to the Latin *scientia* (knowledge). Briefly put, when historians talk about science before the 13th century, they are not talking about the systematic study and pursuit of knowledge obtained by proposing and testing hypotheses subjected to experimental methodology to see whether they are empirically true or false, which has been the task of scientists since approximately the 13th century to the present day.

Science's Christian Connections[1]

Alfred North Whitehead, the renowned philosopher of science and a non-Christian, once said that "faith in the possibility of science, generated antecedently to the development of modern scientific theory, is an unconscious derivative from medieval [Christian] theology."[2] Whitehead, as Rodney Stark has rightly noted, "had grasped that Christian theology was essential for the rise of science in the West, just as surely as non-Christian theologies had stifled the scientific quest everywhere else."[3] In a similar vein, Lynn White, a historian of medieval science, has stated that "the [medieval] monk was an intellectual ancestor of the scientist."[4] And the German physicist Ernst Mach remarked: "Every unbiased mind must admit that the age in which the chief development of the science of mechanics took place was an age of predominantly [Christian] theological cast."[5]

Crediting Christianity with facilitating the rise of modern science probably sounds incredible to many, including scientists. The reason for this, in part, seems to go back to Andrew Dickson White who in 1896 published *A History of the Warfare of Science with Theology in Christendom*. Christianity and science, as the book's title indicates, were portrayed as enemies, or at least highly incompatible. But even before White's negative portrayal of some Christians and their view of science appeared, "methodological atheism" (to use Peter L. Berger's term) had already become the accepted epistemology of countless scientists and professors in colleges and universities. Thus, when biographies of past noteworthy scientists appear in books or journals, their Christian background and its influence on their scientific work, which was true of virtually every scientist from the 13th to the 19th century, is never mentioned. Thus, it seems unthinkable to many today that Christianity could have fostered and aided the arrival of modern science.

Christian Presuppositions Underlying Modern Science

Christianity, with its Judaic heritage, has always taught and insisted that there is only one God, and that he is a rational being. Without these two presuppositions, there would be no modern science. To cite Whitehead again, experimental science required Christianity's "insistence on the rationality of God."[6]

If God is a rational being, then should not human beings, made in his image, also employ rational processes to study and investigate the world in which they live? That question was answered in the affirmative when some Christian natural philosophers linked rationality with the empirical, inductive method of acquiring knowledge. One such philosopher was Robert Grosseteste (ca. 1168–1253), a Franciscan bishop and the first chancellor of Oxford University, who first proposed the inductive, experimental method.[7] This approach was further developed by his student Roger Bacon (1214–1294), also a Franciscan cleric, who argued that "all things must be verified by experience."[8] Bacon was a devout believer in the truthfulness of Scripture, and being empirically minded, he even saw the Bible in the light of sound reason and as verifiable by experience. Brian Clegg, a physicist and historian of science, in a recent biography of Roger Bacon, called him "the first scientist."[9] Another natural philosopher was William of Occam (or Ockham, 1285–1347), also a member of the Franciscan Order, who, like Roger Bacon, believed knowledge needed to be derived empirically.

Almost 300 years later, another Bacon, Francis Bacon (1561–1626), gave additional momentum to the empirical method by actually recording his experimental findings. He has been called "the practical creature of scientific induction."[10] In the context of rationality, he stressed careful observation of phenomena and collecting systematic information in order to understand nature's secrets.[11] His scientific interests, however, did not deter him from also devoting time to theology, for he also wrote treatises on the Psalms and on prayer.

By introducing the inductive-empirical method, guided by rational procedures, these four men departed considerably from the ancient Greek perspectives of Aristotle (384–322).

Aristotle's natural philosophy, which had a stranglehold on the world for more than 1,500 years, held that knowledge was only acquired through the deductive processes of the human mind; the inductive method, which required manual activity was taboo because such physical or manual activities were seen as appropriate only for slaves, not for thinkers or freemen. The ancient world had complete confidence in the deductive method (*a priori* or arm-chair reasoning) as the only way of arriving at knowledge and understanding. And even after the empirical method had been suggested, the scholastic world, for the most part, continued to adhere to Aristotle's deductive approach.

In addition to the presuppositions that God is a rational being and that his created world may be studied in a rational manner, Christianity had another presupposition that was equally important for the development of science. That presupposition said God, who created the world, is separate and distinct from it. Aristotelian philosophy, on the other hand, saw God (or gods) and the universe of nature intertwined. His was a pantheistic, panemanationist conception of the world.[12] Planets, for example, were seen as having an inner intelligence (*anima*) that induced them to move. This pantheistic view of planetary movement was first challenged by Jean Buridan (1300–1358), a Christian philosopher at the University of Paris.[13] He saw Aristotle's philosophy contrary to Christian theology, which said that "in the beginning God created the heavens and the earth" (Genesis 1:1), for Aristotle's theory maintained that the natural world had no beginning, nor was it created by God, according to his work *On the Heavens* (279–284).

"Modern [experimental] science," says Robert Fletcher, "begins in 13th century Europe, based firmly on the plinth furnished by translations from Arabic and Greek."[14] Although some Muslim translations, especially of the Greek classics in natural philosophy, provided some intellectual inducements that later contributed to modern experimental science, Muslims did not invent or encourage it. The real pioneers of science were not Muslims but Christians; four of them have already been mentioned above. There were numerous other early scientists from the 13th century on whose spiritual home was rooted in Christianity and who contributed greatly to modern science. Their contributions can be found in human physiology, biology, astronomy, physics, mathematics, chemistry, and medicine. For a more detailed look at the lives and works of some of these scientists, see Appendix. B.

Islam's Alleged Connection to Science

Given that many Muslims live in the shadow of Christianity, they often try to counter or gainsay any credit assigned to Christianity; often this is done by asserting that Islam was there first, so the speak. One such example is that Muslims and many of their apologists argue that Islam was the first to provide a home for science. Here is how one writer puts it: "As regards the origins of science, it was a widely held belief in the period from the ninth to the eleventh centuries that almost all ancient nations had developed a body of scientific wisdom, a wisdom that 'migrated' from one region of the earth to another until it found a final home in Islam."[15] This same author also says that Islam has been "unlike Christianity, which was said to have nearly succeeded in snuffing out the sciences in the lands over which it ruled."[16] This assertion, of course, is contrary to well-established facts in the history of science, which the present chapter shows in its brief survey below.

What Do Muslims Mean by "Science"?

As already indicated, before the 13th century natural philosophers did not advocate or employ the testing of theoretical hypotheses in order to confirm or reject them in the pursuit of reliable, valid knowledge. This, of course, is also true when Muslims and others credit Islam with having provided a home for science. The latter claim is false for a number of reasons.

First, the discussions of Islam's alleged scientific contributions commonly pertain to the Arabic translations of Greek literature that dealt with the philosophy of nature, natural phenomena, and mathematics. In this context, the Muslim Arabic capture of Jundishapur in Persia in 638, a city that became a center for translating and disseminating Greek writings, is sometimes cited as an example of having advanced scientific information.[17] Another example sometimes refers to Haroun al-Rashid, caliph of Baghdad in 786, who "scoured the known world for Greek and Syriac texts to translate into Arabic."[18] Still another example is one that occurred in the ninth century, when under the Muslim Arabic Umayyads and Abbasids dynasties, translations were made from Greek writings dealing with medicine and astronomy (*WI*, 262). Referring to these Greek translations, Max Meyerhof says, "scientists of the Islamic world stood on a firm foundation of Greek science."[19] Again, as already noted, these Arabic translations did not contain knowledge derived from the empirical-experimental method, which came several centuries later.

190

Second, although a great deal of Greek "science" was translated into Arabic, it was not just Muslims who deserve credit for this. Many of the translations were made by Nestorian Christians who worked for Muslims.[20] The Nestorians knew Greek and Syriac, and after the Arabic Muslim conquests in the latter part of the seventh and early eighth century, they also mastered Arabic. These Nestorians, says one scholar, "more than any other people helped raise Islam to leadership in culture and science."[21] They also translated Greek works in mathematics and medicine into Syriac.[22] And Christians translated for Muslims in Spain, as George Sarton, the historian of science, informs us. He also notes that Christians in Spain were assisted by Jews.[23]

It should further be noted that some translations of Greek literature into Arabic occurred a couple of centuries before Muhammad founded Islam. Probus, a Christian priest-physician in Antioch, made Aristotle available to the Arabic world through his translations in the early fifth century.[24] Thus, before or after Islam came into being, much of the credit for many translations from Greek into Arabic must be shared by both Muslims and Christians.

Third, the Muslim Arabs were not the first to translate Greek "science" into Latin either. History shows that, two to three centuries before Islam was founded, translations of Greek writings were made into Latin by Christians in Europe. Ulfilas (ca. 311–381), a Christian bishop and missionary to the Goths, translated some of Aristotle's works. In the early part of the fifth century, Boethius (ca. 480–ca. 524), often called a founder of the Middle Ages because of his influence on medieval Europe, also translated Greek writings into Latin. And in the fifth century, Cassiodorus (ca. 485–ca. 580), a monk, translated numerous Greek classics for Christians to read. Finally, in the latter part of the sixth century the Benedictine monks in Monte Cassino, Italy, also translated Greek texts into Latin.

Fourth, some of the translations from Greek into Arabic were in higher mathematics—a Greek invention. This early exposure to higher math gave the Arabs the advantage in mathematics for almost a thousand years before the subject became well known to the Europeans during the Renaissance.[25] At first, Arabs in the ninth century resisted accepting the Indian numerals of the Hindus (now known as Arabic numerals), which made higher mathematics possible. But they resisted them less than did the Europeans when they first encountered them.[26] Apparently, this early and relatively long exposure to mathematics from the Greeks enabled Muslims to become proficient in algebra and algorithm before these two subjects spread to the West. Al-Kwarizmi (born ca. 825), a Persian, has been credited with having invented algebra and algorithms.[27] But Charles Singer, a historian of science, says: "The mathematics of Al-Kwarizmi shows little originality."[28] He further says: "In general the achievement of the Arabs in pure mathematics is below the Greeks in geometry and below the Hindus in algebra."[29] However, Singer does say "the Arabs exhibited great skill in applying their mathematics to physical and to a lesser extent to astronomical problems."[30] Given this skill, they taught Western Europeans mathematics up to the 16th century.[31] Furthermore, while Muslims possessed advanced mathematical knowledge, it is important to note that mathematics is not a science. It is the language of science.

Fifth, in the 13th century Robert Grosseteste, the first chancellor of Oxford University in England, found that "the Arabic translations of Greek authors were so inaccurate, and in consequence misrepresented the original meaning of the authors, that he introduced Greeks from the Near East as instructors in their own language, so that the works could be studied in the original language."[32] Can bad translations be credited with providing a home for science?

A sixth reason has to do with the fact that much of the historical discussion of science among Muslims usually pertains to mechanical devices that were effectively employed, but ordinarily not invented by them in Islam's so-called "Golden Age" (900-1100). Muslims were no technological innovators. For instance, Rodney Stark points out that Muslims, similar to the ancient Romans, did not know how to harness a horse so it could pull from the shoulder with a collar instead of a yoke around the horse's neck. This relatively simple but highly important technology was first developed by the Europeans in the so-called "Dark Ages." [33]   And although the Muslim Arabs knew how to breed fine Arabian horses, they had to learn from the Europeans how to equip their horses with saddles and stirrups, noted in Chapter 2.

One scholar, Eugene Myers, says, "Islam did not go beyond the achievements of Hellenistic mechanics; no new inventions of importance were made."[34] A major reason for the lack of new inventions lies in the following explanation: "In philosophy and the sciences, the Muslims were the pupils of the Greeks, so much so that they regarded the books of the Greek masters as fixed systems laid down once for all as the final truth."[35]

Seventh, even in astronomy, often cited as an example of scientific know-how among Arab Muslims, Islam did not provide a home for science either. Although the astronomy of the Arabs was more practical than that of the Greeks, "they made no advance in principles over Ptolemy (ca. A.D.100–170), whose work, known to them as the *Almagest* (superior to all books) the foundation of all their theory."[36] While the Arabic Muslims made considerable use of and improved the astrolabe (an instrument used by navigators and astronomers to determine latitudinal and longitudinal positions as well as determine time), it was not their invention. The Greeks had already invented it in the second century before Christ.[37]

Eighth, Muslims also did not make any innovative strides in physiology or medicine, even though Ibn Sina (Avicenna in the West) in the early 11th century wrote his *Canon of Medicine*, an encyclopedia of treating diseases. This work has often been cited as one of Islam's great achievements in medicine. But as Flornian Cajori has shown, "In Syria," for instance, "the sciences, especially philosophy of medicine, were cultivated by Greek Christians."[38] And Bernard Lewis has remarked that among the Ottoman Turks—Muslims all—as late as the mid-1600's, "There [was] no attempt to follow new discoveries and little awareness even of the existence of such a process. The great changes in anatomy and physiology occurring at the time pass unnoticed and unknown."[39]

Ninth, Islam sometimes persecuted some of its thinkers who wrote and discussed natural philosophy. Pro-Islamic writers often cite Avicenna as one of their greatest thinkers— "the Prince of Philosophers" in the Islamic world. Indeed, he deserves this honor, but what Muslim writers commonly fail to mention is that he was severely persecuted by Islamic religious authorities.[40] The dislike for Avicenna and his works resulted in the Caliph of Baghdad in 1150 committing to the flames his philosophical writings, along with the writings of some others.[41] And in the 12th century Ibn Rushd (Averroes in the West), a judge, philosopher, and physician in Muslim-occupied Spain was exiled to Morocco three years before he died.[42]

Finally, Islam was not a home for science because it never produced any individuals who employed the inductive or experimental method. In this regard, the assessment of Bernard Lewis regarding the Ottoman Muslims is appropriate: "The basic ideas of forming, testing, and, if necessary, abandoning hypotheses remained alien to a society in which knowledge was conceived as a corpus of eternal verities which could be acquired, accumulated, transmitted, interpreted, and applied but not modified or transformed."[43] Although these remarks by

194

Lewis describe the Ottoman Muslims, they are also quite descriptive of other Muslims. For the "eternal verities" he mentions were (and are) in the eyes of devout Muslims found in the Koran, which they say cannot be "modified or transformed" by any scientific findings.

"Islamic Science"?

When one reads about science in Islamic circles, a rather strange term appears very frequently, namely, "Islamic science." This term is found in numerous articles and books. There are even books that have the words "Islamic science" in their titles. *The Oxford History of Islam* (1999), which has a chapter on science, uses the term "Islamic science" a number of times. The term "Islamic science," however, is false and biased.

Science is never Christian, Jewish, or Islamic. Scientific work may be done by Christians, Jews, or Muslims, but that does not make it Christian, Jewish, or Islamic. Just as mathematics or physics is not and cannot be Islamic or Christian, likewise science is not and cannot be Islamic or Christian. Writers who use "Islamic science" would never use the term "Christian science," and rightly so. In fact, if any historian or any other writer were to use the term "Christian science" in an article or book dealing with science, editors of reputable journals or publishing houses would reject it. Why then do writers and editors not rule out the term "Islamic science"?

During the Hitler era in Germany, the Nazis disparagingly spoke of "Jewish physics." When they did so, they not only were terribly wrong, but they also revealed their anti-Semitic prejudice. In response, reputable scholars and others rightly rejected the Nazi term "Jewish physics." Thus, it must be asked: Why have respectable scholars and others not rejected the term "Islamic science"? Do the writers who use

195

this erroneous expression not see that not only is it a false term, but, as in the case of the Nazis, it also conveys a definite bias? Even though in using the term "Islamic science" the bias is not anti-Islamic, it is still a false and misleading term.

The equally unfortunate terms of "Islamic medicine" and "Islamic technology" also appear quite often in literature discussing science in Muslim circles, and they are no more acceptable than "Islamic science." Clearly, a double standard exists among many historians and publishers.

In my research on science and Islam, I have found only one writer, Pervez Hoodbhoy, a Muslim and a physicist in Pakistan, who finds fault with the term "Islamic science." His book *Islam and Science* (1991) has a chapter titled "Can There Be An Islamic Science?" He answers his question. "No, there cannot be an Islamic science of the physical world, and attempts to create one represent wasted effort."[44]

Concerning Islamic Contributions

In the context of natural philosophy, one does indeed find some Arabic-Muslim contributions in the areas of astronomy, physics, mathematics, optics, physiology, and medicine, all before the 13th century. Islam had furnished some noteworthy natural philosophers. In addition to Avicenna (980-1037) and Averroes (1126-1198), it had men like Jabir Ibn Hayyan (ca. 760–ca. 815), Al-Kindi (813–880), and Al-Razi (ca. 865–925)..

Jabir was a physician who has been called "the father of Arabic alchemy." One source says that "a hundred alchemical works ascribed to Jabir are extant."[45] However, there is some evidence that the works bearing his name are not his, but "are in all probability the work of a sect dedicated to the pursuit of alchemy as a science with power both to give and control over the forces of nature and to purify the soul."[46] Although his reputed work was in alchemy, now no longer a reputable pursuit, some of it "did contain genuine chemical knowledge."[47] And aside from a few chemical terms, derived from these writings (such as alkali, antimony, realgar, tutania, ammonia), modern chemistry is not indebted to Jabir.

Al-Kindi, often called "the first Arabic philosopher," wrote numerous works dealing with meteorology, optics, and physics. Some have argued that the Latin translation of his *Optics* influenced Roger Bacon, 400 years later.[48] Reportedly, he wrote over 200 works, but most of them have been lost.[49]

Al-Razi (Rhazes in the West), a Persian physician who spoke Arabic, wrote a text on small pox and measles. He was chief physician in Baghdad around 900,[50] and he also wrote a multivolume medical encyclopedia, which was translated into Latin in the 15th century.[51] Theology, mathematics, astronomy, nutrition, and alchemy were some of his other topics. Some have likened him to the Greek Hippocrates in regard to his writings in medicine. There is no evidence, however, that his medical insights advanced the cause of scientific medicine that came several centuries later. In fact, one medical historian has said: "Rhazes, the Persian, was a talented clinical observer, but not a Harvey."[52]

When the published works of Avicenna are considered, it is obvious he surpassed other Arabic Muslim thinkers. Given that many in his day pursued alchemy, it also attracted his interests, but he disagreed with most alchemists, for he argued that base metals could not be transmuted.[53] He also wrote about botany, geology, and Islamic theology. In the West he is best known for his *Canon of Medicine,* a medical digest of five books, which leaned heavily on Galen's work and hence perpetuated his errors. However, it must be noted that because "Muslims were strictly prohibited from dissecting either human bodies or living animals"[54] it was not possible for Avicenna or other Muslims in medicine to correct Galen's many errors.

Before Vesalius and Paracelsus in the 16th century, Avicenna's *Canon* was widely used as a text in European medical schools as well as by physicians. But when Europe's empirically minded medical scientists appeared, they found much of the *Canon's* contents in conflict with the empirical findings of science, and it was no longer used or respected. Paracelsus tossed the *Canon* into the fire, and Leonardo da Vinci had already rejected it a few years earlier (see Appendix B). However, since new knowledge is rarely accepted quickly, the *Canon's* use in some regions lingered on into the early 17th century.

Averroes, born on the Muslim-occupied Iberian peninsula, studied medicine and philosophy, as well as law. Like Rhazes, he too published a medical encyclopedia, titled *Liber Almansoris*. Muslims credit him with discovering the importance of physical exercise on human health. He also speculated about astronomy, magnetism, and colors.

While Muslim writers and their apologists cite Avicenna and Averroes as brilliant thinkers, these writers are rather taciturn by not mentioning that their written works were not well received by the Islamic religious authorities. As already noted, Avicenna was persecuted, and a hundred years after his death his works were burned by the caliph in 1150 in Baghdad. Even before his writings were burned, they were regarded as heretical by al-Ghazali (1058–1111), who is seen by many Muslims as Islam's most influential philosopher since Muhammad. But al-Ghazali is also seen as the man with whom the decline of Islam's reputed Golden Age began.[55] Averroes was banished by orthodox Muslims in 1195, three years before he died. His works, like those of Avicenna, were seen as being out of tune with orthodox Islam. And before both Avicenna and Averroes came under suspicion, Jabir, the natural philosopher and physician, had been exiled in the ninth century for his unorthodox views. Here is more evidence that Islam did not provide a home for science.

Islam and Science Today

Not just when modern science began in the 13th century, but even today Islam lags behind the West in the world of science. Recently, Aaron Segal wrote, "the Muslim world produces a disproportionately small amount of scientific output, and much of it relatively low in quality."[56] Islam has 20 percent of the world's population, but it generates less than five percent of the world's scientific output.[57] Moreover, Sudan and Iran have no interest in science, and in countries like Libya, Syria, and Afghanistan science has been crippled, says Segal.[58]

The Islamic lag in science is neither new nor surprising. Writing his monumental volumes in the history of science some 70 years ago, George Sarton said that Muslims, for the most part, were not interested in matters concerning the order of nature. They were primarily interested in religious implications of the world in which they lived.[59] This Muslim anti-scientific attitude, Meyerhof argues, has its roots in the 11th century thinking of al-Ghazali (d. 1111), whose influence and importance in Islam has often been ranked next to Muhammad. It was al-Ghazali who argued that scientific pursuits led to unbelief and hence were not activities for devout Muslims to pursue.[60] In support of Meyerhof's observ-ation, David C. Lindberg, another historian of science, says, "[T]he foreign sciences never ceased to be viewed by the great majority of Muslims as useless, alien, and perhaps dangerous ... [these]sciences were never deeply integrated into Islamic culture, but survived on the margins."[61] Thus, as Bernard Lewis has noted, "The Renaissance, the Reformation, even the Scientific Revolution, and the Enlightenment, passed unnoticed in the Muslim world."[62] This helps explain the current and continuing lag in science in Islamic countries.

Conclusion

Although Islam produced some noteworthy natural philosophers among the Arabs, they never attained the intellectual stature of the Greeks. They received much of their knowledge from the ancient Greeks, whose books they read and translated into Arabic. In the words of one historian of science, "The legacy of the Islamic world in medicine and natural science is the legacy of Greece, increased by many additions, mostly practical."[63] Speaking about medicine among Muslim Arabs, another scholar has been even more critical, saying: "Arabian medicine was little better than superstition."[64]

It also needs to be noted that although Islam's natural philosophers produced some noteworthy works in physiology and medicine from about the ninth through the 11th century, "Islamic medicine and science came to a standstill, about 1100. ... "[65] It was Christianity, not Islam, which provided the necessary presuppositions, the motivation, and the men who launched modern science. Thus, from the 13th century on, Islam's influence in science, if one can call it science, in contrast to Christianity's influence, has been conspicuously lagging. In support of this claim, Lindberg in his *The Beginnings of Western Science* (1992), says that in regard to the study of nature, "the church was one of the major patrons—perhaps the [sic] major patron—of scientific learning."[66]

Finally, it is well to remember that Muslims discovered no scientific laws, such as Kepler's three laws in astronomy, Newton's law of gravity, Pascal's law of liquid pressure, Ohm's law in the field of electricity, Boyle's law in chemistry, Kelvin's absolute zero, Faraday's electromagnetic induction, Dalton's atomic weights, Lavoisier's law of the conservation of energy, or Mendel's laws pertaining to heredity. Nor did any Muslims discover bacteria, introduce chloroform, inoculate against diseases, discover circulation of the blood, introduce antiseptics, or encourage the dissecting of human cadavers.

200

These and other great moments in science were by-products of Christianity's influence, all outside the context of any Islamic influence or motivation. Hence, as noted by Ibn Warraq at the beginning of the present chapter, it is a "myth that Islam has encouraged science."

9

CHURCH AND STATE

OR

UNION OF MOSQUE AND STATE

"Congress shall make no law respecting an establishment of religion. ... "
(First Amendment of the Constitution of the United States)

Between Western democratic countries and Islamic countries another great divide appears. This divide concerns the manner in which governments relate themselves to the social institution of religion, and how religious organizations in turn relate themselves to state governments. Although there are differences in the various Western countries with regard to the separation of church and state, they all have some clear lines of distinction between the two. For instance, some European countries (England, Sweden, Italy, and some others) still have state churches, some of which even receive some tax-based support from their government, whereas in the United States there is no state church and no direct support is given by government to any religious group. Even where state churches exist in Europe, the church may not dictate policies to the state, and the state ordinarily may not dictate policies to the church. But in Islamic countries the state and the Islamic religion are inseparable because "Islam is a religion and a state."[1]

Separation of Church and State[2]

Does the concept of separation of church and state reflect a Christian influence? When one listens to the secular media today, especially in the United States, the impression is given that the separation of church and state is a phenomenon totally divorced from any Christian influence. This does not reflect the facts of history. Here the words of Bernard Lewis, an expert in Islamic studies, are instructive. In speaking about the separation of church and state vis-à-vis Islam's concept of the state and religion, he said: "The notion of the church and state as distinct institutions, each with its laws, hierarchy, and jurisdiction, is characteristically Christian with its origins in Christian scripture and history. It is alien to Islam."[3]

Contrary to the current faulty perception, there is considerable evidence that the separation of church and state has substantial Christian roots harking back to the response Jesus gave to the Pharisees. They tried to entrap him by asking whether it was lawful to give tax money to the Roman Caesar, whom they despised. Jesus asked them to show a Roman coin. "Whose likeness and inscription is this?" he asked. "Caesar's," they replied. Then Jesus responded: "Render therefore to Caesar the things that are Caesar's, and to God the things that are God's" (Matthew 22:21).

Three hundred years after Jesus made this statement, Hosius, bishop of Cordoba, Spain, from 353–356, reprimanded Emperor Constantius II for meddling in ecclesiastical matters by trying to get the Western bishops to condemn Athanasius for opposing the Arian heresy. So Hosius said: "Intrude not yourself into ecclesiastical affairs ... God has put into your hands the [secular] kingdom; to us [bishops] He has entrusted the affairs of His Church."[4] In support of his reprimand, he cited the example set by Jesus that was discussed above.

During their first 300 years of bloody persecutions, the early Christians neither sought nor expected the government to support them in their religious activities. Their religious activities were divorced from any ties to the government of Rome. They differed remarkably from the pagan Romans for whom religious activities were linked to a particular city or the state. The Latin word *religare* (from which we get the word religion) meant that there was a bond between the Roman people and the state. The Christian idea of "an association of people bound together by a religious allegiance with it own traditions and beliefs, its own history, and its own way of life, independent of a particular city or nation was foreign to the ancients."[5]

The fact that Christian religious practices were not linked to a city or state was one of the things that irritated Celsus, a second-century pagan critic of Christianity. He saw Christians as separatists or sectarians. But after Constantine the Great (d. 337) legalized Christianity in 313 and soon involved himself in many of the church's affairs, the separation of church and state among Christians slowly began to blur, and for more than a thousand years after Constantine the church and state were often intertwined.

When Bishop Hosius chided the emperor, it was the government that was attempting to make ecclesiastical decisions. But by the early Middle Ages the situation had reversed itself. Now the church increasingly intruded in the affairs of secular government. This fusion of church and state, for example, was one of the things that angered Martin Luther in the 16th century. He especially criticized the pope for involving himself in secular government, which he saw as a violation of what he called the concept of two kingdoms (realms). It was the church's task solely to preach and teach the gospel of Jesus Christ. This he called the spiritual kingdom or realm. The government's task was to keep peace and order in society by restraining and punishing the unlawful. This he called the worldly kingdom or realm. The secular government could only compel people to behave outwardly; it could never make a person's heart spiritually righteous. Only the preaching of the Christian gospel (an activity of the spiritual realm) could do that. In the spiritual realm the Christian operates as a disciple of Christ; in the secular realm he functions as a citizen of his country. Although the two realms are separate, the Christian as an individual is active in both because God is active in both. In the spiritual realm he is active in proclaiming the gospel, whereas in the secular kingdom he supports government's use of the law and the sword without injecting elements of the gospel. In order to buttress his concept of two realms (kingdoms), Luther cites Jesus' statement about giving to Caesar what is his and to God what belongs to him. Briefly put, the two realms (church and state) have separate functions and are not to be merged or intermingled.[6]

When America's Founding Fathers in 1791 wrote the First Amendment to the Constitution—"Congress shall make no law respecting an establishment of religion, or prohibiting the free exercise thereof"—they not only intended to provide freedom of religion for the individual, but in effect also said the two realms or kingdoms, to use Luther's terminology, were to be kept separate even though the words "separation of church and state" are not in the First Amendment.

The words "separation of church and state" (which in recent years have become a national preoccupation with many secular Americans) are the result of an inference made from a letter Thomas Jefferson sent to the Danbury Connecticut Baptist Association on January 1, 1802. In that letter he used the phrase "building a wall of separation between church and state." When he used these words, he had no intention of curtailing religious practices. Neither he nor the drafters of the First Amendment had even the remotest thought of outlawing governmental support for religion. He, like Luther, merely wanted to keep the government from making religious decisions or the church from making governmental decisions. This is evident from some of the acts he performed when he was president of the United States. For instance, he used federal money to build churches and establish missions for the purpose of bringing the gospel to American Indians. In short, "What the federal government was prohibited from doing, in Jefferson's view, was prescribing a particular set of religious rites or promoting a particular sect at the expense of others."[7] Jefferson also sent a treaty to the Congress that provided a "Catholic church building" for the Kaskaskia Indians in 1803.[8] Note that this was after his "wall of separation" speech in Connecticut.

America's Founding Fathers, including Jefferson, wanted the nation to have freedom *of* religion, not *from* religion. The latter is currently being promoted by groups such as the American Civil Liberties Union and its anti-Christian allies. In order to achieve freedom from religion, secularists have been using the state, with the help of the United States Supreme Court, to "free" the people *from* religion. Outlawing Christmas crèches, banning prayers in public schools, and removing the Ten Commandments from tax-supported buildings are three present-day American examples. When Jesus spoke to the Pharisees he only indicated that the two realms were separate, not that Caesar (the government) and religion were in conflict or that religion or God had to be jettisoned from public life.

So, returning to the question asked earlier, does the doctrine of separation of church and state reflect the influence of Christianity? The answer is a definite yes, especially in light of the American experience. The American Founding Fathers—all well-read individuals—were familiar with the teachings of Jesus Christ. They knew about Jesus' statement about Caesar and God, about the church–state conflicts in history, and about the monopoly state churches had in Europe. Moreover, as is well known, they were also conversant with John Locke's writings, which reflected much Christian thinking. In light of Locke's scholarly bent, it is quite likely that he also was familiar with Luther's doctrine of the two realms. This latter point is not mere speculation, for in *A Letter Concerning Toleration*, Locke wrote: "All power of civil government relates only to men's civil interests, is confined to the care of things of this world, and hath nothing to do with the world to come."[9]   These words sound remarkably similar to Luther's two-realms doctrine. So it is quite plausible that the Founding Fathers, via this   Luther-like statement by Locke, together with Christ's Caesar-and-God teaching, imported this Christian understanding of the separation of church and state as they hammered out the First Amendment's freedom-of-religion clause.

Freedom of Religion
As discussed in Chapter 2, the early Christians, in the spirit of the Christ's teaching, which they emulated and reflected, never coerced or forced anyone to join their ranks even though they wanted people to become followers of Jesus Christ. During the church's first 300 years, Christians always and only gained new converts in a context of religious freedom, even though that freedom was often not extended to them. They suffered frequent and severe persecutions at the hands of Roman authorities.

Despite the many persecutions, the numbers of Christians continued to grow and increase. Their stalwart and faithful adherence to Christ's teachings of love and forgiveness appealed to many pagans, who became Christians even at the possible cost of persecution. Then after three centuries of persecution, Christianity attained legal status in 313 when Emperor Constantine, together with co-emperor Licinius, signed the Edict of Milan.

Christianity continued to flourish and thrive after 313. Soon even the emperors joined the church. But, as is often true, with success comes abuse of power. Thus, in 380 Emperor Theodosius, a Christian emperor, compelled all government officials to embrace Christianity, an act that violated Christ's and early Christianity's posture of religious freedom. The next year the emperor proclaimed Christianity to be the Roman Empire's official religion. And as noted in Chapter 2, Emperor Justinian in the sixth century brought many into the church by involuntary means. In the eighth century, Charlemagne the Great also forced many to join the church, and in the 11th century King Haroldsson compelled the pagans in Norway to become "Christians."

As much as Christ wanted people to follow him, these leaders, and others like them, obviously forgot that he had never forced anyone to follow or believe in him, even though it pained him to see people in their spiritual obstinacy spurn him and his message. He wept over Jerusalem's hard-headed rejection of him. His method of gaining converts was by teaching and preaching, not by coercion. Thus, when people were brought into the church by compulsion or through enticements of various kinds, both the method and the spirit of religious freedom practiced by Christ and the early Christians were grossly abused and violated.

Freedom of religion and religious beliefs were also transgressed when individuals were decapitated or burned at the stake for believing or teaching what some leaders in the church at times called heresies. Only 72 years after Christianity had gained legal status in the 313, Priscillianus, a Spanish bishop with Gnostic leanings, in 385 under Emperor Gratian's direction, was the first man in the church to be decapitated. But it must also be noted that St. Ambrose and Pope Siricius denounced the execution and refused fellowship with the accusers.[10] In 844 Charles the Bald began the Inquisition by enjoining bishops to interrogate teachers in the church to see whether they were teaching heresies. Space does not permit mentioning the inquisitions that followed. In 1480 the frequently cited Spanish Inquisitions began, lasting until the early 1800's. Incinerating the bones of John Wycliffe (30 years after his death) for questioning the doctrine of transubstantiation, the burning of John Hus at the stake in 1416, and putting Jerome Savonarola to the flames in 1498 were all equally horrible and unChristian.

These are a few examples of how the organized church before the Reformation at times violated freedom of religion. Unfortunately, some major injustices also occurred among some of the Protestants. John Calvin, for instance, approved the execution of Michael Servetus for heresy in 1553, and the Dutch Calvinists hanged John of Oldenbarneveldt in 1619 for rejecting Calvin's doctrine of double predestination.

On the other hand, there were always prominent Christian leaders who proclaimed the right of individuals to believe according to their consciences. These leaders maintained this position even though they held firmly to Christ's teaching that there is no salvation outside of faith in him. Tertullian in the early third century said that "it is a fundamental right, a privilege of nature, that every man should worship according to his own convictions ... to which free-will and not force should lead us" (*Ad Scapula* 2). Similarly, Lactantius (d. ca. 335) defended the freedom of religious belief. According to him, "It is religion alone in which freedom has placed its dwelling. For it is a matter which is voluntary above all others, nor can necessity be imposed upon any, so as to worship that which he does not wish to worship" (*The Epitome of the Divine Institutes* 49). In the fifth century St. Augustine, although an ardent defender of the Christian faith, never forced the pagans to accept Christianity.[11] And in the 16th century, Martin Luther (1483–1546) told the German princes in a letter that it was not the function of government to "forbid anyone to teach or believe or say what he wants—the Gospel or lies."[12]

A number of other Christian theologians and leaders could be cited to document that the freedom of religious beliefs stems from biblical Christianity. To the skeptics who deny this fact, perhaps because many in the church often violated this principle, one need only ask: Where does one find the greatest amount of religious freedom?   Is it in countries where Christianity has had the greatest and longest presence, or is it in societies where Christianity has had little or nor presence? The answer decidedly favors Christianity.

Despite some of the flagrant violations of religious freedom that occurred in the history of the church, the will and spirit of Christ eventually prevailed. God did not let evil have the last word. Thus, at various times in history, God would raise up stal-wart advocates of religious freedom in men like Tertullian, Lactantius, Wycliffe, Hus, and Savonarola, as noted above. He did so again in the person of Martin Luther, who before Charles V and the Diet of Worms in 1521 defied the authority and power of popes who had all but eliminated religious freedom.   He wanted to be free to follow his conscience. As historians know, a number of territorial princes sided with Luther, and a new era of religious freedom dawned with the arrival of the Protestant Reformation. So powerful was Luther's breakthrough for religious liberty and freedom of conscience that Thomas Bailey, a secular historian, in his massive volume on American history credits him as one of the "indirect founding fathers of the United States."[13]

The separation of church and state is, of course, closely linked to freedom of religion. And the most clearly formulated example of religious freedom is found in the First Amendment of the American Constitution, which states: "Congress shall make no law respecting an establishment of religion or prohibiting the free exercise thereof."   Briefly said, the government keeps its hands off religion, and religion keeps its hands off government.

Mosque and State: Siamese Twins of Islam

When one examines the history of Islam and its relationship to government or state, it soon becomes evident that, as Bernard Lewis has remarked: "In the traditional Islamic order, there is in principle no secular law but only the God-given Holy Law of Islam."[14] So closely joined is the state to the religion of Islam that they are in effect like Siamese twins.

The close bond between the religion of Islam and state governments in Islamic countries has been in existence without interruption for almost 1,400 years, and little or no attempt has been made in Islamic countries to separate the two. During the past 14 centuries, Turkey is so far the only exception where religion and the state have been separated, but even in Turkey there has in recent years been a strong move by Islamist forces to undo this separation.

Separation of Mosque and State: An Islamic Heresy

Given that the separation of church and state (religion and the state) has been a strong cultural norm for Americans and also for many Europeans for over 200 years, largely since the American War of Independence and the French Revolution, it is difficult for many to understand the total fusion of religion and the state as it exists in Muslim countries

The fusion of religion and the state began with Muhammad in the 620's. Ardent Muslims strenuously defend this fusion. This is well illustrated by Maryam Jameela, a convert from Judaism and a zealous defender of everything that is traditionally Islamic. In opposition to some liberal Muslims, who point to Turkey as a model for Muslims to imitate, she writes: "[F]rom the day Muhammad migrated from Mecca to Madinah Islam was a state as well as a religion. Muhammad was ruler as well as Prophet. Madinah was the capital of a sovereign state by every definition of that term. The Prophet raised armies, declared war, concluded peace, signed treaties, received and sent ambassadors, levied taxes, and dispensed justice as did all the Khalifs who succeeded him."[15]

211

For Islamic countries to adopt the separation of the Islamic religion from the state would obviously be a revolutionary reform. The very thought is repulsive to Muslims like Jameela. She declares: "Islam can never be 'reformed' for it is perfect in itself."[16]

Jameela's strong opposition to separating religion from the state is not an isolated exception among Muslims. Countless Muslims, probably the vast majority, similar to Jameela, defend the fusion of religion and the state relentlessly. That is why to date "Only one Muslim country, the Turkish Republic, has formally adopted the separation of religion and state as law."[17]

It appears that the vast majority of Muslims firmly believe it is Allah's will to have the state and religion combined. Some Muslims argue that the practice of not separating the spiritual from the temporal exists because Islam subordinates everything to God, unlike Christianity, which gave to the West the separation of church and state, the latter being the result of Christ's teaching that says Caesar should get what is Caesar's and God what is God's.[18] The Islamic argument, theologically speaking, implies that in the realm of politics Islam is better or superior to Christianity, and thus only if everything is not subordinated to God can religion be separated from the state.

Islamic purists see the separation of religion from the state as heretical. This is clear when one reads comments like the following. Mohmad Elhachmi Hamdi, who does not favor the West's model of separation of religion and state, has said: "The heart of the matter is that no Islamic state can be legitimate in the eyes of its subjects without obeying the main teachings of the *sharia*. A secular government might coerce obedience, but Muslims will not abandon their belief that state affairs should be supervised by the just teachings of the holy law."[19]

212

Expressed another way, "In the Muslim perception, there is no human legislative power and there is only one law for the believers—the Holy Law of God, promulgated by revelation."[20] In line with this thought is the statement once uttered by Iran's Ayatollah Khomeini: " 'Islam is politics or it is nothing.' "[21] Religion and the state are Islam's Siamese twins. As Bernard Lewis has pointed out, the separation of religion and the state in the eyes of Islam is a Christian disease.[22]

Separation of Religion and State in Turkey

When Mustafa Kemal, better known as Ataturk ("Father of the Turks"), became the head of Turkey in 1923 he began implementing a number of major changes. He abolished the longstanding Muslim caliphate, the Arabic alphabet, and the Muslim lunar calendar. But most significantly, he also separated religion from state activities, which meant abolishing the Shariah. He took these actions in order to emulate the West, for he was convinced if Turkey was to progress, and not regress, in the modern world, these reforms were vital.

In 1924, Turkey's constitution removed the article that said Islam was the country's religion.[23] This was the first time this kind of action happened in any Islamic country. To complement this action Kemal even outlawed turbans for men, replacing them with brimmed hats. (For this change the Isalmic purists attacked him saying it was his clever way of preventing men from praying in the accustomed prostrate position because the brimmed hats kept their heads from touching the ground or floor.) Another act brought about "the abolition of chattel slavery, the emancipation of women and restriction of polygamy and granting, in principle, equal rights to non-Muslims."[24]

Given these liberating acts one wonders whether in part they were acts of repentance on Kemal's part. For it was he who rejoiced when his men in Smyrna went house to house, breaking down the doors of Greek and Armenian Christian residences and killing family by family and then setting the 2,000-year-old city ablaze,[25] annihilating thousands of innocent people a couple of years before he became Turkey's leader in 1923. Seeing the inferno, he reportedly said: " 'It is a sign that Turkey is purged of the traitors, the Christians, and the foreigners, and that Turkey is for the Turks' " (*JW*, 407).

Islamic purists, from the beginning, have been irate with Kemal's reforms, often referred to as Kemalism. They have accused him of being an atheist, not only because he compelled men to wear brimmed hats, even in a mosque, but also because he converted some mosques into museums, closed some Islamic religious schools, banned religious organizations, and prohibited Muslims from making pilgrimages to Mecca and Medina.[26] Pilgrimages, however, are now permitted again.

Given the strength and longevity of traditional Islamic doctrine and ideology, it might be surmised that Turkey's separation of religion and state, given the events that have occurred in the 1980's and 1990's in Iran, Pakistan, Sudan, and Afghanistan, where the Shariah has been revived, would come under attack by the purists. Now that possibility does exist, for in the last 10 years two Islamist-minded governments have been elected.[27] The reforms, including the separation of religion from the state, could in the future be annulled in favor of the Shariah laws. Here it is well to remember that "The logic of Islamic law ... does not recognize the permanent existence of any polity outside Islam. ... In the meantime, it is a religious duty of Muslims to struggle until this end is accomplished."[28]

Fear of Kemalism in Muslim Countries

Although the Shahs in Iran from the mid-1930's to the late 1970's had never established the separation of religion from the state, they did try to introduce some other reforms, for example, giving women greater freedom by outlawing the veil

214

and the chador and permitting women to go out in public among men. These so-called secular acts frightened purist Muslims like Ayatollah Khomeini, who squelched the Western-like reforms in 1979 when he came out of exile and returned to power and restored the Shariah, which became the law of the land in 1980.

The fear of Kemalism is not confined to Iran. It is also present in Pakistan, where in 1977 the country moved to implement the Shariah, which it did not have when it became independent in 1947. But now the Shariah has been declared to be "above Pakistan's civil law."[29] The Islamic purists see this as assurance against a Kemal-like invasion that occurred in Turkey in the 1920's and is still present today. And of all Muslim countries, Saudi Arabia is most strongly innoculated against the Kemalist virus.

The forces opposed to Kemalism have also made progress in Africa. Sudan in 1983 declared Shariah to be the law of the land, and in 1989 it proclaimed itself to be an Islamic nation. When Shariah becomes the law of the land, there is no separation of religion and state.

Conclusion

The separation of religion and state does not seem to have much promise in most Islamic countries. Muhamed Elhachmi Hamdi, cited above, put his finger on the problem when he said that devout Muslims will not abandon their belief that state laws must be subordinate to Shariah laws. The tenacious clinging to the Shariah makes it impossible for Muslims to separate religion and the state. Thus, in order for religion and the state to be separate, the Shariah laws have to be rejected, as happened in Turkey in the 1920's under the leadership of Kemal Ataturk. For this to happen again in an Islamic country would mean a major revolution, one that is not likely to occur in the near future. In fact, as noted earlier, traditionalist Muslims in Turkey are working to dismantle Kemalism, and in recent years they have been able to elect more representatives in Turkey's unicameral legislative body.

There are at least two reasons that the separation of religion and state is not likely to occur in Islamic countries. First, it would mean abandoning the Shariah laws, which to the majority of devout Muslims is unthinkable. Second, to most Muslims it would be capitulating to a Christian value, and since Muslims have for centuries had a strong dislike, if not an outright hatred, for Christianity, it is extremely unlikely to happen.

The separation of religion and state is something Westerners are obviously talking about and would like to see in Muslim societies, but one hears virtually nothing from Muslims about this. Not even in Western Europe or in America, where thousands of Muslims now live, do we hear them extolling the separation of religion and the state. Their silence and its significance does not seem to be noticed by Westerner leaders who often have a naïve view of Islam. Instead, one hears Muslims in recent years, especially in France, Italy, and England, saying that they want the West to permit them to live under Shariah laws.[30] Clearly, this situation seriously calls into question the West's heritage of the separation of religion and the state.

10

ISLAM: A RELIGION OF PEACE?

"Peace, peace, when there is no peace" (Jeremiah 8:11)

In spite of the shocking events on September 11, 2001, Americans and other Westerners are being told that "Islam is a religion of peace." A corollary to this statement tells the public that these Muslim terrorists "hijacked Islam." But the public never hears whether the teachings of Islam might have hijacked the terrorists.

"The Bible Also Teaches Violence"

When certain passages from the Koran are cited that advocate violence, Muslims and their apologists are quick to reply that the Bible in the Old Testament has such passages, too. This is a flawed response. While the Old Testament does indeed have such passages, including some that advocated violence against ancient Israel's enemies, the New Testament has none. There is not a single verse in the entire New Testament that advocates violence. Neither Jesus nor his disciples ever uttered one word advocating or condoning violence. Instead, Jesus said: "If any one strikes you on the right cheek, turn to him the other also" (Matthew 5:39).

As indicated in Chapter 2, when Christians were severely persecuted during the first 300 years after Christ's resurrection, there is no evidence that any of them engaged in any form of violence, not even in self-defense. Unfortunately, after Christ-ianity attained legal status, some emperors and other Western leaders, who paraded as Christians, did indeed carry out some acts of violence. Those acts, however, clearly violated Christian principles. Those leaders soiled the name of Christianity, and their acts were not Christian acts.

When defenders of Islam cite examples of "Christian violence" in history, two things need to be noted. First, those Western leaders who engaged in non-defensive battles were often nominal or pseudo-Christians, or at best Christians horribly flawed. Second, unlike Muslims who were —and continue to be—urged by numerous passages in the Koran and the Hadith to carry out violent (jihad) behavior, the so-called Christians who engaged in violence did not have a single passage in the entire New Testament to support their violent behavior. The latter point is a vitally important difference when the violence done by Muslims is compared to that done by nominal Christians.

In regard to the violence found in the Old Testament, there is this to remember. Unlike Muhammad who called himself a prophet, who used the sword himself to kill people, and who directed numerous bloody battles, not one of the Old Testament prophets ever advocated using the sword, much less employed it themselves. This was true of Isaiah, Jeremiah, Ezekiel, Daniel, Micah, Amos, Malachi, and all the Hebrew prophets. Moreover, the violent commands found in the Old Testament that were directed against certain groups are all in the past tense, 3,000 years ago. Moreover, neither Christians nor Jews use the violent or warlike passages of the Old Testament to promote or justify violence or killing of people today.

What the Koran, Hadith, and Shariah Say About Violence

To examine the question of whether Islam is a "religion of peace," it is necessary to look at the Koran, the Hadith, the Shariah, and historical evidence regarding Islam's 1,400-year record. Chapter 1 already discussed a number of verses from the Koran relative to the battles that were fought under

218

Muhammad's direction, and how he frequently had individuals executed in cold blood.

The House of Islam vs. the House of War

To answer the question of whether Islam is a religion of peace, it must be noted that Islam from its beginning has divided the world into two irreconcilable spheres. There is *Dar al-Islam* (House or Land of Islam) and *Dar al-Harb* (House or Land of War). The *Dar al-Islam* is populated with the followers of Islam, the territory where "Muslim government rules and Muslim law prevails."[1] The *Dar al-Harb,* on the other hand, is the house or land of non-Muslims. It is any territory occupied by non-Muslims ("infidels"), who are "destined to come under Islamic jurisdiction, either by conversion of its inhabitants or by armed conflict" (*ID*, 43). Briefly put, "All acts of war are permitted in the *Dar al-Harb*" (*WI*, 218).

Clearly, the concept of the *Dar al-Harb* does not mesh with the assurances one hears these days in the West that Islam is a religion of peace. Bernard Lewis sees the implications of the *Dar al-Harb* rather clearly: "In Muslim writings, the Christian world becomes the House of War par excellence, and the war against Christendom is the very model and prototype of the jihad."[2]

The concept of the *Dar al-Harb* is not only held or believed by "radical Muslims." It is an integral part of Islam. It is an ideology that helps one understand the following verse in the Koran. "And kill them wherever you find them, and drive them out from whence they drove you out ... " (Sura 2:191). Numerous other verses could be cited to show that Islam is not a religion of peace (see Appendix A). It is only peaceful if everyone submits to its ideology and control—that is, when everyone becomes a member of the House of Islam, which could be called the House of Submission, consistent with the meaning of the name "Islam."

The Concept of Jihad

As noted in Chapter 1, the Shariah manual for Sunni Muslims, *Reliance of the Traveller*, states: "*Jihad* means to war against non-Muslims, and is etymologically derived from the word *mutahada*, signifying warfare to establish the religion" (o9.0). Chapter 2 noted that a considerable amount of false information is presently being propagated about the Islamic concept of jihad. Some Muslims and apologists are trying to tell the public that jihad does not mean holy war, but that it means struggling or striving to improve oneself in one's personal or spiritual life. They call this "the greater jihad." One apologist for Islam, John Kaltner, has recently even stated that "*jihad* is a concept that cannot be linked to violence or war in any way."[3] He cites a verse from Sura 22:78 to support his argument. That lengthy verse says in part: "'And strive for Allah with the endeavor which is His right. He hath chosen you and hath not laid upon you in religion hardship; the faith of your father Abraham (is yours) . . .'"[4]

Although the word "jihad" can indeed mean struggle or strive, it is quite another argument to say that it only means a personal struggle to improve one's spiritual life. Such an argument contradicts the majority of statements that speak about jihad in the Koran, the Hadith, and the Shariah, where the word almost exclusively means physical fighting and warlike activities done to advance a holy war(s) against the "infidels."

A jihad command in the Koran, noted earlier in another context, is relevant here and needs to be cited again. "Fight those who do not believe in Allah, nor in the latter day, nor do they prohibit what Allah and His Apostle have prohibited, nor follow the religion of truth, out of those who have been given the Book, until they pay the tax in acknowledgement of

220

superiority and they are in a state of subjection" (Sura 9:29). Sura 9:123 further underscores the physically combative nature of jihad: "O you who believe! Fight those of the unbelievers who are near to you and let them find in you hardness; and know that Allah is with those who guard (against evil)."

In fact, the Koran also says that jihad refers to subduing the whole world in order to bring about only one, universal religion: "And fight with them until there is no more persecution and religion should only be for Allah; but if they desist, then surely Allah sees what they do" (Sura 8:39). Interestingly, this particular verse appears in the chapter titled: "The Spoils of War."

One section of the Hadith talks about keeping a horse "for the purpose of Jihad in Allah's Cause" (*Sahih Al-Bukhari* 52:45). This passage obviously has nothing to do with struggling to improve oneself personally or spiritually. Another Hadith passage talks about "Participation in Jihad after the consummation of marriage" (*Sahih Al-Bukhari* 52:115). And still another Hadith reference refers to obtaining permission from an imam "if one wishes to participate in a holy battle" (*Sahih Al-Bukhari* 52:113). Clearly, these references talk only about physical fighting, not about personal or spiritual striving or struggling.

Reliance of the Traveller (o9.0) cites three verses from the Koran in support of jihad: "Fighting is prescribed for you" (Sura 2:216); "Slay them wherever you find them" (Sura 4:89); and "Fight the idolaters utterly" (Sura 9:36). Muslims are also urged to "undertake jihad against enemies, dividing the spoils of battle among the combatants, and setting aside a fifth ... for deserving recipients" (o25.9.8). Preceding o9.4, it has a section titled "WHO IS OBLIGED TO FIGHT IN JIHAD" [sic] in which it spells out some aspects of jihad. And under the caption "THE RULES OF WARFARE" [sic] it notes: "It is not permissible to kill women or children unless they are fighting against the Muslims" (o9.10). It further declares: "It is permissible in jihad to cut down the enemy's trees and destroy their buildings" (o9.15). Again, these references have only one meaning—to fight the "infidels."

The argument that jihad is a personal struggle to improve oneself spiritually receives very little support from the Koran, the Hadith, or the Shariah. Moreover, numerous scholarly books and articles written by Muslims do not provide this nonviolent concept of jihad. *The Concise Encyclopedia of Islam* (1989), for example, states that jihad is "a Divine institution of warfare to extend Islam into the *dar al-harb* (the non-Islamic territories which are described as the 'abode of struggle,' or of disbelief) or to defend Islam from danger."[5]

The notion that jihad only means personal striving is a belief derived from the Sufi Muslims. But Sufi Muslims are a mystical sect and only a small minority. Thus, when some Muslims are redefining jihad, they are drawing their arguments from a sect within Islam, not from Islam as a whole. In doing so, they are basically casting aside the evidence in the Koran, the Hadith, and the Shariah; they are also ignoring the facts of history. As Bernard Lewis recently stated, "Mohammad himself led the first jihad in the wars of the Muslims against the pagans in Arabia."[6]

In another of his works on Islam, Bernard Lewis notes that recently Muslims in Iran, in their attempt to justify Khomeini's 15-year-old *fatwa* that condemned Salman Rushdie to death for writing *Satanic Verses*, have found evidence in Muhammad's life to support Khomeini's condemnation. Researchers have found that Muhammad, after the Battle of Bedr in 624, had two Arab poets executed for lampooning him.[7] He also had Kab ibn al-Ashraf, a half Jew, brutally murdered by one of his sycophants, as noted in Chapter 1. These and many other murderous acts of the jihad by Muhammad and by his associates have been imitated by Muslims for hundreds of

222

years. Yet the myth that Islam is a religion of peace is repeated again and again, especially in recent years.

Jihad and Patronizing Non-Muslim Politicians

There have recently been a number of high-ranking governmental officials in the United States and Britain perpetuating the myth that Islam is peaceful in their public statements. Their comments, especially since September 11, have been heard so often that one hesitates to repeat them. Many of them sound as though they were taken from the same politically correct "playbook," repeated almost robotically. Here are some examples.

President Clinton once said it was unfair to identify Islam with "the forces of radicalism and terrorism."[8] President George W. Bush, in a speech to the United States Congress, declared that Islam's "teachings are good and peaceful, and those who commit evil in the name of Allah blaspheme the name of Allah."[9] On another occasion he said: "Islam is peace."[10] Similarly, Secretary of State Colin Powell, at a State Department's Ramadan Iftaar, stated: "I have learned about Islam as a religion of peace and caring."[11] Regarding those Americans who do not see Islam in this light, President Clinton's Secretary of State, Madeline Albright, chastised them for their "appalling degree of ignorance" about Islam.[12] And on April 1, 2004, the American ambassador Paul Bremer in Baghdad, in response to the attack that brutally killed and burned four American civilians in Fallujah the day before, said on television that this atrocity was "contrary to all religions, including Islam."

These appeasing comments are not limited to governmental officials of the United States. In England, Prime Minister Tony Blair has voiced similar statements. Speaking about Muslim terrorists, even before September 11, he once said, "Islam is not about terrorism or extremism." To this he added that acts of terrorism "have nothing to do with the teachings of the Qur'an. ... "[13]

If Islam is a peaceful religion, how does one explain the countless acts of terror and aggression of its jihads that transpired during its history from the seventh century on, including those of Muhammad? Those jihads, some of which were noted in Chapters 2 and 6, make it difficult to say Islam is a peaceful religion.

Given the relentless efforts that are being made to present Islam as a religion of peace, in spite of the documented evidence to the contrary, the following questions need to be asked.

1. Why is it a capital crime in most Islamic countries to make critical or negative comments about Muhammad, question the Koran, or renounce Islam?

2. Why have so many writers, especially former Muslims, who have written works critical of Islam had their lives threatened, forcing them in many instances to have guards, adopt pseudonyms, and keep their addresses secret?

3. How does one explain the following words of Irshad Manji, the Canadian critic of Islamic teaching? She says:

> Pick a Muslim country, any Muslim country, and the most brutal humiliations will grab you by the vitals. In Pakistan, an average of two women every day die from 'honor killings,' often with Allah's name on the lips of the murderers. ... In Mali and Mauritania, little boys are seduced into slavery by Muslim hustlers. In Sudan, slavery happens at the hands of Islamic militias. In Yemen and Jordan, Christian humanitarian workers have been shot point-blank. In Bangladesh, artists who advocate for the rights of religious minorities have been locked up or driven out of the country altogether. It's all documented.[14]

4. How does one explain the comment by Oriana Fallaci? She says: "From Afghanistan to Sudan, from Palestine

to Pakistan, from Malaysia to Iran, from Egypt to Iraq, from Algeria to Senegal, from Syria to Kenya, from Libya to Chad, from Lebanon to Morocco, from Indonesia to Yemen, from Saudi Arabia to Somalia, the hate for the West swells like a fire fed by the wind."[15]

5. Why have the jihad passages in the Koran not been abrogated under the Islamic so-called doctrine of abrogation?

6. Why, as Robert Spencer has noted, are there no verses in the Koran or Hadith that mitigate the violent passages?

7. Finally, two additional questions, as asked by Reza F. Safa, an ex-Shiite Islamist, are pertinent. "If Islam is peaceful, why are there so many verses in the Koran about killing the infidels and those who resist Islam? If Islam is peaceful, why isn't there even one Muslim country that will allow freedom of religion and speech?"[16]

When politicians and apologists say that Islam is a peaceful religion, one wonders whether they have ever read the Koran. Granted, it is not an easy book to read. One could call it a verbal collage. George Sale, a British scholar of Islam, who first translated the Koran into English in 1734, said, "it is a motley jumble of inconsistencies, for what is a crime in one chapter is a commendable action in another."[17] Edward Gibbon, the British historian, said it was "an incoherent rhapsody of fable, and precept, and declamation, which sometimes crawls in the dust, and is sometimes lost in the clouds."[18] Even Cyril Glasse's *The Concise Encyclopedia of Islam* (1989), a volume favorable to Islam, speaks of the Koran's "disjointed and irregular character."[19] Nevertheless, if politicians really want to understand the present Islamist terrorist threats, they need to—in fact they must—read the Koran as well as the Hadith.

If national leaders and statesmen do not read these Islamic sources, they may bring upon themselves and their nations a tragedy similar to what happened in the 1930's when

225

freedom-loving leaders failed to read Hitler's book *Mein Kampf*. Many did not believe Hitler and his Nazis were all that bad. Had Neville Chamberlain, Prime Minister of England, read *Mein Kampf*, he probably would not have seen Hitler as a man of peace and he would not have appeased him in Munich in 1938. One year later, this false perception of peace resulted in World War II. Given that experience, along with centuries of Islamic jihads in the Middle East, Africa, and Europe, when Americans are told Islam is a religion of peace, they would do well to heed George Santayana's counsel: "If we do not learn from the mistakes of history, we are destined to repeat them."

"Americans," says Gene Edward Veith, "tend to be in a state of denial about the religious dimensions of this war [Christian vs. Islamic worldviews], thanks to our habit of political correctness and our omni-tolerant religious relativism. We insist that Islam is a benign religion of peace and tolerance."[20] What could be more favorable to the Islamic jihad—which is centuries old—than to throw the *kuffar* (infidels) off guard by having them believe that Islam is a peaceful religion?

Those continuing to perpetuate America's state of denial need to listen to C. Iqbal, a Muslim, who has resided in the United States for 35 years. Recently, he stated "I will not deny that the Qur'an promotes violence against non-Muslims and that history proves it." He continued: "I feel that it is stupid to deny, lie, justify or defend something which is not acceptable by the standards of today's civilized world and human rights."[21]

What Is So Hard About Understanding the Jihad?

In spite of the above documentation of what jihad is and does, it is clear that many, including many key European and American officials and much of the public, do not seem to understand the nature of Islam's jihad. Hence, some seemed surprised when, since September 11, some Muslims, within and outside of the American military, were arrested as alleged spies or enemy combatants.

When Americans are surprised that some Muslims are found as spies or men aiding the Islamic terrorists, there are probably at least two reasons for it. First, Americans, who have been reared in an environment of liberty and freedom, have come to believe that everyone growing up in a context of freedom has internalized these values. So why would someone raised in America's free society, for example, James Walker, Yaser Esam Hamdi, Jose Padilla, James Ujaama, and Ryan Anderson allegedly betray his country to aid Islamists whose religion advocates jihadic violence against the very country that gave them freedom and liberty? Similarly, why would an American Muslim soldier throw a grenade into an army camp injuring 13 fellow American soldiers in Kuwait during the early stages of the Iraq War in March 2003 if his religion is a religion of peace?

Second, because most Americans have grown up in a society where the Judeo-Christian ethic is still to some degree a part of the American culture, they find it difficult to imagine that a religion with over one billion members worldwide and which many call a peaceful religion could teach its followers to adopt the philosophy of jihad. When Americans think this way, they forget that non-Muslims live in *Dar al-Harb*, the House of War.

"Radical Muslims": A Valid Concept?

We hear a lot in the media and from politicians, especially since September 11, that the Muslim terrorists are "radical Muslims." Sometimes the term "Muslim extremists" is used as well. Both labels are used to convey the idea that these individuals are a small fringe group of Muslims who have hijacked Islam, as it has been expressed. The concept of radical Muslims, however, is not without some major conceptual or definitional problems. The following discussion notes some of them.

First, what distinguishes radical Muslims from those who are not radical? Do radical Muslims believe in the Koran and see Muhammad as their prophet, whereas the non-radical Muslims do not? From all indications they both believe in the Koran and see Muhammad as Islam's prophet.

Second, do radical Muslims fully believe and totally commit themselves to the teachings of the Koran and the Hadith? On the other hand, do non-radical Muslims not fully believe and not totally commit themselves to the teachings of the Koran and the Hadith? If the answer to both questions is yes, then radical Muslims are true-believing Muslims and the non-radical Muslims are only nominal Muslims. As nominal Muslims, they apparently are selective in what they believe or accept in the Koran and the Hadith, similar to nominal Christians who are selective regarding what they believe or accept in the Bible. This raises the question of whether nominal Muslims are really Muslims just as it does whether nominal Christians are really Christians. Nominal Muslims may call themselves Muslims just as nominal Christians call themselves Christians, but does that make either group what it says it is? Logically, it cannot be denied that so-called radical Muslims are really true Muslims, but whether nominal or non-radical Muslims are really true Muslims appears open to debate. Does merely calling one self a Muslim make one a Muslim?

Third, if radical Muslims are those who engage in terror and killing of innocent people, then, in order to be consistent, the definition must include Muhammad. Given the prevailing concept of "radical Muslims," he certainly fits that definition. He was Islam's first warrior. History shows he ordered numerous massacres and even killed some individuals himself, as noted in Chapter 2. His successors (caliphs) did much the same; they too killed scores of innocent people as they pursued their jihads, and they did so for centuries.

Fourth, how do "radical Muslims" become radical? Is it perhaps because the Koran, the Hadith, and the Shariah contain radical precepts? As one authority on Islam has recently said, "Informed Muslims *know* [sic] that the Koran does not advocate moderation!"[22]

Finally, the concept of radical Muslims, as used by the media and politicians, implies these Muslims are only a small minority or a fringe group. But this ignores the fact that there are millions of terrorist-minded Muslims in al-Qaeda, Hamas, Islamic Jihad, Hezbollah, and other like-minded Islamist groups. Estimates indicate that the "radical Muslims" have a following of approximately 150 million members in the various terrorist groups listed above.[23] A recent report (January 2004) noted that Hamas, which advocates the destruction of the State of Israel, has been growing steadily in numbers and power by attracting middle-class professionals. It now offers social services such as day camps and summer schools for children of these professionals. The report further stated that Hamas may soon be able to replace the Palestinian Authority in Palestine.[24]

In December 1988, in Bolton, England, about 7,000 Muslims publicly protested and burned Salman Rushdie's novel, *Satanic Verses.* Then on January 14, 1989, Muslims imitated this protest by burning Rushdie's book in Bradford, England.[25] And 30,000 Muslims gathered in protest outside the British Parliament in London on May 27, 1989.[26] Were these only small groups of radical Muslims?

In response to the idea that radical Muslims are only a fringe group, the words of Oriana Fallaci, a former Muslim, seem relevant: "Their yells Allah-akbar [God is great], Allah-akbar [God is great]. Jihad, Jihad. ... Extremist fringes?! Fanatical minorities?! They are millions and millions, the fanatics. The millions and millions for whom, dead or alive,

Osama Bin Laden is a legend similar to the legend of Khomeini."[27]

Conclusion

After viewing the evidence of Islam's numerous non-peaceful jihads, along with what has been noted and discussed in the preceding chapters, it is difficult to call Islam a religion of peace. Historically speaking, it seems that calling Islam a peaceful religion is a relatively recent phenomenon. In the past historians understood and recognized that the Judeo-Christian values of liberty, justice, and truth were threatened every time Muslims launched their jihads in various geographic regions. Scholars and historians did not hesitate to depict Islam as a non-peaceful religion. For example, Sir William Muir, a 19th century British scholar of Islam and Muhammad, without hatred or animosity felt compelled to write: "The sword of Mahomet and the Coran [sic] are the most fatal enemies of Civilization, Liberty, and Truth, which the world has yet known" (*LM*, 4:322).

When Bertrand Russell, the British philosopher, published his book *Why I Am Not A Christian* in 1927, he did not have to take a pseudonym. There was no high-ranking Western official who condemned him to death, nor was there a group publicly protesting and burning his book. There is a tremendous difference between Judeo-Christian morality and the morality of Islam. As Ali Bhutto, a former prime minister of Pakistan, said: "No religion is as oppressive as mine."[28]

When many in the media and apologists for Islam criticized Franklin Graham in the fall of 2001 for saying Islam was an "evil and wicked religion," they should have evaluated his comments in the light of Islam's history before denouncing him. The fact that Graham's comments were politically incorrect does not mean they were also historically incorrect.

In regard to Islam being a religion of peace and that only a few radical Muslims are the problem, columnist Don Feder has recently written a telling statement, one that every governmental leader in the West and all freedom-loving Westerners seriously need to ponder. "Imagine," he says, "in 1940, Winston Churchill taking to the airwaves to announce that Nazism was an ideology of peace which, regrettably, had been perverted by a few fanatics like Hitler and Goebbels. But most storm troopers and SS men are fine fellows, your friends and neighbors."[29]

11

POLITICAL CORRECTNESS AND APOLOGISTS:

ISLAM'S BEST FRIENDS

"For lying is thy sustenance, thy food; yet thou pretend'st to truth" (Milton)

In previous chapters occasional references were made regarding apologists for Islam. The phenomenon of political correctness has been mentioned as well. Given that defenders of Islam are greatly aided by the current milieu of political correctness in the West, this chapter shows that together they are, in effect, Islam's best friends.

In spite of voluminous evidence showing that Muhammad and his followers have from the inception of Islam engaged in numerous wars and acts of violence, often massacring scores of innocent people, there are today numerous apologists—both Muslim and non-Muslim—for Muhammad and the religion he founded. As Ibn al-Rawandi has noted, it is understandable that Muslims, born and raised as Muslims, with family ties and so on, would defend Islam. But why "educated Westerners voluntarily adopt it and actively promote it is a phenomenon in need of explanation."[1] Surely, non-Muslim apologists must know some of the documented history of the acts of violence that occurred in the name of Allah since the time of Muhammad..

In today's *Weltanschauung* of political correctness, apologists, as Al Sina says, are "expediently lying when the truth is hurtful."[2] Both Muslim and non-Muslim apologists try to put a positive spin on Muhammad's many blood-stained activities. Some try to deny the countless jihads, such as the numerous unprovoked invasions and occupations of countries and regions that occurred from the seventh century on. Others ignore Islam's complicity in slavery, forced conversions, punishing apostasy by execution, and treating non-Muslims as second-class (*dhimmi*) citizens. Some non-Muslim apologists even engage in patronizing Islam, something they would not do in regard to Christianity or Judaism.

Praising Muhammad

Ever since Muhammad died in 632, there have been some Muslims who have served as apologists or polemicists for him. But since approximately the early 20th century, apologists for Muhammad have become especially prominent. As Daniel Pipes reminds us, they now have even invaded the ivy halls and classrooms of Western universities.[3] In addition, many are found in politics, in the textbook publishing industry, and in the liberal left-wing media. The astonishing fact is that many apologists are not Muslims.

Although non-Muslim apologists for Muhammad and Islam are a relatively recent phenomenon in Islam's 1,400-year history, the apologetic seeds were planted in the latter part of the 1700's by the well-known British historian Edward Gibbon, who wrote the six volumes of *The Decline and the Fall of the Roman Empire,* completed in 1788. Until then, as apologist Caesar E. Farah says, "[T]hrough the Middle Ages and up to the Age of Enlightenment [eighteenth century] Muhammad's prophethood and message remained the object of suspicion and controversy."[4]

Earlier, we saw that one of the earliest non-Muslim critics of Muhammad was John of Damascus (d. ca. 750), a Christian priest and monk who said Muhammad was influenced and misled by the Nestorians and Arians, two heretical sects of Christianity. In Chapter 1 we saw that Alighieri Dante (d. 1321) placed Muhammad in the lowest circle of hell. These men were not alone in their critical view of Muhammad.

Ramon Lull (ca. 1232–1315), a convert to Christianity in his adult life, at age 45 began to study Arabic and Islam, and at age 50 became a Christian missionary to the Muslims in North Africa. He challenged Muslims to prove that Islam was superior to Christianity, and his teachings pointed out that Muhammad had broken every one of the Ten Commandments. For this he was imprisoned twice, flogged, and ultimately stoned to death in June of 1315.[5]

Another early critic of Muhammad, a contemporary of Lull, was Riccoldo de Monte Croce (1243–1320), a Dominican priest, who lived for a time in the Middle East, including Baghdad. He too learned Arabic, studied the Koran, and in 1300 he published his *Confutatio Alcoran* (Refutation of the Koran). In this book's foreword, Riccoldo stated: "During the reign (611–641) of Emperor Heraclius there appeared a man, indeed a devil, a first-born child of Satan, opposed to the truth and the Christian church. He was intoxicated with carnal lust and engaged in crafty evil—his name was Muhammad."[6]

Martin Luther (1483–1546) came upon Riccoldo's book 200 years later. When he first read it he doubted that Muslims believed what Riccoldo said. Later, after he had read Ketton's Latin Koran in 1541, he changed his mind and agreed that Riccoldo was correct about the evils of Islam.[7] He later wrote saying: "Muhammad martyred many innocent children and Christians by cruelly executing them."[8] Luther considered Riccoldo's work so valuable that he translated it from the Latin into German in 1542. Recently (2003), this book has been translated for the first time into English by Thomas C. Pfotenhauer by the title *Islam in the Crucible: Can it Pass the Test?*.[9]

Space does not permit citing numerous other critics of Muhammad from the Middle Ages to the present day. But the comments of two more observers are worthy of note. George Sale, a 19th-century British biographer of Muhammad, said "the

234

greatest advocates of the mission of Mohammad have never been able to deny that he was extremely wicked. ... "[10] Edward Augustus Freeman, also a 19th-century scholar of Islam, argued that Muhammad "was clearly blameworthy in not fully informing himself on such important questions [e.g., who Christ really was]. Consequently, his system became one of mere retrogression and bitter antagonism to the truth."[11]

Even though Gibbon described Muhammad as an "illiterate barbarian," who operated "with the sword in one hand and the Koran in the other," [12] he oddly enough extolled him in a number of ways. He tried to make Muhammad look good in regard to his multiple wives by contrasting him to King Solomon who had 700 wives. He also spoke well of him for "despising the pomp of royalty."[13] For the most part, he said positive things about Muhammad and Islam. His relatively positive portrayal of Muhammad and Islam left its mark in the West. "Gibbon's influence on the Western perception of the Prophet and Islam," says Bernard Lewis, "and their place in history is enormous."[14]

Gibbon's influence, however, was not immediate. As already noted, it was not until after World War I that one finds a growing number of non-Muslim apologists in the West casting the best possible light on Muhammad. Tor Andrae, a biographer of Muhammad at the University of Upsala in Sweden, was one such apologist. In 1936, he authored his book in German, *Mohammad, Sein Leben und Sein Glaube* (Mohammad, the Man and His Faith). He tries to justify Muhammad's numerous violent and warring activities by saying; "One must see Mohammed's cruelty toward the Jews against the background of the fact that their scorn and rejection was the greatest disappointment of his life, and for a time they threatened completely to destroy his prophetic authority."[15] He further states, "Mohammed's religious integrity rests ... upon the fact that he himself was one of those great personalities who are expressions of the creative life of God. ... "[16]

This is a rather strange ethic on Andrae's part to see mere scorn and rejection as justification for Muhammad's atrocities. One wonders whether this same charitable comment would have been extended to Jesus Christ had he acted like Muhammad, for he was also rejected by people, and on more than one occasion. The Gospel informs us that they also tried to stone him.

Another non-Muslim apologist, Arthur Gilman, after noting that Muhammad's religious role was tarnished by polygamy (polygyny) and blotted by slavery, nevertheless tries to put Muhammad in a good light by saying, "but in both of these respects, it was an improvement upon what had preceded it."[17] He also tries to exonerate him by making him appear as a victim of false information: "It was his [Muhammad's] misfortune not to have seen Christianity in its full brightness, and it has been a misfortune of his followers ever since. To him Isa [Jesus] was not the perfect man that Jesus was. ... "[18] Thus, we are told that the evil things Muhammad did were really not his fault.

Some apologists even defend and justify Muhammad's brutal assassinations, as does John Bagot Glubb. He argues that Muhammad's assassinations can only be seen as "indefensible in a country that possesses a constitution, laws, a judicial system and a police force. In seventh century Arabia, however, none of these things existed."[19] Another apologist for Muhammad is the recently deceased and well-known American novelist James A. Michener. Contrary to what history shows concerning Muhammad's 10 blood-drenched years (622–632), Michener ignores these facts by saying he was "a saintly man ... [who] preached that slaves should be set free ... that peace is better than war, that justice prevails."[20]

236

It is difficult to understand how Michener, who reportedly did extensive research for his many novels, failed to do adequate research regarding the life and actions of Muhammad. Michener's comment that Muhammad preached against slavery is contradicted by Muhammad not only having taken slaves captive in his battles, but also dispensing slaves to his fellow Muslims and keeping slaves himself. Some of his slaves were females whom he kept as concubines. One of them was Mary, a Coptic Christian.[21] Another was Rihana, mentioned below. Moreover, in Sura 24:33 of the Koran Muhammad instructs Muslims as to how they may keep slaves. This verse in the Koran still stands.

Other apologists, similar to Gibbon, defend Muhammad's lifestyle of having multiple wives and a number of concubines as well. One scholarly report, published by an Iranian Muslim, states he had 20 wives and several concubines.[22] Yet, Desmond Stewart says: "Whatever sensuality he may have had, however, was tempered by kindness and loyalty."[23] This comment reminds one of the old adage: "No man is so evil that there is not some good in him."

There have, of course, always been some Muslims who have publicly defended Muhammad. Muhammad Husayn Haykal (1888–1956), an Egyptian biographer of Muhammad, was one of them. In his *The Life of Muhammad* (1976) he defends the founder of Islam to such an extent that he even maintains that when Muhammad consummated his marriage with nine-year-old Aisha, she was "fully grown," even though she still "loved amusement and play."[24] And although he notes the decapitation of the half-Jewish man Kab ibn al-Ashraf, he says nothing about the role Muhammad played in this execution. He also says nothing about what Muhammad commanded in regard to Ibn Khatal, a captive who clung to the curtains in the Kaaba. "Kill him," said Muhammad (*Sahih Al-Bukhari* 52:169).

Apologists for Islam have not only appeared in American universities and colleges, but they have also invaded the arena of public grade schools, where they skew stories in favor of Muhammad, making him look good and noble in the eyes of young, malleable pupils. For instance, one kindergarten textbook states: "Muhammad had always been a thoughtful man, and there were evidently times when he needed to be by himself. He needed time to meditate about his life and the things that were happening in the world around him."[25] This sentence fails to note that many of the things happening in the world around him pertained to his bloody battles. Reading this sentence, no kindergarten child would even remotely imagine, much less learn, about the many atrocities that Muhammad directed. The apologists, emboldened by the multiculturalist ethic of political correctness, are not teaching facts about Muhammad, but spreading patronizing propaganda that unequivocally contradict the facts of history.

Ignoring Muhammad's Anti-Semitism

In addition to putting the best possible "face" on Muhammad's many bellicose ventures, apologists also ignore his anti-Semitic actions. Chapter 1 noted that Muhammad angrily changed the direction of prayer for Muslims from Jerusalem to Mecca after he was rejected by the Jews. He had also asked Muslims and Jews to observe Yom Kippur, but when the Jews also rejected this effort, he made the month of Ramadan a time for Muslim fasting.

These rejections caused him to hate Jews. He showed and exercised his hatred right after he won the Battle of Bedr. He "deported one of the three major Jewish groups from Medina and confiscated its property. The second Jewish group later suffered a similar fate; and because the third Jewish group was reputed to be hostile to Islam, Mohammad had the men [about 700, noted earlier] killed and the women and children sold into slavery."[26] This particular vindictive action shocked even his wife Aisha.[27] With actions such as these, within three years he had eliminated the Jews from Medina (*ID*, 37).

Muhammad's anti-Semitism is also evident in the Koran: "Certainly you will find the most violent of people in enmity for those who believe (to be) the Jews ... " (Sura 5:82). He also blamed the Jews for "hiding and dislocating the prophecies of himself" (*LM*, 71). Another verse in the Koran reads: "Wherefore for the iniquity of those who are Jews did We disallow to them the good things which had been made lawful for them, and for their hindering many (people) from Allah's way" (Sura 4:160).

As Tor Andrae has stated in defense of Muhammad: "For him it was a fixed axiom that Jews were sworn enemies of Allah and his revelation. Any mercy toward them was out of the question."[28] Thus, after Muhammad had conquered Medina and later Mecca, it is not surprising that no Jew or Christian without special permission has been allowed to set foot in either city (*JW*, 75).

Yet it is not politically correct to criticize Muhammad. On the other hand, as Serge Trifkovic has pointed out, "Jesus Christ is freely 'deconstructed' and 'contextualized' in the same Western institutions of higher learning—and often by the same people—who defer uncritically to Muslim sensibilities and obsessions."[29] There is obviously a double standard in vogue, one that benefits neither Muslims, non-Muslims, nor the pursuit of truth.

In regard to telling the truth about Muhammad, Ibn Warraq's comments are fitting: "Muslims do not need patronizing liberals to meet them 'half way.' Muslims need to write, for example, an honest biography of the Prophet that does not shun the truth, least of all cover it up with dishonest subterfuge of condescending Western scholars."[30]

Extolling Islam

If Muhammad is praised, the religion that he founded receives even more praise from apologists—or Islamophiles, as some critics call them. This praise is no longer confined to articles or books. Public schools, which in recent years have been barred from saying or implying anything favorable about Christianity, are now increasingly extolling Islam and some of its practices.

Criticism of Islam is not permitted today because it is defined as "mean-spirited." But it was not always so, as we have seen from some of the criticisms that go back at least to the eighth century. And it needs to be noted that the critics were by no means motivated by hatred toward Muslims or Islam, but rather they could not close their eyes to the hard facts of history, as so many defenders of Islam are doing today.

Extolling Islam in America's Public Schools

Recently (2003), the Excelsior Elementary School in Byron, California, required its seventh-grade students to role-play being Muslims, such as choosing Muslim names, dressing in Muslim garb, reading from the Koran, and praying to Allah. In order to obtain a passing grade, students were also required to give assent to statements saying that the Koran was God's word as revealed to Muhammad. When some parents took the case to court, a federal judge ruled that the school did not violate the United States Constitution.[31] In New York, according to the *New York Post* (December 1, 2003), one Brooklyn high school gives permission for Islamic students "to turn the auditorium into a makeshift mosque for their daily prayer vigil."[32] And "prayer rooms," said the *New York Post*, are provided at other high schools, including Brooklyn Tech and International HS [sic] in Long Island City, Queens."[33]

In the summer of 2002, the University of North Carolina in Chapel Hill, North Carolina, announced that 3,500 freshmen

240

in the class of 2006 for the fall semester would be required to read Michael Sell's book *Approaching the Qur'an: The Early Revelations* (1999). In typical apologetic fashion, Sell, a professor of religion at Haverford College in Pennsylvania, sanitizes Islam by omitting the Koran's passages that command violent behavior or jihad.

Interestingly, the American Civil Liberties Union (ACLU), which frequently challenges the display of Christmas crèches, Christian crosses, or the Ten Commandments on public property, has come to the defense of the University of North Carolina. In response to the ACLU's decision, an editorial in the *Wall Street Journal* said it well: "Finally, it seems, the ACLU has found a religion it can tolerate."[34]

The ACLU's defense of the University of North Carolina would seem to indicate that its longstanding opposition to the display of Christian symbols or the Ten Commandments on public property has apparently never really been about the alleged violation of the separation church and state. Rather, it seems that the issue at hand is the ACLU's great dislike of Christianity. In its Christophobic stance, the ACLU has become Islamophilic.

"Muslims Also Believe In Jesus"

In efforts to extol Islam, it is quite common to hear Muslims and some of their defenders say: "Muslims also believe in Jesus." Apparently this statement is intended to make Christians in the West feel at ease with the idea that Muslim beliefs are not that different from their own. In a similar vein, Professor Rollin Armour, Sr. in his book *Islam, Christianity and the West* (2003), states: "Islam and Judaism are closer to Christianity than other religions, and Islam would seem closer of the two because of the high esteem in which it holds Jesus."[35] The latter part of this statement is similar to what a Muslim imam, Fisal Hammouda, proclaimed to a large gathering of

241

Christians at the Willow Creek Community Church in South Barrington, Illinois, in October 2001, soon after the events of September 11. He declared: "We believe in Jesus more than you do."[36]

Meant to extol Islam, this imam's statement was really disingenuous and an insult to informed, committed Christians. Why? Because the Koran and Islam deny the crucifixion of Christ, and therefore his physical resurrection from the dead is also denied. Both of these historical events form part of the foundation of Christianity. To deny either one of these doctrines has for centuries *ipso facto* placed a person or group outside the pale of Christianity. Thus, Muslims do not believe more in Jesus, but far less than do informed, committed Christians.

It also necessary to note that, when Muslims speak of Jesus, they never speak of "Jesus Christ." It is always "Jesus" without the name "Christ." For instance, every time the Koran mentions Jesus, the name of "Christ" is conspicuously absent. There is a definite reason for this omission. If Muslims said "Jesus Christ," they would be admitting, at least tacitly, that he was the Messiah predicted in the Old Testament. As many readers know, the name Christ is the English translation for the Greek word *Christos*, the Hebrew equivalent of the word Messiah, meaning the anointed one of God.

To repeat, Muslims do not "believe in Jesus more" than do Christians. As the renowned scholar, J. Muehleisen Arnold, said more than a century ago: "The last events of our Lord's life are singularly perverted in the Koran."[37] Hence, Islam does not hold Jesus in "high esteem," as Armour said above.

"Muslims also Recognize Jesus as a Prophet"

This is another statement heard today when Islam is discussed and extolled in public gatherings. Unfortunately, it reveals a lot of ignorance in regard to what Christianity teaches

242

concerning Christ as prophet. Unlike Muhammad, who said he was Allah's prophet and messenger who revealed his word, Christ *was the Word*. In him the Word became flesh (John 1:14). The source of his message was not inspiration but incarnation. He was not inspired, but the Inspirer.[38] "For in him dwelt the fullness of the Godhead bodily" (Colossians 2:9 KJV). Moreover, Christ's primary mission was not as a prophet—important as that was—but to suffer, die, and rise from the dead so that all who believe in him would attain eternal life.

Thus, for Muslims to refer to Jesus as a prophet in no way strikes a note of harmony or agreement with orthodox Christians, who adhere to the teachings of historic Christianity. For Muslims or their supporters to say they also believe in Jesus as a prophet extols Islam at the expense of the truth.

"Jews Fared Well In Islamic Areas"

"Jews within Islamic areas," says Armour, "usually fared well."[39] This statement ignores what Muhammad did to the Jews in the Medina area when he had hundreds of prisoners brutally decapitated not long after the Battle of Bedr, mentioned earlier. The statement also overlooks the anti-Semitic edict of 1148 in Muslim-occupied Spain, which resulted in Muslims expelling the Jews from Spain unless they converted to Islam. To say Jews were "usually treated well" also overlooks that in 1159 Jews, together with Christians, in Tunis, as noted in Chapter 2, were given the choice of converting to Islam or face death (*DE*, 89). Armour's statement further ignores that in 1066 an entire Jewish community of approximately 3,000 in Granada, Spain, was annihilated by Muslims (*DE*, 89).

Regarding the anti-Semitism that existed in Muslim-occupied Spain, Rodney Stark has recently made a poignant observation. "Western historians, especially textbook writers, have given considerable coverage to the fact that in 1492 ...

Ferdinand and Isabella forced all Jews to leave Spain within three months, except for those willing to convert to Christianity. Almost without exception these writers do not report that this merely reimposed the Muslim edict of 1148 that expelled all Jews from Spain, upon penalty of death, unless they embraced Islam."[40]

One of the noteworthy victims of the anti-Jewish edict in 1148 was Maimonides, the renowned Jewish scholar and philosopher. He had to flee to the city of Fez, where he disguised himself as a Muslim before he found asylum in Egypt (*DE*, 88).

Even today, Jews do not fare so well in Islamic countries. Alan Dershowitz says that "every single Muslim and Arab state, including the Palestinian Authority, relegates Jews to a position that is far inferior to that of non-Jews in largely secular Israel."[41]

Ignoring Anti-Semitism in Non-Islamic Countries

Apologists for Islam are adept at ignoring anti-Semitism on the part of Muslims in non-Islamic countries. As Daniel Pipes has recently stated, "If anti-Semitism lurks furtively in the Christian countries, in the Muslim world it proudly rules."[42] Anti-Semitism also rules proudly in the rhetoric of the Nation of Islam in the United States, whose leader, Louis Farrakhan, has in recent years openly and publicly expressed his anti-Semitic convictions on numerous occasions. Nor is anti-Semitism among Muslims in the United States confined to the Nation of Islam. In March 1977, the Hanafi Muslims (black converts) seized the headquarters of B'nai B'rith in Washington, D.C., where they held some occupants hostage for 39 hours.[43] But apologists for Islam were strangely silent. More recently, in 1994 a Lebanese Muslim immigrant opened fire on a van carrying Orthodox Jewish boys across the Brooklyn Bridge in

New York.[44] And Israeli embassies have in recent years been bombed in France, Argentina, and other countries.

Anti-Semitism is also virulently present in the current Islamic organization known as Hamas. One of its leaders recently stated: "God brought Jews together in Palestine not to benefit from a homeland, but to dig their grave there and save the world from their pollution."[45] It is worth noting that the Islamic anti-Semitic posture is also very much present in the anti-Zionist ideology, which seeks to eliminate the current State of Israel. Anti-Zionism, says Bat Ye'or, has its roots in the Islamic concept of jihad. (*DE*, 208).

The Facts be Damned

Apologists, with all the efforts they have put forth in recent years in the name of political correctness, have laid an egg that already appears to have hatched a monster, at least in one Australian state. In 2001, the state of Victoria in Australia passed the Racial and Religious Tolerance Act. This law makes it an offense to "humiliate" or "denigrate" a "class of persons" (religious and ethnic groups) by any means of communication. Regarding this law, Tom White of *The Voice of the Martyrs* newsletter, says:

> None of us wish to be humiliated, so the terminology in this law sounds noble. But Muslim lawyers, in concert with the Australian court, are now bringing Christians to hearings simply for stating facts about Islam and for referring Muslims to specific references in their own Koran. Facts or the truth cannot be offered as a defense in this court. Basically, this law is written so that if the truth, including a historical document, causes someone of another religion to feel humiliated, then this offense is grounds for a hearing, trial and possible six-month imprisonment. The offended person may have never met the offender. One Christian stated that this act 'upholds ignorance as a virtue.'[46]

In October 2003, two Christian pastors (Danny Nalliah and Daniel Scott) were charged under this law and had to appear before a tribunal in the state of Victoria in response to Muslims who accused them of having incited hatred in a seminar they had conducted for Christians. Their offense was having cited references from the Koran and other Islamic texts that speak about Islam's jihad. Fortunately, Michael Higgins, the judge in this case, did not agree with the Muslim accusers, saying: "It cannot be regarded as controversial that there are passages in the Quran ... which could and do incite believers in Islam to violence and hatred of non-Muslims. These passages are well-known and widely cited by terrorist groups."[47] He further stated: "Exposing the roots of this problem within Islam is not the same thing as inciting hatred. Since Christians are one of the named targets of *jihad* fighting in the Quran, they have a right and a duty to be well informed about this aspect of Islam."[48]

Whether the State of Victoria's law and its formulators were of the same mind as the Muslim accusers is not known. The Victoria judge, however, had the good sense to recognize that at issue in this Scot-Nalliah case was whether one may still cite facts—no matter how unwelcome they might be to a given person or group—and not be legally punished. This judge did not sanctify the German philosopher Friedrich Hegel's infamous remark—"the facts be damned"—which this law comes perilously close to enshrining. What the future holds regarding this law or similar ones that will likely be passed elsewhere, no one knows. One cannot help but wonder whether all judges, given the prevailing and pervasive social and cultural pressures of political correctness, will have the wisdom or the courage to rule as Judge Higgins did.

It is rather ironic that Daniel Scot, who fled Islamic Pakistan in 1987 after facing accusations under Pakistan's

246

blasphemy laws, found himself accused of similar charges in a non-Muslim country that sees itself as a free and open society. This law in Victoria is an example of good intentions gone awry, intentions that in large measure are a by-product of apologetic propaganda in a sea of political correctness. If the price of liberty is eternal vigilance, it seems that vigilance, at least in Victoria, Australia, deferred to political correctness and to the apologists, who, in their paranoia about the possibility of anyone defaming Islam, were able to influence lawmakers to enact a law that has frightening consequences for freedom-loving people.

Facts are also damned elsewhere. In Canada a Christian recently handed out leaflets protesting documented Muslim persecutions in different parts of the Islamic world. He was accused by Muslims of "inciting hatred" and taken to a Canadian court. He was found guilty of breaking Canada's hate speech laws and sentenced to 240 hours of community service and six months of probation time in jail.[49] The facts did not matter. "At the United Nations," says Daniel Pipes, "the decidedly non-diplomatic epithets 'blasphemy' and 'defamation of Islam' have become part of normal discourse, serving as convenient instruments for shutting off discussion of such unpleasant matters as slavery in Sudan or Muslim anti-Semitism."[50]

The Power of Fear and Intimidation

In Chapter 7 we saw that any comment or remark considered unfavorable to Islam, Muhammad, or the Koran is a crime of apostasy (*irtidad*) and severely punished, often by death, in many Islamic countries. Laws that make it a crime to voice comments deemed unfavorable naturally create fear and intimidate people from freely expressing themselves. Although Muslims in non-Islamic or Western countries do not have the power to silence critics by Shariah law, many have nevertheless been quite effective in silencing many individuals by employing tactics of fear and intimidation.

Paul Fregosi cites a French Muslim who said: "Our greatest strength is that people are afraid of us" (*JW*, 411). Fregosi also mentions that a British publisher declined to publish his book *Jihad in the West* (1998). The publisher, fearing Muslim reprisals, said: "'We have to play the game according to Muslim rules' " (*JW*, 412).

Given the current atmosphere of fear and intimidation, it is extremely rare, even in Western countries, to find discerning Muslims who voice any criticism of Islam. Hence, it is highly unusual to hear someone like Irshad Manji, a Muslim woman in Toronto, Canada, questioning some of the teachings and precepts of Islam. In so doing, however, she has acquired a guard to protect her and installed bulletproof windows in her home.

Fear and intimidation are used with the intent of silencing not only Muslims such as Manji, but also non-Muslims who would say anything considered uncomplimentary regarding Islam or Muhammad. In November 1999, Daniel Pipes published an article titled "How Dare You Defame Islam." The article shows how Islamists in various non-Muslim countries use the tactics of fear and intimidation to silence their critics.[51]

Unfortunately, non-Muslim apologists have kept silent regarding these tactics. Some have even sided with Muslims who use these methods. For instance, after Ayatollah Khomeini on February 14, 1989, issued his *fatwa* condemning to death Salman Rushdie for writing *Satanic Verses,* British historian Hugh Trevor-Roper saw nothing wrong with Khomeini's *fatwa*, saying: "I would not shed a tear if some British Muslims, deploring the manners, should waylay him in a dark street and seek to improve them. If that should not cause him thereafter to control his pen, society would benefit and literature would not suffer."[52]

Freedom-loving individuals must have been stunned to hear this professor contradict his society's value of free speech, which has made it possible for him to speak and teach freely as a university professor. They must have been equally stunned to hear him contradict a basic moral value by saying he had no problem with someone "waylaying" Rushdie. In addition to the British professor, John Simpson of the British Broadcasting Corporation said Rushdie held hostage "those of us who care for and respect Islam. ... "[53] The public must also have been shocked by the remarks of another British resident, Australian-born Germaine Greer, a radical feminist who authored the book *The Female Eunuch* in 1971. She called Rushdie "a megalomaniac," and then added, "I approve of the behavior of the Muslims."[54] Her criticism of Rushdie was especially ironic, not only because of her radical feminism, which clashes with Islam's view of women, but also because she previously had herself "photographed in the nude chopping down a six-foot penis."[55]

In response to the English history professor's statement, Ibn Warraq asks "Will that 'closet hooligan' Trevor-Roper wake up from his complacent slumber, when those 'poor hurt Muslims' begin demanding the withdrawal of those classics of Western literature and intellectual history that offend their Islamic sensibilities but must be dear to Professor Trevor-Roper's heart?" (*WI*, 9).

But the British professor was not alone. John L. Esposito, a longtime apologist for Islam and now a professor at Georgetown University in Washington, D.C., also expressed his disgust with Rushdie's novel by saying that he knew "of no Western scholar of Islam who would not have predicted that [Rushdie's] kind of statement would be explosive."[56] Exposito's comment unwittingly and ironically really indicts

249

Islam, for in effect it says that, given the nature of Islam with its theology of jihad, what else would one expect?

Other silencing effects are used as well. After Rushdie was condemned by Khomeini, Revenue of Canada banned importing *Satanic Verses*. Coles Book Stores, a large Canadian bookstore chain, took the book off the shelves in its 198 stores, "citing concern for the safety of its employees."[57] Some American bookstore chains, including Barnes and Noble, also pulled Rushdie's book from their shelves, and in India and South Africa the book was banned.[58]

The silence of apologists, intentionally or unintentionally, lends support to the tactics of Islamist forces. For example, in 1998 the Council on American-Islamic Relations (CAIR) was able to get National Public Radio to blacklist Steven Emerson for his efforts in uncovering the terrorist organization Hamas in the United States. When Jeff Jacoby, a columnist at the *Boston Globe*, protested the involvement of CAIR in the matter, it launched a letter-writing campaign against him. The following is a partial quote from one of the letters: " 'Dear JEW [sic] ... How dare you defame Islam. ... ' "[59]

In 1999, CAIR turned its verbal guns on Daniel Pipes, the author of a number of articles and books that have exposed the tactics of Islamists.[60] A couple of years earlier, CAIR asked the Roman Catholic Church to investigate Father Richard Neuhaus, the editor of *First Things*. In the October 1997 issue of this periodical he published an article about Islam's many military conquests, rapine, slavery, etc.

The tactics of successfully intimidating and thereby silencing writers and media outlets, as Daniel Pipes correctly notes, is in effect "a first step toward the application of Islamic law, for it is a basic premise of that law that no one, and especially not non-Muslims, may openly discuss precisely those subjects that CAIR wishes to render taboo. ... Permitting the

Sharia to trump the [American] Constitution in even one arena signals to Islamists that they have a chance to turn non-Muslims in the United States into a sort of *dhimmi* population, where *dhimmis* (according to Islamic law) are non-Muslims who accept a range of Islamic restrictions in return for being left alone." Pipes continues, saying that it is "absurd ... that Muslims who make up a tiny proportion of the U. S. population, can impose their will on the majority of Americans." But the apologists in today's culture of political correctness have said nothing about this unfortunate phenomenon.

In regard to Wahhabism, the Islamic ideology of Osama bin Laden and his al-Qaeda network and the dominant form of Islam in Saudi Arabia, Stephen Schwartz in *Two Faces of Islam* (2002) says: "There are many critics of Wahhabism among American Muslims, but few are willing to speak out for the record. Most have been intimidated into silence."[61]

In regard to this Muslim silence, Robert Spencer says: "Ominous as all this is, even more so is the silence of the so-called 'moderate' Muslim clerics—that is, clerics who are about as far from Wahhabism as an imam can get." He further states: "An alarming number of imams in the Western world simply said nothing about September 11 attacks, or sent out a vague statement that could be interpreted favorably by both sides."[62]

Recently, Stephen L. Carter, in his book *Civility* (1998), has noted: "Nowadays lots of Americans seem reluctant to join public moral conversation, seeming to fear what others might say in return. This is a tragedy. A society that refuses to speak the language of morality is more fearful than free."[63] It reminds one of the words of Greek playwright Euripides: "a slave is one who may not speak his thoughts."

"Islam—Our Religion Today, Your Religion Tomorrow"

In response to Rushdie's *Satanic Verses*, Muslims took to the streets protesting in Pakistan, India, Saudi Arabia,

Bangladesh, England, and other places. One report, as noted in the previous chapter, says 30,000 angry Muslims gathered outside the British Parliament in London on May 27, 1989.[64] In this gathering some protesters carried banners that read: "Islam—Our Religion Today, Your Religion Tomorrow." The message of these banners may seem far-fetched and even absurd to some. But if political correctness continues unabatedly, along with the ever-increasing Muslim migration to the West, the high birth rates among Muslims, and the pandering to Muslims by Western politicians, the words on the English banners may someday become a reality. In France, the Muslim population already comprises seven percent (some reports say 10 percent) of the country's 60 million residents. In Granada, Spain, which in the 1960's had no Muslim population, now (in 2004) has 15,000. Some Muslims call Granada the Islamic capital of Europe.[65] In Germany, Muslims make up at least five percent of the country's 83 million inhabitants. And estimates indicate that in the 15 nations of the European Union there are between 12 and 16 million Muslims. Some estimates note that if the countries of Eastern Europe are included, there are twice that many Muslims in Europe. Moreover, the continuous pro-Islamic propaganda voiced by the apologists impedes Westerners, including Americans, from getting the facts about the true nature of Islam. Thus, Westerners may someday find the words "Islam—Our Religion Today, Your Religion Tomorrow" to be a painfully true reality. Some events are already pointing in that direction.

In Manchester, England, "a radical Muslim who does not even speak English has been elected to the city council."[66] In Italy a secret Shariah court has evidently been meting out Islamic "justice," as noted in Chapter 9. On December 20, 1999, the Muslim Shariah court in England issued a *fatwa* "prohibiting all Muslims from participating in Christmas or Christian New Year celebrations taking place in the Millennium

Dome" (*ID*, 330). In France, it is estimated that every year some 35,000 Muslim girls illegally are subjected to clitoridectomies, also known as female genital mutilation.[67] A recent poll in France found that half of the country's 86 public universities reported some problems threatening their secular status as a result of Muslim agitation.[68] One analyst recently said "the idea of France itself is eroding [and its] key pillars of the secular republic are cracking."[69]

Nor is the Islamic goal of bringing Shariah law into the West confined to England, Germany, Italy, or France. Siraj Wahaj, a top figure in the Council of American-Islamic Relations, has recently said that "the implementation of sharia in the U. S. is approaching fast."[70] In May 2004, Hamtramck, Michigan, approved the Shariah's public call to prayer.

Another indicator of the growing presence and power of Islam is the proliferation of Muslim mosques. France in 1974 had only one mosque, but now has approximately 1,500. Recently (January 2003) French governmental officials were considering Muslim demands for federal subsidies for the construction of additional mosques. To meet this request the government would have to change or repeal a 1905 law, which prohibits governmental financing for religious purposes. At least one governmental official has already said the law needs to be updated.[71] Presently, French public opinion does, however, not favor such a change.[72] Germany now has about 2,000 mosques.[73] And according to one report, Bradford, England, sometimes called the "Islamic capital of England," in the late 1990's had "forty mosques and many Koranic schools."[74]

Mosques are also multiplying in the United States, in disproportion to the growth of the Muslim population. Thirty percent of the 1,200 American mosques have been built since the early 1990's. Stephen Schwartz cites Shaykl Muhammad Hishan Kabbani, a critic of Islamic Wahhabism, who estimates that 80 percent of the known 1,200 American mosques are under the political control of Wahhabi imams and are directly subsidized by Saudi Arabia's oil money.[75]

It is sobering to know that before the mid-1980's, according to Schwartz, there was no "Muslim establishment" in America. But now Wahhabism in the United States, aside from operating in most American mosques, is also interlocked with Muslim groups such as CAIR, the American Muslim Council (AMC), the American Muslim Alliance (AMA), and the Islamic Society of North American (ISNA). With these and other Islamic groups, Schwartz says, Wahhabism has achieved the "conquest of American Islam." Wahhabism's network has even spread to American college and university campuses by the infiltrating Muslim Student Association (MSA).[76]

Westerners, including Americans, familiar with the spiritual, non-political functions of churches and synagogues, cannot be falsely lulled into thinking that mosques serve similar purposes, and that they are therefore politically harmless. Many mosques, as already shown, serve both religious and political purposes. "Mosques are not only centers for spirituality; they are now bases for political and social mobilization." So says Nihad Awad, the executive director of the Council of American-Islamic Relations.[77] Hence, behind the veneer of religion, many mosques are functioning as ideal meeting places for planning and inspiring jihad (terrorist) activities against America and the West.

In March 2003, *World* magazine published an article providing additional evidence that mosques in the United States are not only used for religious functions but also for political purposes. The article cited a reporter from the *Los Angeles Times* who found a mosque in Culver City, California, displaying political banners.[78] The latter is not what one finds in mainline churches.

Western countries constitutionally provide freedom of religion. That freedom could ironically be the West's Achille's heel. Muslims, who have little or no such freedom in Islamic countries, are able to use this freedom as they work toward achieving their goal to Islamize the West, including America, in part by using mosques.

In the context of Muslims seeking to Islamize the West, it is wise to remember the words of Ibn Khaldun (1332–1406), the brilliant Islamic philosopher. Khaldun, according to Robert Payne, argued that "kings and empires will always fall before small groups of fanatics armed with *asabiyya* [instinctive group cohesion]."[79] As an example, Payne cites Ibn Saud of the Wahhabis and how he rose to power in the early 1930's in Saudi Arabia.[80] Ibn Saud's small-but-fanatical group caused the previous government of King Husayn in Arabia to fall. The Saudi dynasty still rules today, and the Wahhabic influence is no longer confined to the sandy soil of the Arabian Peninsula. Payne also cites Ibn Khaldun to remind us that Muhammad, the founder of Islam, similar to Ibn Saud, also used *asabiyya* to gain power.[81]

Given Ibn Khaldun's historic insights, which Payne uses to shed light on what transpired in Arabia 500 years later in the 1930's, Americans and others in the West cannot afford to be at ease thinking the Islamist terrorists with their determination and *asabiyya* do not have the potential of making their religion the religion of the West. According to Khaldun, smallness of a group (today's terrorists) does not minimize the danger. Moreover, the "smallness" of the Islamist groups is not really so small, given that they comprise, as noted earlier, about 150 million, and perhaps more, according to some reliable estimates. This significant number, plus their fanaticism together with *asabiyya*, makes them capable of not only carrying out acts of terror, but of also accomplishing far greater objectives.

It is not just fanaticism and *asabiyya* that aid the Islamist terrorists. The West's climate of political correctness aids them as well in that it gives Westerners a false, irenic picture of

Islam, lulling them to complacency and perhaps even to indifference. When the tragedies of September 11 occurred one could not help but ask: "Given the pervasiveness of political correctness, will it allow America and other Western countries to fight and win the war on terrorism?"

If the Islamic terrorists someday were to accomplish their objective of making their religion the religion of the West, it would mean more than a change in religion. It would also mean a revolutionary cultural change, for Islam, as noted earlier, is both a religion and a state. It would not be a mere clash of cultures, but the defeat and destruction of Western culture. As Robert Morey notes, "Whenever Islam becomes the dominant religion in a country, it alters the culture of that nation and transforms it into the culture of seventh-century Arabia."[82] This brings to mind the changes Islam has brought about elsewhere over the centuries, as described by Sir William Muir: "Many a flourishing land in Africa and Asia, which once rejoiced in the light of light and liberty of Christianity, is now crushed and overspread by darkness gross and barbarous" (*LM*, 522).

It would also corroborate Islam's belief that its culture is superior to that of the West, as noted in Samuel P. Huntington's portrayal of Islamic thinking in his book *The Clash of Civilizations and the Remaking of World Order* (1997). Gone would be the West's culture and its numerous institutions of freedom, liberty and justice, not the least of which is the separation of religion and the state.

If the messages on the banners in England still seem like a far cry, Westerners, especially Americans, need to ponder the plans Shamin A. Siddiqi, a Muslim strategist, proposes for Muslims in America. His book *Methodology of Dawah Ilallah in American Perspective* (1989) lays out a blue print with step-by-step di-rections on how Muslims in America must proceed to make Islam the religion and government of United States, at least by about the year 2015.[83]

Siddiqi argues that Americans are hungry for the religion of Islam because they live in "a Godless society and [are] purely materialistic in every walk of life."[84] American society resembles *Jahiliyah* (state of religious ignorance), similar to what Muhammad found in Arabia in 622 when he began to fabricate the religion of Islam.[85] If Siddiqi is right—and he may well be—it would largely be because Americans, exposed to years of relativism and secularism in their schools and the media, have lost their biblically based moral beliefs and values. This phenomenon has gained momentum in recent years through the dogma of political correctness, which portrays all religions as having equal value. Truth, religious or any other, lies only in the eyes of the beholder. What is true for you is not necessarily true for me. If this is what Westerners, including Americans, have accepted—and research shows many have—then what harm could there possibly be if Islam became the religion of the West and the United States? If that someday should happen, America and the rest of the West will have traded their Christian heritage for a mess of religious pottage concocted by a man who on the Arabian sands, 1,400 years ago, distorted the work and teachings of Jesus Christ and replaced them with his own man-made religion.

Conclusion

Truth and freedom are never served by people overlooking well-corroborated facts in history. Western democracy and its accompanying freedoms are based on people being free to hear and learn the truth and facts of history without other individuals ignoring, denying, or slanting those facts as is done by apologists for Muhammad and Islam. To be permitted to know and learn the truth is one of the highest values of a free society. With the aid of political correctness,

257

apologists for Islam, knowingly or unknowingly are undermining this great bulwark of freedom in the West.

To know the truth requires freedom of speech so it can be expressed without having to skew the facts or intimidating those who seek to make it known to others. Freedom of speech may at times affect the sensitivities of a given people or group, and thus not be politically correct, but it must be remembered that when this fundamental right was enshrined in Western democracies, especially in the American Constitution, free speech was not intended to be confined to polite after-dinner speeches. For as the economist Henry George once said: "He who sees the truth, let him proclaim it, without asking who is for it or who is against it."

APPENDIX A

THE KORAN'S JIHAD (HOLY WAR) VERSES

In order that readers might gain a better understanding of the fact that jihad does indeed refer to physical, warlike behavior, the present appendix quotes 35 jihad passages from the Koran. Some scholars count over 100 jihad passages in Islam's sacred book. Don Richardson in his book, *Secrets of the Koran* (2003), lists 109 "war verses." For the sake of brevity, the present appendix quotes only 35 of these passages.

1. "O you who believe! retaliation is prescribed for in the matter of the slain; the free for the free, and the slave for the slave, and female for the female, but if any remission is made to any one by (aggrieved) brother, then prosecution (for the bloodwit) should be made according to usage, and payment should be made to him in a good manner. ..." (Sura 2:178).

2. "And there is life for you (in the law of) retaliation, O men of understanding, that you may guard yourselves" (Sura 2:179).

3. "And fight the way of Allah with those who fight with you, and do not exceed the limits, surely Allah does not love those who exceed the limits" (Sura 2:190).

4. "And kill them wherever you find them, and drive them out from whence they drove you out, and persecution is severer than slaughter, and do not fight with them at the Sacred Mosque until they fight with you in it, but if they fight you, then slay them; such is the recompense of the unbelievers" (Sura 2:191).

5. "And fight with them until there is no persecution, and religion should be only for Allah, but if they desist, then there should be no hostility except against the oppressors" (Sura 2:193.

6. "Fighting is enjoined on you, and it is an object of dislike to you, and it may be that you dislike a thing while it is good for you, and it may be that you love a thing while it is evil for you and Allah knows, while you do not know" (Sura 2:216).

7. "And fight in the way of Allah, and know that Allah is Hearing, Knowing" (Sura 2:244).

8. "And when did go forth early in the morning form your family to lodge the believers in encampments for war and Allah is Hearing, Knowing" (Sura 3:121).

9. "And if you are slain in the way of Allah or you die, certainly forgiveness from Allah and mercy is better than what they amass" (Sura 3:157).

10. "And if indeed you die or you are slain, certainly to Allah shall you be gathered together" (Sura 3:158).

11. "Those who said of their brethren whilst they (themselves) held back: Had they obeyed us they would not have been killed" (Sura 3:168).

12. "O you who believe! take your precaution, then go forth in detachments or go forth in a body" (Sura 4:71).

13. "Therefore let those fight in the way of Allah, who sell this world's life for hereafter; and whoever fights in the way of

Allah, then he be slain or he be victorious. We shall grant him a mighty reward" (Sura 4:74).

14. "Those who believe fight in the way of Allah, and those who disbelieve fight in the way the Shaitan [satan]. Fight therefore against the friends of the Shaitan; surely the strategy of the Shaitan is weak" (Sura 4:76).

15. "Our Lord! why hast Thou ordained fighting for us?" (Sura 4:77).

16. "Fight then in Allah's way; this is not imposed on you except in relation to yourself, and rouse the believers to ardor; maybe Allah will restrain the fighting of those who disbelieve, and Allah is strongest in prowess and strongest to give an exemplary punishment" (Sura 4:84).

17. " ... then seize them and kill them wherever you find them, and take not from among them a friend or a helper" (Sura 4:89).

18. " ... if they do not withdraw from you, and (do not) offer you peace and restrain their hands, then seize them and kill them wherever you find them; and against these We have given you clear authority" (Sura 4:91).

19. "The punishment of those who wage war against Allah and the apostle and strive to make mischief in the land is only this, that they should be murdered or crucified or their hands and feet should be cut off on opposite sides or they should be imprisoned; this shall be a disgrace for them in this world, and in the hereafter they shall have a grievous chastisement" (Sura 5:33).

20. "I will cast terror into the hearts of those who disbelieve. Therefore strike off their heads and strike off every fingertip of them" (Sura 8:12).

21. "And whoever shall turn his back to them on that day—unless he turn aside for the sake of fighting or withdraws to a company—then he, indeed, becomes deserving of Allah's wrath, and his abode is hell; and an evil destination shall it be" (Sura 8:16).

22. "So you did not slay them, but it was Allah Who slew them, and you did not smite when you smote (the enemy), but it was Allah Who smote, and that He might confer upon the believers a good gift from Himself . . ." (Sura 8:17).

23. "And fight with them until there is no more persecution and religion should only be for Allah; but if they desist, then surely Allah sees what they do" (Sura 8:39).

24. "O Prophet! urge the believers to war; if there are twenty patient ones of you they shall overcome two hundred, and if there are a thousand of you they shall overcome a thousand of those who disbelieve, because they are a people who do not understand" (Sura 8:65).

25. "It is not fit for a prophet that he should take captives unless he has fought and triumphed ..." (Sura 8:67).

26. "So when the sacred months have passed away, then slay the idolaters wherever you find them, and take them captives and besiege them and lie in wait for them in every ambush ..." (Sura 9:5).

27. "And if they break their oaths . . . then fight the leaders of unbelief . . ." (Sura 9:12).

28. "Fight them; Allah will punish them by your hands and bring them to disgrace, and assist you against them and heal the hearts of a believing people" (Sura 9:14).

29. "Fight those who do not believe in Allah, nor in the latter day, nor do they prohibit what Allah and His Apostle have prohibited, nor follow the religion of truth, out of those who have been given the Book, until they pay the tax in acknowledgement of superiority and they are in a state of subjection" (Sura 9:29).

30. "O you who believe! fight those of the unbelievers who are near to you and let them find in you hardness; and know that Allah is with those who guard (against evil)" (Sura 9:123).

31. "So when you meet in battle those who disbelieve, then smite the necks until when you have overcome them, then make (them) prisoners ..." (Sura 47:4).

32, "You shall soon be invited (to fight) against a people possessing mighty prowess; you will fight against them until they submit; then if they obey, Allah will grant you a good reward; and if you turn your back as you turned before, He will punish you with a painful punishment" (Sura 48:16).

33. "We have made the iron, wherein is great violence and advantages to men, and that Allah may know who helps Him and His apostles in the secret; surely Allah is Strong, Mighty" (Sura 56:25).

34. "Surely Allah loves those who fight in His way in ranks as if they were a firm and compact will" (Sura 61:4).

35. "O Prophet! strive hard against the unbelievers and the hypocrites, and be hard against them; and their abode is hell; and evil is the resort" (Sura 66:9).

Appendix B

Christian Pioneers in Science

The scientists mentioned below were all greatly influenced by their Christian beliefs and values. These values and beliefs often complemented and motivated their scientific pursuits. For the most part, only the more prominent scientists, the ones who are commonly mentioned in school textbooks, are cited.

Human Physiology and Biology

Leonardo da Vinci (1452–1519). Most people think of Leonard da Vinci as a great artist or painter, but he was also a scientific genius. He analyzed and theorized in the areas of botany, optics, physics, hydraulics, and aeronautics, but his greatest contributions to science lie in the study of human physiology. He made meticulous drawings of the human body based the cadavers he dissected. One historian says that "his drawing and comments, when collected in one massive volume, present a complete course of anatomical study."[1] This was a major breakthrough because, before his time, and for some time after, physicians really had very little valid knowledge of the human body. They were largely dependent on the writings of the Greek physician Galen (ca. 130–200), whose propositions on human physiology were in large measure extrapolated from lower animals such as dogs and monkeys. Leonardo's anatomical observations led him to question, for example, the belief that air passed from the lungs to the heart. He used a pump to test his hypothesis and found that it was impossible to force air into the heart from the lungs.[2]

Lest one think that Leonardo's scientific theories and experiments were divorced from his Christian convictions, it is well to recall his other activities. His paintings—for example, *The Baptism of Christ, The Last Supper*, and *The Resurrection of Christ*—are enduring reminders of his strong Christian beliefs.

Andreas Vesalius (1514–1564). The anatomical work of Leonardo was not forgotten. The man who followed in his footsteps was Andreas Vesalius, a young, brash anatomist from Belgium. At age 22, he began teaching at the University of Padua. In 1543 he published his famous work, *De humani corpis fabrica* (Fabric of the Human Body). The book mentions over 200 errors in the physiological writings of Galen, the revered Greek physician. The errors were found as a result of dissecting human cadavers, as Galen's knowledge was based only on dissecting animals.[3]

When Vesalius exposed the numerous errors of Galen, he received no accolades. His contemporaries, like his former teacher Sylvius, still wedded to the Greek physician's writings, called him a "madman."[4] Others saw him as "a clever, dangerous free thinker of medicine." He encountered more than his share of troubles. While in Spain, as the physician of Charles V, he was not permitted to dissect any corpses. Yet, after Charles' reign, he did perform an autopsy on a nobleman. Unknown to Vesalius, the nobleman was not quite dead. Opening his chest, according to reports, Vesalius and his assistants witnessed a beating heart. His enemies accused him of impiety and murder, and the Inquisition sentenced him to death. However, King Philip II intervened and reportedly commuted his sentence on the condition he would take a pilgrimage to the Holy Land. He did, but on his way back he became seriously ill, and while his ship rested in the harbor of the island of Zante, he died.

Although he questioned much of the existing physiological knowledge, he never questioned God's role in the construction of the human body. On one occasion, he said: "We are driven to wonder at the handiwork of the Almighty."[5] He was not condemned as a heretic, as some church critics have implied, for at the time of his death he had an offer waiting for him to teach at the University of Padua, where he first began his career. Whatever was the cause of his death, he greatly advanced the knowledge of medicine and physiology, for which he is rightly known as "the father of human anatomy."

William Harvey (1578–1657). Here we find another pioneer on the forefront of science, in this instance, scientific physiology. Harvey was born and baptized in the Folkestone parish church in England. Like Vesalius, he studied medicine at the University of Padua. Following in the footsteps of Vesalius and Pare, he engaged in observations and experiments on deceased human bodies after returning to his home in England. He dared to question the still-revered Greek physician, and so in 1628 he published *On the Motion of the Heart and the Blood,* a treatise demonstrating that blood circulated through the arteries of the body by the ventricles of the heart contracting simultaneously. His findings corroborated the biblical statement that "the life of the flesh is in the blood" (Leviticus 17:11).

Gregor Johann Mendel (1822–1884). Where would the study of the science of heredity be had the world not been blessed with this brilliant Augustinian monk and scientist? As often stated in science texts, it was his work on cross-fertilization of garden peas that led him to the concept of genes and the discovery of his three laws: the law of segregation, the law of independent assortment, and the law of dominance. The first law states that a sperm or an egg may contain either a shortness or tallness factor (gene); the second law asserts that characteristics are inherited independently of one another; and the third law says that one gene always dominates, for example, tallness over shortness of an organism.

He spent most of his life in a monastery in Brno, Moravia, and other than being a monk not much is known about his Christian beliefs. It is known, however, that he studied Charles Darwin's theory of evolution and rejected it. Whether the rejection was prompted by his Christian convictions is not clear.

Astronomy and Physics

It was Ptolemy (A.D. 100–170), the Egyptian, who in his multivolume work *Almagest* put forth the theory that the earth was a stationary object. This theory, not derived from the Bible, ironically came to be regarded as the Gospel truth by scientists and many Christian theologians for 1,400 years. Ptolemy and some other natural philosophers from Arabia, Persia, and India, who came after him, are often called scientists. Without impugning these thinkers, who tried to understand natural phenomena, they did not, as noted in Chapter 8, utilize the experimental-empirical methodology. Hence, they were not able to provide empirically reliable, verifiable knowledge. It was only after empirical methods, advocated by Grosseteste and Roger Bacon in the 13th century, had become an integral part of science that such knowledge became a reality.

In the early stages (16th and 17th centuries) of modern, empirical astronomy four names loom large: Copernicus, Brahe, Kepler, and Galileo, all professing Christians. But it is an undeniable fact that the Christian theology and values that motivated and influenced by these men in their pioneering scientific work are conspicuously omitted in school textbooks.

Nicolaus Copernicus (1473–1543). He was born in Torun, West Prussia. His parents were German, as was his language and his family name—Niklas Koppernigk. He even belonged to a German fraternity at the University in Cracow, where he Latinized his name to Copernicus.

He earned a doctor's degree and was also trained as a physician; however, his uncle, with whom he had been staying since his childhood years, also had him study theology, which resulted in his becoming a canon (not a priest) in the Frauenburg Cathedral in East Prussia. But the world knows him best for having introduced the heliostatic theory that says it is not the sun that rotates around the earth, but the earth that rotates around the sun. This concept is often called the "Copernican Revolution." His theory was not entirely new, for in the third century B.C. Aristarchus of Samos suggested a somewhat similar theory. And in the Middle Ages some thought the earth might be in motion, "but nobody had troubled to work out the details of such scheme."[6] Copernicus did, and therein lies his contribution to science.

Copernicus received a published copy of his *De revolutionibus orbium coelestium* (Concerning the Revolutions of the Celestial Bodies) on his deathbed in 1543. He had hesitated to publish it earlier, not because he feared a charge of heresy from church officials, as has often been falsely reported without any documentation, but because he wanted to avoid the ridicule of other scientists, who were still loyal to Aristotle and Ptolemy. It was this characteristic that prompted Arthur Koestler, a scientific chronicler, to call him "the timid canon."[7]

It was his Christian friends, especially Georg Joachim Rheticus and Andreas Osiander, two Lutherans, who persuaded him to publish his findings. Before its publication, Rheticus was so interested in Copernicus' research that he took a two-year leave from his mathematics professorship at Wittenberg

University (where Martin Luther taught) in order to work with Copernicus in Frauenburg.

Thus, although Copernicus remained a moderately loyal son of the Roman Catholic Church, it was his Lutheran friends who made his publication possible. As one modern scholar has said: "No historian will cover up the facts that a Lutheran prince [Duke Albrecht of Prussia] subsidized the publication of his [Copernicus'] work, that a Lutheran theologian [Andreas Osiander] arranged for the printing, and that a Lutheran mathematician [Georg Joachim Rheticus] supervised the printing."[8]

Tycho de Brahe (1546–1601). This Danish Christian is another man who advanced the cause of scientific astronomy. In 1572 he published *De nova stella* (Concerning the New Star). As a Lutheran, he once wrote that it is "the divine works that shine forth everywhere in the structure of the world."[9] In 1577, one year after he had built an observatory, he published a paper describing a newly sighted comet. In 1599, Emperor Rudolph II summoned Tycho from Denmark to Benatak (near Prague) to be his chief astronomer. Less than two years into his tenure, he died of a bladder infection brought on by his delaying to relieve himself because he did not want to leave a royal banquet.

Johannes Kepler (1571–1630). When Tycho died in 1601, Kepler, who had been his assistant, succeeded him. Kepler, who had once studied for four years to become a Lutheran pastor, turned to astronomy after he had been assigned to teach mathematics in Graz, Austria, in 1594. Unlike Tycho, who had not yet accepted the heliostatic theory, Kepler wholeheartedly accepted it. In fact, Owen Gingrich, a Harvard University astronomer, says Kepler, not Copernicus, deserves the real credit for the heliocentric theory. "Copernicus gave the world a helio*static* system, [but] it was Kepler who made it into a helio*centric* system." Gingrich further states: "We have grown so accustomed to calling this [heliocentric theory] the Copernican system that we usually forget that many of its attributes could better be called the Keplerian system."[10]

Kepler's mathematical calculations contradicted the old Aristotelian theory that said planets orbited in perfect circles, an assumption that Copernicus still continued to hold. Kepler's calculations led him to hypothesize and empirically substantiate that planets orbited elliptically, a finding known as his first scientific law. Later, he discovered that planets move faster in their orbits when closer to the sun and more slowly when farther from the sun. This became his second scientific law, which he discovered before his first law. Next he discovered that the squares of the time it takes for any two planets to revolve around the sun are "as the cubes of their mean distances from the sun."[11] This finding is his third scientific law.

These three laws alone, often called the first "natural laws" in science, were enough to make Kepler famous. But he did much more. In 1597, at the young age 26, he published *Mysterium cosmographicum* (Mystery of the Universe), and in 1604 his *Optics* was published. His most famous work, *Astronomia nova* (The New Astronomy), appeared in 1609. It spelled out his first two laws. Both laws contradicted the old Aristotelian doctrine, and Kepler made it known that he had done so empirically.[12] In 1618, he published *Harmonice mundi* (Harmony of the Earth), in which he stated his third law.

He was the first to define weight as the mutual attraction between two bodies, an insight that Isaac Newton used later in formulating the law of gravity; and Kepler was the first to note that tides were affected by the moon. Some 300 years after he stated the inverse square law in optics, photometry confirmed his hypothesis.[13] He also published an astronomy book, *Tabulae Rudophinae*, in honor of Emperor Rudolph II, who conferred on him the title of Imperial Mathematicus. *Tabulae*

Rudolphinae contained tables and rules that were used for more than a 100 years to predict planetary positions.[14]

Many people know that Dionysius Exiguus (d. 544), a Scythian monk, gave the world the Western calendar dating system based on the time of Christ's birth. But he calculated Christ's birth several years too late. Kepler was the first to discover this error. His calculations placed Christ's birth between 4 and 5 B.C., a date commonly accepted today. Along with his many discoveries, Arthur Koestler also credits him with being the first to pioneer differential calculus.[15]

Kepler's scientific thoughts and works were never divorced from his Christian convictions. In his first publication, *Mysterium cosmographicum,* he revealed his Christian faith in the book's conclusion wherein he gave all honor and praise to God.[16] Later, with reference to discovering his first law, he said: "I believe it was an act of Divine Providence that I arrived just at the time when Logomontanus [Brahe's assistant] was occupied with Mars."[17] Stressed and overworked, as he often was, he would sometimes fall asleep without having said his evening prayers. When this happened, it bothered him so much that the first thing he would do in the morning was to repent.[18] He once said: "I have constantly prayed to God that I might succeed in what Copernicus had said was true."[19] In one letter he wrote, "I am serious about the Christian faith, and I do not trifle with it."[20]

Galileo Galilei (1564–1642). Effectively using the telescope, the invention of Johann Lippershey, Galileo was the first to discover that the moon had valleys and mountains, that the moon had no light of its own but merely reflected it from the sun, that the Milky Way was composed of millions of stars, that Jupiter had four bright satellites, and that the sun had spots. He also determined, contrary to Aristotelian belief, that heavy objects did not fall faster than light ones.

Unfortunately, Galileo's observations were not well received by his Roman Catholic superiors, who saw Aristotle's theories—not the Bible—as the final word of truth. Even letting Pope Paul V look through the telescope at his discoveries did not help his cause. His masterpiece, *A Dialogue on the Two Principal Systems of the World* (1632), resulted in a summons before the Inquisition, where he was compelled to deny his belief in the Copernican-Keplerian theory and was sentenced to an indefinite prison term. For some reason the sentence was never carried out. In fact, four years later he published *Dialogues on the Two Sciences.* This work helped Isaac Newton formulate his three laws of motion.

Galileo was less of a Copernican than Kepler, with whom he often disagreed. He largely ignored Kepler's discoveries, apparently because he was still interested in keeping the Ptolemaic theory alive.[21] He also criticized Kepler's idea that the moon affects tides.[22] If he was less Copernican than Kepler—and he was—then why did he get into trouble with theologians who placed his books on the Index's forbidden books? The answer seems to be because he was a Roman Catholic, while Kepler was a Lutheran. The Catholics had no authority over Kepler. And as noted earlier, it was the Lutherans, not the Catholics, who encouraged and even financially underwrote the publication of Copernicus' work. Thus, when modern critics condemn the church or Christianity for its opposition to Galileo and the Copernican theory, it must be underscored that it was not the entire Christian church, or all of its theologians, that did so. The Calvinists also did not condemn the Copernican theory. It is therefore quite appropriate to credit Christianity with lending support to the findings of Copernicus and Kepler, not only because men like Copernicus, Osiander, Rheticus, Duke Albrecht, Brahe, and Kepler were devout Christians, but also because Christianity, at least 300 years earlier, had spawned individuals like

273

Grosseteste, Buridan, Oresme, Roger Bacon, and Francis Bacon, who introduced and promoted the empirical method that made it possible to discover and corroborate the heliocentric theory.

In the 16th and early 17th centuries Lutherans bolstered science, and after that the Calvinists (mostly Puritans) did their part when they founded the Royal Society of London in 1645. Seven of its 10 scientists were Puritans. After receiving royal recognition in 1661, this organization became the world's most prestigious scientific association.

Physics and Mathematics

Isaac Newton (1642–1727). In the area of astronomy and physics, the findings of Kepler reverberated after his death in 1630. One scientist who caught the reverberations was Isaac Newton, who, like Kepler, was highly gifted in mathematics and especially in astronomical physics. It was Kepler's planetary laws that helped Newton devise the inverse square law of gravitation. Without these laws, says Arthur Koestler, Newton "could not have arrived at his synthesis."[23] The discovery of the laws of gravity finally buried Aristotle's theory that each planet had an internal intelligence. Newton's *Mathematical Principles of Natural Philosophy* is considered "one of the greatest single contributions in the history of science."[24] One can even argue that his discovery of gravity also confirmed the biblical statement that God "hangs the earth upon nothing" (Job 26:7).

Although some have argued that Newton was not an orthodox Christian, there is no doubt that he was highly influenced by Christian beliefs. In fact, some of his writings sound like an echo of the Apostles' Creed. For example, "God governs the world invisibly, and he has commanded us to worship him, and no other God ... he has revived Jesus Christ our Redeemer, who has gone to the heavens to receive and prepare a place for us, and ... will at length return and reign over us ... till he has raised up and judged all the dead."[25] Newton revered the Bible to such a degree that he searched it for a hidden code that would reveal the future.[26]

Blaise Pascal (1623–1662). In the world of physics the name Blaise Pascal stands out prominently, both for his scientific contributions and for his Christian convictions. Science knows him for Pascal's law, which says liquid in a container exerts equal pressure in all directions; for his pertaining to measuring barometric pressures at different altitudes; for inventing the syringe and the hydraulic press; for constructing the first adding machine; and for Pascal's triangle. A few years ago computer scientists honored him by naming a computer language after him, and Christian theology honors him for his strong defense of Christianity's veracity. He boldly said: "It is not only impossible but useless to know God without Jesus Christ."[27] He also argued he would rather believe the writings of the Apostles, who died for their testimony, than the words of those who did not.[28] Many also know him for what has come to be known as Pascal's Wager. Expressed in simple language, his wager says: "If I believe Christianity to be true and it turns out to be false, I have lost nothing, but if I believe it to be false and it turns out to be true, I have lost everything."

Gottfried Leibnitz (1646–1716). Both Leibnitz and Newton are credited with having developed a theory of differential calculus, and because physics is so dependent on higher mathematics (the language of science), it can be argued that Leibnitz's mathematical contribution was vital to science. Leibnitz saw the Bible as God's authoritative word. As a Lutheran, he spoke of God's grace and maintained that there was no conflict between true Christian faith and valid reason.

He even remarked that, after having studied various theologians, he accepted the doctrines of the Augsburg Confession (the official Lutheran position presented to Charles V in Augsburg, Germany, in 1530). He said it strengthened his faith because of its irenic formulations.[29]

Alessandro Volta (1745–1827). Nearly a hundred years after Pascal, this Italian scientist discovered current electricity. He is honored every time the term *volt* or *voltmeter* is used by electricians or mechanics. Without pretense, Volta reflected his Christian convictions as he participated in Catholic masses and various devotional activities. In one of his letters he wrote: "I am not ashamed of the Gospel, may it produce good fruit."[30]

Georg Simon Ohm (1787–1854). A dedicated physicist and Christian, this man formulated the equation that measures electrical resistance, which today is known as Ohm's law. The Ohmmeter instrument is named in honor of him. The nature of his Christian faith is apparent from what he said while writing his first volume on *Molecular Physics*. He indicated that he was planning to write additional volumes, "if God gives me the length of days."[31]

Andre Ampere (1775–1836). This savant of science has his name enshrined in the language of electrical measurements. Electricians and motor mechanics regularly use the term "ampere" (or "amp"), a unit that measures the strength of an electric current. They also know that amperes equal volts divided by ohms.

After an early lapse in his Christian faith, Ampere returned to it with additional strength. He firmly believed that one sees the existence of God in nature. For example, he wrote: "One of the most striking evidences of the existence of God is the wonderful harmony by which the universe is preserved and living beings are furnished in their organization with everything necessary to life."[32]

Michael Faraday (1791–1867). This scientist discovered electromagnetic induction, thus making electricity available for varied applications. This, however, was not his only contribution to science and technology. He was the first to make a liquid out of gas, and he also invented the generator. Although he was an Englishman, one year after his death the French Academy of Science honored him as "the greatest scientist the Academy had ever counted among its members." In his religious life, he was a member of the Sandemanians or Glasists, a small Christian group that firmly believed in the Bible and in Jesus Christ as God's only Son. He not only read the Bible daily, but he also "donated a significant portion of his income to the church and frequently visited and tended the sick."[33]

William Thompson Kelvin (1824–1907). Here we have another devout Christian and a renowned scientist as well. Better known as Lord Kelvin, he made his mark in science by establishing the scale of absolute zero, by first conceptualizing energy, and by founding thermodynamics. The Kelvin scale, which measures absolute zero, bears his name. As a Christian, he saw the Christian religion and science as highly compatible. This stance was by this time no longer common, as it was, for example, with Kepler, Newton, Robert Boyle, and virtually all of the scientists before the mid-1800's. Thus, some of his peers did not take kindly to his Christian convictions. In response to them, he said: "If you think strongly enough, you will be forced by science to the belief in God."[34]

Chemistry

Robert Boyle (1627–1691). Most high school or college students encounter the name Robert Boyle in chemistry classes when they learn about Boyle's Law, which states that the pressure of gas is inversely proportional to the space allotted to it. In addition to his work on gases, he was the first scientist to separate chemistry from alchemy and to formulate "a precise definition of a chemical element."[35] He is credited with discovering that sound does not travel in a vacuum, and he was the first to espouse the mechanical theory of matter, a concept that posited the existence of atoms moving in empty space.[36]

In 1645, Boyle helped found the Royal Society of London for the Improvement of Natural Knowledge. As already noted, it soon became the most respected scientific association of its kind. In light of these and other achievements in the science of chemistry, he is recognized as "the father of chemistry."

His many scientific accomplishments did not deter him from his avocation, the study of Christian theology. His interests in theology resulted in his becoming a highly respected biblical scholar. He wrote and presented a number of theological essays and was even offered a bishopric, which he declined. Unlike many secularists and some scientists of today, he did not see Christianity and science as being in conflict. In fact, he tried to show that Christianity and science not only were compatible but also "integrally related to one another."[37] As a Christian, he had a lifelong interest in Christian missionary work. He served as governor of the Corporation for the Spread of the Gospel in New England, and he left money to support Bible translations. In his final will he left money for foreign missionary work and also for the "Boyle Lectures," which he wanted to be given to convert unbelievers.[38]

Antoine Lavoisier (1743–1794). Half a century after Robert Boyle, another prominent chemist appeared in the person of Antoine Lavoisier. Like so many other scientists, he too was a Christian, though he had lapsed for a while during his career. Being the observant Frenchman that he was, he showed the world that oxygen was a necessary component to burn materials. He also demonstrated the law of the conservation of energy. For these contributions and others, the French Academy of Sciences awarded him a gold medal. Tragically, as part of the aftermath of the French Revolution, the revolutionaries captured and guillotined him in 1794, a mere five years after the revolution had begun. Many of his biographers note he died confessing his belief in Jesus Christ.

John Dalton (1766–1844). He was the first to publish the atomic weights of some elements. This earned him the title "father of the atomic theory." He also formulated the law of partial pressure relative to gases. In 1831 he helped organize the British Association for the Advancement of Science.[39] Medical science honors him to this day with the term Daltonism, the alternate name for color-blindness, which he discovered and with which he himself was afflicted. His Christian beliefs, say Karl Kneller, were never in doubt.[40]

George Washington Carver (1864?–1943). This scientist, born of black slave parents, became one of America's top authorities on peanuts and sweet potatoes, but he also developed over 300 by-products from peanuts, ranging from instant coffee to soap and ink. From the sweet potato he made over 100 by-products, including floor polish, shoe polish, and candy. He also used his scientific knowledge to persuade farmers that they could grow peanuts, sweet potatoes, and pecans instead of cotton. This advice greatly diversified and enriched American agriculture, especially in the South.

Carver received numerous awards and honors, one of which was the Roosevelt Medal in 1939. This award read: "To a scientist humbly seeking the guidance of God and a liberator to men of the white race as well as the black." These were fitting words, for Henry Morris writes that Carver was "a sincere and humble Christian" who never hesitated to "to confess his faith in the God of the Bible and attribute all his success and ability to God."[41]

Medicine

The ancient Greeks believed their god Aesculapius used serpents and dogs to heal sick people by having them lick patients with their tongues. Thus, in ancient Greek art a dog is often seen pictured standing beside Aesculapius.[42] (Even today the serpent is a symbol of modern medicine.). Obviously, this Greek concept of healing was far removed from any scientific methods.

Although the medical writings of Avicenna (980–1037), a Muslim, were widely used by Western physicians, the first noteworthy progress in the art and science of healing (medicine) occurred in the Abbey of Monte-Cassino (Italy), founded by the Benedict of Nursia in 528. From here, says Gabriel Compayre, the monks studied medicine "with marked devotion," and from here "the taste of medical studies spread as far as Salerno, and by the 11th century, the little town had become an intellectual center that attracted students from all parts of Western Europe."[43] Two hundred years later, Salerno's medical studies attached themselves to the University of Naples. By the mid-1300's the medical school at Montpellier, France, performed dissections on human cadavers once every two years, and at the University of Paris at the rate of two per year.[44] In this context, it is important to note that none of the Muslim physicians dissected any human bodies, for as Howard R. Haggard says, "their religious beliefs forbade this practice."[45]

The early science of medicine, however, like the studies in astronomy, did not always proceed smoothly. One can find negative comments regarding the study of human anatomy in the writings of the church father Tertullian (d. ca. 220) and also in what St. Augustine (354–430) said. There were also some synods (regional gatherings) in the church that prohibited monks from studying medicine. The Synod of Clermont (1130) and the second Synod of Lateran (1139) are two such examples.[46] These two synods were largely reacting to a practice by some of the Crusaders in which they boiled off the flesh of dead Crusaders so that their skeletal remains could be brought home.

The negative reactions on the part of some church fathers and regional synods have often been exaggerated by secular critics to imply that the whole Christian church was anti-medicine or anti-science. Not so! For at no time did the entire church ever oppose, much less condemn, medical science or any other branch of science.

With regard to these negative attitudes, at least two factors are usually overlooked. First, as in the case of Copernicus and Galileo, some of the church's theologians were so firmly wedded to Aristotle's deductive philosophy and Galen's medical writings that they saw the new empirical methodology of science, such as dissecting human cadavers, as wrong. To question the work of Aristotle and Galen was unacceptable. Thus, it was not biblical or Christian doctrines that prompted opposition to science, but rather it was the pagan Greek theories that some theologians and synods saw as the only acceptable authority.

Second, cadavers were usually obtained by robbing graves. Some of the bodies Vesalius used were acquired that way. Grave robbing, or even disturbing graves, is still a major taboo—and illegal as well. Even secularists oppose it. Thus, the opposition to dissecting human bodies, in part, pertained to robbing graves and was not simply the result of theological obstinacy. In fact, there is evidence to the contrary. For instance, in 1556, as dissections became more common, some complaints reached Charles V. He referred the issue to the theological faculty at the University of Salamanca. The response was positive: "The dissection of human cadavers serves a useful purpose, and therefore permissible to Christians of the Catholic Church."[47] And it should be remembered that dissecting cadavers had been legally performed in at least three universities since the 1300's. These universities were Bologna, Montpellier, and Padua. Hence, there never was a total ecclesiastical ban on dissections. It is well to remember that with the appearance of Christian universities, as Rodney Stark reminds us, there came "with them a new outlook on dissection."[48]

Paracelsus (1493–1541). His medical opponents did not like him. Disparagingly, they called him *Lutherus medicorum* (the Luther of medicine) because he criticized many existing medical practices. In response to some of his critics he once said: "I am a Christian. I am no sorcerer, no pagan, no gypsy."[49]

He argued that external agents attacked the human body to produce illness, thus foreshadowing the modern germ theory. This idea was contrary to the established doctrines of Galen that held disease resulted from internal imbalances of the body's humors. Fellow physicians objected to Paracelsus' empirical methods and did not agree that chemicals should treat diseases. Once he horrified them by burning the revered medical writings of the Greek physician Galen and also the *Canon of Medicine* by Avicenna.[50]

By stating that illnesses were the result of external and natural causes, he spurned the belief that God or the saints inflicted diseases (some diseases were named after the names of saints). He once said: "We dislike such nonsensical gossip as it is not supported by symptoms."[51] As a Christian, he argued it was God's will that people should live long lives, and physicians were to work to achieve that end.[52] One historian stated that Paracelsus was a man "destined to awaken the scientific spirit among physicians and to spread the contagion of the Renaissance to the field of medicine."[53] This was indeed a significant step forward for medical science.

Ambroise Pare (1509?–1590). Medicine, specifically surgery, received a gigantic boost from this French physician, whom one medical historian has called "the greatest of all time."[54] Until Pare's day, surgery was performed by barbers, executioners, bathhouse keepers, and vagabonds.[55] Physicians saw it beneath their dignity. Pare was particularly adept in treating gunshot wounds received by soldiers in battle. Rather than stop a wound's flow of blood by cauterizing it with a red-hot iron, he used ligatures to stop the bleeding, as surgeons do today. He also introduced artificial eyes, improved existing artificial arms and legs, and implanted teeth.[56] On one occasion, an elderly woman told him that he should apply chopped onion to skin burns. Being experimentally minded, he not only accepted the woman's suggestion, but he also applied the chopped onion to one side of the burn and left the other side untreated. The side with the onion application did indeed heal more rapidly. This experiment revealed his scientific bent, and he apparently was the first physician to use the experimental-control method in modern medicine. He was said to be a man of tough fiber, but this did not diminish his Christian humility. When complimented on his success in healing a soldier's wounds, he would say: "I dressed his wounds, but God healed them."[57]

Louis Pasteur (1822–1895). Although Pasteur was a chemist and microbiologist, he made his mark in science by discovering bacteria, which has enabled physicians to save millions of lives. Working in the laboratory, this talented scientist showed how bacteria caused fermentation, spoiled food, and infected wounds. He also demonstrated the effective use of antiseptics; successfully treated hydrophobia; introduced inoculation; and gave the world the method of pasteurization, named after him. His research also led him to annul the old false hypothesis of spontaneous generation, which he replaced with the concept of biogenesis—that is, life comes from life. Like so many other Christians in the development of science, his scientific findings did not eclipse his faith. He once said: "The more I know, the more does my faith approach that of the Breton peasant."[58] And when he lay dying on his bed, "one of his hands rested on that of Mme. Pasteur [his wife], the other held a crucifix."[59]

James Simpson (1811–1870). Similar to other scientists discussed so far, Simpson, a Scottish citizen, was another scientifically minded Christian. He was an obstetrician and gynecologist who discovered chloroform in 1847. His suggestion that chloroform be used to alleviate pain in childbirth brought strong resistance from his medical colleagues. But after Queen Victoria received it at the birth of her seventh child (Peter Leopold), the medical establishment soon conformed.[60]

The discovery of chloroform laid the foundation for modern anesthesiology. Reportedly, it was the biblical account that God put Adam in a deep sleep to create Eve from one of his ribs that inspired Simpson to discover chloroform.[61] If this account is correct, it is not the only evidence of his biblical convictions. He also wrote a gospel tract in which he confessed his faith in Jesus Christ, and he told a friend that his greatest discovery was "that I am a sinner and Jesus Christ is the Saviour."[62]

Joseph Lister (1827–1912). Building upon Pasteur's discovery that fermentation was caused by bacteria, medical science was fortunate to have had Lister, a Quaker from England, who later became the physician of Queen Victoria. He introduced and applied antiseptics to keep germs (bacteria) from multiplying in surgical or accidental wounds. Teaching physicians to wash their hands and to use only sterile instruments greatly reduced infections and the mortality rate of patients. Before Lister's time, even minor surgeries resulted in high death rates. With his contributions, surgery became divided into two periods—before and after Lister.[63]

NOTES

CHAPTER 1

1. Philip Schaff, *History of the Christian Church* (New York: Scribner's Sons, 1895), 4:171.

2. George Sale, "The Life of Mohammad," in *The Koran* (New York: A. L. Burt, 1894), 41.

3. Robert Spencer, *Islam Unveiled: Disturbing Questions About the World's Fastest-Growing Faith* (San Francisco: Encounter, 2002), 175.

4. Ibid., 56.

5. In *Reliance of the Traveller* the alphabetical symbol in this reference refers to the book in the volume, and the first numeral refers to the chapter; the second numeral refers to a given verse.

6. John Gilchrist, *Is Muhammad Foretold in the Bible?* (Cape Town, Africa: Roodepoort Mission, 1985), 27.

7. Gustave E. von Grunebaum, *Medieval Islam: A Study in Cultural Orientalism* (Chicago: University of Chicago Press, 1962), 16.

8. A. J. Arberry, *The Koran Interpreted, II* (New York: Macmillan, 1950), 345.

9. Emile Dermenghem, *The Life of Mahomet,* trans. Arabella Yorke (New York: Macmillan, 1930), 60.

10. Ibid.

11. Sir William Muir, *Mahomet and Islam: A Sketch of the Prophet's Life From Original Sources And A Brief Outline Of His Religion* (London: The Religious Tract Society, 1895), 32 (hereafter cited in text as *MI*).

12. Dermenghem, *The Life of Mahomet*, 61.

13. Sir William Muir, *The Life of Mohammad: From Original Sources* (Edinburgh: John Grant, [1861], 1923), 55 (hereafter cited in text as *LM*).

14. Henry Treece, *The Crusades* (New York: Barnes and Noble, 1962), 31.

15. Milton Viorst, *In the Shadow of the Prophet* (Boulder: Westview, 2000), 102.

16. Treece, *Crusades*, 31.

17. Viorst, *In the Shadow*, 102.

18. A. Guillaume, *The Life of Mohammad* (translation of Ishaq's Sirat Rasul Allah) (London: Oxford University Press, 1955), 212.

19. Sale, "Life of Mohammad," 20.

20. Al Dashti, *Twenty Three Years: A Study of the Prophetic Career of Mohammad,* trans. F. R. C. Bagley (London: George Allen and Unwin, 1985), 81.

21. Sale, "Life of Mohammad," 192.

22. Paul Fregosi, *Jihad in the West: Muslim Conquests from the 7th to the 21st Centuries* (Amherst, NY: Prometheus Books, 1998), 58 (hereafter cited in text as *JW*).

23. Philip Yancey, *The Jesus I Never Knew* (Grand Rapids: Zondervan, 1995), 196.

24. Anis A. Shorrosh, *Islam Revealed: A Christian Arab's View of Islam* (Nashville: Thomas Nelson, 1988), 182.

25. Martin Lings, *Muhammad: His Life Based on the Earliest Sources* (New York: Inner Traditions, 1983), 229–233.

26. Ibn Warraq, "Dramatis Personae: Explantory List of Individuals and Tribes," in *The Quest for the Historical Muhammad,* ed. Ibn Warraq (Amherst, NY: Prometheus Books, 2000), 542.

27. Tor Andrae, *Mohammad: The Man and His Faith,* trans. Theophil Menzel (London: George Allen and Unwin, 1956), 149.

28. Samuel M. Zwemmer, *Islam: A Challenge To Faith* (London: Darf, 1985), 9.

29. Treece, *Crusades,* 31.

30. Ibid.

31. Ahmed Rashid, *Jihad: The Rise of Militant Muslims in Central Asia* (New Haven: Yale University Press, 2002), 265.

32. Ergun Mehmet Caner and Emir Fethi Caner, *Unveiling Islam* (Grand Rapids: Kregel, 2002), 185.

33. Ibid.

34. Sale, "Life of Mohammad," 5.

35. Dashti, *Twenty Three Years,* 129.

36. Andrae, *Mohammad:The Man,* 242.

37. Ibid., 153.

38. Regarding sexual temptation, the New Testament never explicitly says that Jesus was sexually tempted, but given that he was a real flesh-and-blood human male it would seem highly unlikely that he was not tempted sexually. Importantly, the writer of the Epistle to the Hebrews says Jesus was "tempted as we are, yet without sin" (Hebrews 4:15). Jesus himself said: "Which one of you convicts me of sin?" (John 8:46).

39. John Bagot Glubb, *Life and Times of Muhammad* (New York: Stein and Day, 1970), 195.

288

40. Cited in Arthur Gilman, *The Story of the Saracens: From the Earliest Times to the Fall of Baghdad* (New York: G.P. Putnam's Sons, 1896), 143.

41. Ibid.

42. L. Gardet, "Allah," in *The Encyclopedia of Islam*, ed. H. A. R. Gibb, J. H. Kramers, E. Levi-Provencal, and J. Schacht (Leiden: E. J. Brill, 1960), 1:406.

43. Malise Ruthven, *Islam in the World* (Harmondsworth, England: Penguin, 2000), 18.

44. Robert Morey, *The Islamic Invasion: Confronting the World's Fastest Growing Religion* (Eugene, OR: Harvest, 1992), 50.

45. "Allah—the Moon God: The Archeology of the Middle East," http://www.biblebelievers.org.au/moongod.htm (accessed February 5, 2004).

46. Ibid.

47. Ibid.

48. Yoel Natan has book manuscript in process that explores in great the possible linkage between the Islamic crescent and the ancient Middle East astral gods, especially the moon-god.

49. D. B. Macdonald, "Allah," in *Encyclopedia of Religion and Ethics*, ed. James Hastings (New York: Charles Scribner's Sons, 1917), 1:326.

50. Ibid.

51. Caner and Caner, *Unveiling Islam*, 104.

52. Morey, *Islamic Invasion*, 64–65.

53. Ibid., 65.

54. Gilman, *Story of the Saracens*, 108. Muhammad's mythical one-night journey (a report of a vision or a dream) allegedly occurred from Mecca to Jerusalem on *al-Buraq*, a winged, mule-like creature with the head of a woman and the tail of a peacock. While in heaven, he prayed with Jewish and Christian prophets, including Jesus. The Koran alludes to this journey in Sura 17:1. The Sufis, a mystical sect of Islam, instead see Sura 53 as pertaining to the night journey; see Karen Armstrong, *Muhammad: A Biography of the Prophet* (San Francisco: HarperSanFransico, 1992), 139.

55. Ibn Warraq, *Why I Am Not A Muslim* (Amherst, NY: Prometheus Books, 1995), 94 (hereafter cited in text as *WI*).

56. R. V. C. Bodley, *The Life of Mohammad* (Garden City, NJ: Double Day, 1946), 101.

57. Karen Armstrong, *Muhammad: A Biography of the Prophet* (San Francisco: HarperSanFrancisco, 1992), 166.

CHAPTER 2

1. Philip Schaff, *The Person of Christ: The Miracle of History* (Boston: American Tract Society, 1865), 40–49.

2. Henri Pirenne, *Mohammed and Charlemagne*, trans. Bernard Miall (New York: W. W. Norton, 1939), 149.

3. Rodney Stark, *The Rise of Christianity: A Sociologist Reconsiders History* (Princeton: Princeton University Press, 1996), 13.

4. T. W. Arnold, *The Preaching of Islam: A History of the Propagation of the Muslim Faith* (Westminster: Archibald Constable, 1896), 6.

5. Richard Wurmbrand, "Don't Judge," *The Voice of the Martyrs*, April 2003, 12.

6. Arthur Gilman, *The Story of the Saracens: From the Earliest Times to the Fall of Baghdad* (New York: G. P. Putnam's Sons, 1896), 249.

7. Youssef Courbage and Philippe Fargues, *Christians and Jews Under Islam*, trans. Judy Mabro (New York: L. B. Tauris, 1997), 6–7.

8. Anis A. Shorrosh, *Islam Revealed: A Christian Arab's View of Islam* (Nashville: Thomas Nelson, 1988), 72.

9. Ali Dashti, *Twenty Three Years: A Study of the Prophetic Career of Mohammad*, trans. F. R. C. Bodley (London: George Allen and Unwin, 1985), 28.

10. L. Veccia Vaglieri, "Ali b. Abi Talib," in *The Encyclopedia of Islam*, ed. H. A. R. Gibb, J. H. Kramers, E. Levi-Provencal, J. Schacht (London: Luzac, 1960), 1:385.

11. In the light the Bible's Ten Commandments, these acts obviously violated the Commandment: "You shall not murder." But the Koran has no Ten Com-mandments. Moreover, it should not be forgotten that Muhammad himself used the sword on numerous occasions without any moral qualms to achieve his goals, and countless followers did likewise.

12. Ergun Mehmet Caner and Emir Fethi Caner, *Unveiling Islam* (Grand Rapids: Kregel, 2002), 49.

13. Jan Reed, *The Moors in Spain and Portugal* (Totowa, NJ: Rowman and Littlefield, 1974), 21.

14. Mark Williams, *The Story of Spain* (Malaga, Spain: Santana, 2000), 50.

15. Ibid., 51.

16. Ibid., 52.

17. Bernard Lewis, *Islam and the West* (New York: Oxford University Press, 1993), 10–11.

290

18. Rodney Stark, *For the Glory of God: How Monotheism Led To Reformations, Science, Witch-Hunts, and the End of Slavery* (Princeton: Princeton University Press, 2003), 131.

19. Richard Fletcher, *Moorish Spain* (New York: Henry Holt, 1992), 172.

20. Ibid., 173.

21. Bat Ye'or, *Islam and Dhimmitude: When Civilizations Collide* (Madison, NJ: Fairleigh Dickinson University Press, 2002), 436 (hereafter cited in text as *ID*).

22. Bat Ye'or, *The Decline of Eastern Christianity under Islam: From Jihad to Dhimmitude*, trans. Miriam Kochan and David Littman (Madison, NJ: Fairleigh Dickinson University Press, 1996), 89 (hereafter cited in text as *DE*).

23. Stark, *Glory of God*, 49.

24. Throughout this book, when the name "Ottoman" is used, it is used synonymously with the name "Turk." Yet, it needs to be noted that not all Ottomans were Turks, for the Ottomans consisted of many ethnic groups. But virtually all Ottomans were Muslims.

25. *WI*, 231.

26. Robert Irwin, "Islam and the Crusades: 1096–1699," in *The Oxford Illustrated History of the Crusades*, ed. Jonathan Riley-Smith (New York: Oxford University Press, 1995), 251.

27. Robert Payne, *The Holy Sword: The Story of Islam from Muhammad to the Present* (New York: Collier, 1962), 272.

28. *WI*, 231.

29. C. W. C. Oman, *The Story of the Byzantine Empire* (New York: G.P. Putnam's Sons, 1895), 324.

30. Peter F. Sugar, *Southeastern Europe under the Ottoman Rule, 1354–1804* (Seattle: University of Washington Press, 1977), 55.

31. C. W. C. Oman, *The Story of the Byzantine Empire* (New York: G. P. Putnam's Sons, 1895), 333.

32. Ibid., 221.

33. William Stearns Davis, *A Short History Of The Near East* (New York: Macmillan, 1931), 195.

34. Tim Judah, *Kosovo: War of Revenge* (New Haven: Yale University Press, 2000), 5.

35. Ibid., 10.

36. Ferdinand Schevill, *The History of the Balkans: From the Earliest Times to the Present Day* (New York: Harcourt Brace, 1922), 83.

37. Ibid., 83.

38. Ibid., 84.

39. Steven Runciman, *The Fall of Constantinople: 1453* (Cambridge: At the University Press, 1965), 144.

40. Norman Itzkowitz, *Ottoman Empire and Islamic Tradition* (Chicago: University of Chicago Press, 1972), 84.

41. Davis, *Short History*, 357.

42. Christopher J. Walker, *Armenia: The Survival of a Nation* (New York: St. Martin's, 1980), 221.

43. Editorial, "Armenia," *Christian Science Monitor*, September 15, 1915, 18.

44. Walker, *Armenia*, 230.

45. Ibid.

46. Ibid., 345.

47. Gary Lane, "Standing for Jesus in the Midst of Jihad," *The Voice of the Martyrs*, June 2002, 6.

48. C. Edwards, "The Gates of Hell Shall Not Prevail," *The Voice of the Martyrs*, May 2000, 8.

49. Gary Lane, "Carrying the Cross in Pakistan," *The Voice of the Martyrs*, February 2002, 3.

50. "Country Summaries," *The Voice of the Martyrs*, Special Issue 2003, 19.

51. A. M. Rosenthal, "Secrets of the War," *The New York Times*, April 23, 1999, A25.

52. "Nigeria: VOM Office Destroyed by Radical Muslims," *The Voice of the Martyrs*, April 2000, 13.

53. Caner and Caner, *Unveiling Islam*, 78.

54. Arnold, *Preaching of Islam*, 172.

55. Abd-al-Rahman Azzam, *The Eternal Message of Muhammad,* trans. Caesar E. Farah (New York: Devin-Adaid, 1964), 191.

56. Pirenne, *Mohammed and Charlemagne*, 151.

57. Azzam, *Eternal Message*, 209.

58. Abul-Fazl Ezzati, *An Introduction to the History of Islam* (London: New and Media Limited, 1976), 10.

59. Cyril Glasse, "Ahl al-Kitab," *The Concise Encyclopedia of Islam* (New York: HarperSanFrancisco, 1991), 27.

60. Many of these examples are taken from Bat Ye'or's two books: *The Dhimmi: Jews and Christians Under Islam* (Rutherford: Fairleigh Dickinson University Press, 1985) and *Islam and Dhimmitude: Where Civilizations Collide* (Rutherford: Fairleigh Dickinson University Press, 2002). Some

were also taken from A. Ghosh, *The Koran and the Kafir: Islam and Infidel* (Houston: Ghosh, n.d.), 85–86.

61. Bernard Lewis, *Islam and the West* (New York: Oxford University Press, 1993), 53.

62. W. Montgomery Watt, *The Majesty That Was Islam: The Islamic World, 666–1100* (New York: Praeger, 1974), 258.

63. C. Edwards, "The Gates of Hell Shall Not Prevail," *The Voice of the Martyrs*, May 2000, 7.

64. "Christian Life Worth Only a Twelfth that of a Muslim," *Pakistan Christian Post*, October 29, 2003, www.pakistanchristianpost.com

65. Kenneth Scott Latourette, *The Thousand Years of Uncertainty*, A.D. *500–A.D. 1500* (New York: Harper and Brothers, 1938), 296.

66. The Brighton and Hove Forum, "Arab v Jew or Israel v Palestine?" http://ms101.mysearch.com/jsp/GGcres.jsp?id (accessed December 26, 2003).

67. Nehemia Levtzion, "Toward a Comparative Study of Islamization," in *Conversion to Islam*, ed. Nehemia Levtzion (New York: Holmes and Meier, 1979), 10.

68. Ibid.

69. F.L. Cross and E.A. Livingstone, "Coptic Church," *The Oxford Dictionary of the Christian Church,* (New York: Oxford University Press, 1997), 416.

70. Murray T. Titus, *India Islam: A Religious History of Islam in India* (New Delhi: Oriental Books Reprint Corporation, 1979), 27.

71. Arnold, *Preaching of Islam*, 214.

72. Titus, *India Islam*, 31.

73. Latourette, *Thousand Years*, 299.

74. Ibid., 72.

75. Richard Gant, "Indonesian Muslims Forcing Christians to Convert," http://www.cin.org/archives/cinjub/200012/0228.html (accessed December 27, 2003).

76. David Littman, "The U.N. Finds Slavery in the Sudan," *The Middle East Quarterly*, September 1996, 94.

77. Rosenthal, "Secrets of War," A25.

78. Marcus Mabry, "The Price Tag on Freedom," *Newsweek*, May 3, 1999.

79. Bertil Lintner, "Ethnic Cleansing and the Rise of Islamic Militancy in Bangladesh," South Asia Tribune, February 17–23, 2003, http://www.satribune

.com/archves/feb17_2303/opinion_bertil.htm   (accessed December 27, 2003).

80. Cited in Washington Irving, *Mahomet and His Successors* (New York: G. P. Putnams Sons, 1860), 153.

81. Martin Lings, *Muhammad: His Life Based on the Earliest Sources* (New York: Inner Traditions, 1983), 230.

82. For a documented history of how Christianity's influence underlies the West's concepts of freedom, liberty, and justice, see Alvin J. Schmidt, *Under the Influence; How Christianity Transformed Civilization* (Grand Rapids: Zondervan, 2001).

CHAPTER 3

1. Portions of this chapter that pertain to how the ancient Greeks, Romans, and Hebrews viewed women, as opposed to how Christianity changed these views, are excerpted from Chapter 4 in my book: *Under the Influence: How Christianity Transformed Civilization* (Grand Rapids: Zondervan, 2001).

2. Farzaneh Milani, "Lipstick Politics in Iran," *The New York Times*, August 19, 1999, A21.

3. J. P. V. D. Balsdon, *Roman Women: Their History and Habits* (New York: John Day, 1963), 283.

4. I. F. Cervantes, "Woman," in *New Catholic Encyclopedia* (New York: McGraw-Hill, 1967), 14:991.

5. Charles Albert Savage, *The Athenian Family: A Sociological and Legal Study* (Baltimore: 1907), 29.

6. C. M. Bowra, *Classical Greece* (Chicago: Ime, 1965), 85.

7. F. A.Wright, *Feminism in Greek Literature: From Homer to Aristotle* (Port Washington, N.Y.: Kennikat [1923], 1969), 1.

8. Q. M. Adams, *Neither Male Nor Female* (Devon, England: Arthur Stockwell, 1973), 192.

9. Balsdon, *Roman Women*, 272.

10. William Smith, *A Dictionary of Greek and Roman Antiquities* (New York: 1871), 635.

11. Balsdon, *Roman Women*, 278.

12. Wilhelm A. Becker, *Gallus* (London: Longmans, Green and Company, 1920), 438.

13. James Wellard, *Babylon* (New York: Schocken Books, 1972), 146.

14. G. R. Driver and Jon C. Miles, *The Assyrian Laws* (Oxford: At the Clarendon Press, 1935), 130.

15. Wellard, *Babylon*, 147.

16. Balsdon, *Roman Women*, 278.

17. Robin Scroggs, "Paul: Chauvinist or Liberationist?" *Christian Century*, March 15, 1972, 308.

18. W. E. H. Lecky, *History of European Morals from Augustine to Charlemagne* (New York: Appleton, 1870), 385 (hereafter cited in text as *HE*).

19. Leopold Zscharnack, *Der Dienst der Frau in den ersten Jahrhunderten der christliche Kirche* (Gottingen: 1902), 19.

20. Max Weber, *Sociology of Religion* (Boston: Beacon Press, 1957), 104.

21. A. C. Headlam, "Prisca or Priscilla?" in *Dictionary of the Bible* (New York: Charles Scribner's Sons, 1911), 102-1-3.

22. William Morey, *Outlines of Roman Law* (New York: G. P. Putnam's Sons, 1894), 150.

23. Jean-Louis Flandrin, *Families in Former Times,* trans. Richard Southern (Cambridge: Cambridge University Press, 1979), 131.

24. Morey, *Roman Law*, 151.

25. Ibid.

26. Keith Hopkins, "The Age of Roman Girls at Marriage," *Population Studies* (1965), 315, 320.

27. "Kenya School Saves Girls from Early Marriage," *Reuters* (Kajaido, Kenya), January 27, 1999 (obtained from Lexis-Nexis Internet Service).

28. Tabibul Islam, "Bangladesh Health: Despite Laws, Many Brides Are Mere Girls," *Inter Press Service News Wire* (Dhaka, Bangladesh), October 8, 1996 (obtained from Lexis-Nexis Internet Serive).

29. Nicholas Pythian, "Moslem Mauritania to Stop Child Brides," *Reuters* (Nouakchott, Mauritania), October 28, 1996 (obtained from Lexis-Nexis Internet Service).

30. Amir Taheri, *The Spirit of Allah: Khomeini and the Islamic Revolution* (New York: Adler and Adler, 1986), 90–91.

31. James Donaldson, *Woman: Her Position and Influence in Ancient Greece and Rome Among Early Christians* (New York: Longmans, Green, 1907), 88.

32. Carl Joseph von Hefele, *A History of the Councils of the Church* (Edinburgh: T & T Clark, 1895), 4:9.

33. Carl Joseph von Hefele, *Conciliengeschichte* (Freiburg: Herder'sche Verlag, 1877), 3:46.

34. Ibid., 4:349.

35. Qasim Amin, *The Liberation of Women: A Document in the History of Egyptian Feminism*, trans. Samiha Sidhom Peterson (Cairo: The American University in Cairo Press, 1992), 83.

36. Dorothy K. Stein, "Women to Burn: Suttee as a Normative Institution," *Signs: Journal of Women, Culture, and Society* (Winter 1978), 253.

37. Lin Yutang, *My Country and My People* (New York: Halcyon House, 1935), 168.

38. Bernard Lewis, *The Muslim Discovery of Europe* (New York: W. W. Norton, 1982), 287.

39. L. F. Cervantes, "Woman," 14:993.

40. George H. Morrison, *Christ in Shakespeare* (London: James Clarke, 1928), 21.

41. Yediha Kalfon Stillman, *Arab Dress: A Short History From the Dawn of Islam to Modern Times* (Boston: Brill, 2000), 158.

42. Amin, *Liberation of Women*, 37.

43. Jan Goodwin, *Price of Honor: Muslim Women Lift the Veil of Silence on the Islamic World* (Boston: Little, Brown, 1994), 56.

44. Fatima Mernissi, *The Veil and the Male Elite*, trans. Mary Jo Lakeland (New York: Addison-Wesley, 1987), 187.

45. Ibid.

46. Gene Edward Veith, "Heart Problems," *World*, May 3, 2003, 13.

47. Ibid.

48. Stephen Schwartz, *The Two Faces of Islam* (New York: Doubleday, 2002), 265.

49. Fatima Mernissi, *Beyond the Veil: Male-Female Dynamics in a Modern Muslim Society* (New York: Schenkman, 1975), xvi.

50. Ibid, 4.

51. Ibid., 13.

52. Nilufer Göle, *The Forbidden Modern: Civilization and Veiling* (Ann Arbor: University of Michigan Press, 1996), 4.

53. Ibid., 83.

54. Cited in Bernard Lewis, *The Emergence of Modern Turkey* (New York: Oxford University Press, 1961), 265.

55. Oriana Fallaci, *The Rage and the Pride* (New York: Rizzoli, 2002), 110.

56. Ergun Mehmet Caner and Emir Fethi Caner, *Unveiling Islam* (Grand Rapids: Kregel, 2002), 225.

57. Anne Sofie Roald, *Women in Islam: The Western Experience* (New York: Routledge, 2001), 226.

58. Mohammad Mazherrddin Siddiqi, *Women in Islam* (New Delhi: Adam Publishers and Distributors, 1980), 108.

59. Raphael Patai, *The Jewish Mind* (New York: Charles Scribner's Sons, 1977), 365.

60. Martin Lings, *Muhammad: His Life Based on the Earliest Sources* (New York: Inner Traditions, 1983), 345.

61. Khaled Abou El Fadl, *Speaking in God's Name: Islamic Law, Authority, and Women* (Oxford: One World, 2002), 182.

62. Cyril Glasse, "Women," *The Concise Encyclopedia of Islam* (New York: HarperSanFrancisco, 1989), 420.

63. Abdulrahman A. Al-Sheba, "Misconceptions on Human Rights in Islam," trans. Mohammad Said Dabas (Riyadh: Islamic Propagation Office, 2001), www.islamcall.com/rights_misco.htm (accessed December 18, 2003).

64. Maurice Gaudefroy-Demombyne, *Muslim Institutions*, trans. John P. MacGregor (London: George Allen and Unwin, 1961), 132.

65. Hugh Pope, "Women's Rights Gain Foothold Amid Saudis' Cautious Evolution," *Wall Street Journal*, January 22, 2004.

66. El Fadl, *God's Name*, 275.

67. Ibid., 224.

68. *Ghazali's Book of Counsel for Kings*, trans. F. R. C. Bagley (London: Oxford University Press, 1964), 163.

69. Ibid.

70. Fatna A. Sabbah, *Woman in the Muslim Unconscious*, trans. Mary Jo Lakeland (New York: Pergamon, 1984), 13.

71. Ibid, 116.

72. Goodwin, *Price of Honor*, 93.

73. Nabid Toubia, "Female Circumcision as a Public Health Issue," *New England Journal of Medicine* (September 15, 1994), 712.

74. Linda Burstyn, "Female Circumcision Comes to America," *Atlantic Monthly*, October, 1995, 32.

75. Toubia, "Female Circumcision," 712.

76. Burstyn, "Female Circumcision," 33.

77. Steve Cleary and Gary Lane, "Indonesia: I Know the Plans I Have for You," *The Voice of the Martyrs*, May 2001, 7. The authors report that men, women, and children who were forced to convert from Christianity to Islam were circumcised.

78. Ruth Lax, "Socially Sanctioned Violence Against Women: Female Genital Mutilation Is Its Most Brutal Form," *Clinical Social Work Journal* (Winter 2000), 404.

79. Ibid., 403.

80. Geraldine Brooks, *Nine Parts of Desire: The Hidden World of Islamic Women* (New York: Anchor Books, 1996), 54.

81. "Fire and Faith," *Time*, September 28, 1987, 41.

82. Eric Winkel, "A Muslim Perspective on Female Circumcision," *Women and Health* (1995), 3.

83. Lax, "Violence Against Women," 405.

84. Ibid.

85. In the popular vernacular, when a man has more than one wife at the same time, people usually call it polygamy, meaning many marriages, but more accurately, as noted above, it is really polygyny, meaning one man has many wives.

86. *Courier International* (March 9–15, 1995), 27.

87. G. H. Jensen, *Militant Islam* (New York: Harper and Row, 1979), 201.

88. Goodwin, *Price of Honor*, 34.

89. Emile Dermenghem, *The Life of Mahomet*, trans. Arabelle Yorke (New York: Dial Press, 1930), 295.

90. Joseph Schacht, "Law and Justice," in *The Cambridge History of Islam*, ed. P. M. Holt, Ann K. S. Lambton, and Bernard Lewis (Cambridge: At the University Press, 1970), 2:545.

91. Ahmed Rashid, *Jihad: The Rise of Militant Islam in Central Asia* (New Have: Yale University Press, 2002), 3.

92. Paul Findley, *Silent No More: Confronting America's False Image of Islam* (Beltsville, MD: Amana, 2001), 127.

93. Rana Kabbani, *Letter to Christendom*, cited in Brooks, *Nine Parts of Desire*, 54.

94. Naheed Mustafa, "Hijab (Veil) and Muslim Women," www.usc.edu /dept/MSA/humanrelations/womeninislam/hijabexperience.html (accessed November 17, 2003).

95. Mernissi, *Beyond the Veil*, viii.

CHAPTER 4

1. David R. James, "Slavery and Involuntary Servitude," in *Encyclopedia of Sociology*, ed. Edgar Borgatta and Marie L. Borgatta (New York: Macmillan, 1992), 4:1792.

2. Portions of this chapter that pertain to slavery in the pre-Christian era and how it later was responded to by Christians and those influence by Christianity are excerpted from Chapter 11 in my book: *Under the Influence: How Christianity Transformed Civilization* (Grand Rapids: Zondervan, 2001).

3. Lisa Anderson, "Paying for Slavery," *Chicago Tribune*, May 17, 1999, 1.

4. Ronald Segal, *Islam's Black Slaves: The Other Diaspora* (New York: Farrar, Straus and Giroux, 2001), 220.

5. "Country Summaries," *The Voice of the Martyrs*, Special Issue 2003, 19.

6. Robin Lane Fox, *Pagans and Christians* (San Francisco: Perennial Library, 1986), 298.

7. C. Schmidt, *The Social Results of Early Christianity*, trans. R. W. Dale (London: Wm. Isbister, 1889), 430.

8. Edward Ryan, *The History of the Effects of Religion on Mankind: In Countries Ancient and Modern, Barbarous and Civilized* (Dublin: T. M. Bales, 1802), 151.

9. Herbert B. Workman, *Persecution in the Early Church* (New York: Abingdon Press [1906], 1960), 71.

10. Kenneth Scott Latourette, *A History of Christianity* (New York: Harper and Brothers, 1953), 558.

11. John Stoughton, *William Wilberforce* (New York: A. C. Armstrong and Son, 1880), 134, 138.

12. Ibid., 79.

13. Ibid., 78.

14. D. James Kennedy and Jerry Newcombe, *What If Jesus Had Never Been Born?* (Nashville: Thomas Nelson, 1994), 21.

15. Kenneth Stamp, *The Peculiar Institution: Slavery in the Ante-Bellum South* (New York: Alfred Knopf, 1956), 85.

16. Sherwood E. Wirt, *The Social Consequences of the Evangelical* (New York: Harper and Row, 1968), 39.

17. Joseph C. Lovejoy and Owen Lovejoy, eds., *Memoir of the Rev. Elijah Lovejoy* (Freeport, NY; Books for Library Press [1838], 1970), 156.

18. James Brewer Stewart, *Holy Warriors: The Abolitionists and American Slavery* (New York: Hill and Wang, 1976), 35, 37.

19. Louis Filler, *The Crusade Against Slavery, 1830–1890* (New York: Harper and Brothers, 1960), 67.

20. Ibid, 163.

21. Ibid., 72.

22. David B. Chesebrough, *Clergy Dissent in the Old South, 1830–1865* (Carbondale: Southern Illinois University Press, 1996), 42.

23. Ibid.

24. Ibid., 46.

25. Ibid., 125.

26. Cited in Barnes, op. cit., 98

27. Cited in Henry Mayer, *All On Fire: William Lloyd Garrison and the Abolition of Slavery* (New York: St. Martin's, 1998), 568.

28. Cited in Stewart, *Holy Warriors*, 153.

29. Annie Fields, *Life and Letters of Harriet Beecher Stowe* (Boston: Houghton Mifflin, 1898), 377.

30. Mayer, *All On Fire*, 423.

31. Albert Bernhardt Faust, *The German Element in the United States* (Boston: Houghton Mifflin, 1909), 1:46.

32. Ibid.

33. See Robert Brent Toplin, *The Abolition of Slavery in Brazil* (New York: Atheneum, 1972), 118. According to this author, Brazil's abolitionists, "interpreted slavery and Christianity to be incompatible and said that the servile institution was ignominious to Christian civilization and condemned in the Bible."

34. Rodney Stark, *For the Glory of God: How Monotheism Led To Reformations, Science, Witch-Hunts, And The End Of Slavery* (Princeton: Princeton University Press, 2003), 291.

35. Ibid., 304.

36. Bertram Wallace Korn, "Slave Trade," *Encyclopedia Judaica* (New York: Macmillan, 1971), 14:1662.

37. Stark, *Glory of God*, 301.

38. Paul E. Lovejoy, *Transformations in Slavery: A History of Slavery in Africa* (Cambridge, MA: Cambridge University Press, 1983), 15–16.

39. Bernard Lewis, *Race and Slavery in the Middle East* (New York: Oxford University Press, 1990), 12.

40. Anis A. Shorrosh, *Islam Revealed: A Christian Arab's View of Islam* (Nashville: Thomas Nelson, 1988), 173.

41. Irshad Manji, *The Trouble With Islam: A Muslim's Call for Reform in Her Faith* (New York: St. Martin's, 2003), 37.

42. Lewis, *Race and Slavery*, 78.

43. Ibid., 80.

44. Marcus Mabry, "The Price Tag on Freedom," *Newsweek*, May 3, 1999, 42.

45. Andrew Bushel, "Sale of Children Thrives in Pakistan," *The Washington Times*, January 21, 2002. According to this report, young girls were sold at auction sales in the year 2000 in Pakistan's Northwest Frontier Province.

46. Brain Eads, "Slavery's Shameful Return to Africa," *Reader's Digest*, March 1996.

47. Catherine Roberts, "Slaves For Sale," *Maclean's*, May 7, 2001.

48. David Littman, "The U.N. Finds Slavery in the Sudan," *Middle East Quarterly* (September 1996), 92.

49. Barry Came, "Freeing the Slaves of Sudan," *Maclean's*, April 10, 2000.

50. Lisa Anderson, "Paying for Slavery," 1.

51. A. M. Rosenthal, "Secrets of War," *The New York Times*, April 23, 1999, A25.

52. Mindy Belz, "Stopping Slavers," *World*, October 16, 1999, 29.

53. Eads, "Slavery's Shameful Return," 81.

54. Deroy Murdoch, "American Stays Mum About Slavery in Africa," *Headway* (October 1996), 21.

55. Samuel Cotton, *Silent Terror: A Journey into Contemporary African Slavery* (New York: Harlem River, 1998), 105.

56. Ibid., 112–113.

57. Ronald Segal, *Islam's Black Slaves: The Other Black Diaspora* (New York: Farrar, Straus and Giroux, 2001), 98.

58. Mabry, "Price Tag," 43.

59. Ibid.

60. Ibid.

61. Segal, *Islam's Black Slaves*, 98.

62. Lewis, *Race and Slavery*, vi.

63. Ibid.

64. Mabry, "Price Tag," 42.

65. Thomas Patrick Hughes, *Dictionary of Islam* (New Delhi, India: Oriental Books Reprint, 1885), 600.

66. Mabry, "Price Tag," 41.

CHAPTER 5

1. Some portions of the present chapter's discussion regarding Christianity's influence on charity are excerpted from Chapters 5 and 6 of my book: *Under the Influence: How Christianity Transformed Civilization* (Grand Rapids: Zondervan, 2001).

2. V. G. Dawe, "The Attitude of the Ancient Church Toward Sickness and Healing," (Published Th.D. thesis, Boston University School of Theology, 1955), 3.

3. Fielding H. Garrison, *An Introduction of the History of Medicine* (Philadelphia: W. B. Saunders, 1914), 118.

4. Gerhard Uhlhorn, *Christian Charity in the Ancient World* (New York: Charles Scribner's Sons, 1883), 38.

5. Ferdinand Schenck, *Christian Evidence and Ethics* (New York: YMCA Press, 1910), 92.

6. Uhlhorn, *Christian Charity*, 7, 9.

7. Robert Banks, "The Early Church as a Caring Community," *Evangelical Review of Theology* (October, 1983), 318.

8. Ibid., 319.

9. Edward Ryan, *The History of the Effects of Religion on Mankind: In Countries Ancient and Modern, Barbarous and Civilized* (Dublin: T. M. Bates, 1802), 132.

10. Christopher Dawson, *Medieval Essays: A Study of Christian Cultures* (Garden City, NY: Image Books, 1959), 46.

11. Nathaniel W. Faxon, *The Hospital in Contemporary Life* (Cambridge: Harvard University Press, 1949), 7.

12. Roberto Margotta, *The Story of Medicine: Man's Struggle Against Disease—From Ancient Sorcery to Modern Miracles of Vaccines, Drugs, and Surgery* (New York: Golden Press, 1968), 102.

13. With regard to the latter two, the Apostle Peter told the recipients of his Epistle: "Practice hospitality ungrudgingly to one another" (I Peter 4:9). Similarly, the Apostle Paul told the bishops (spiritual overseers) they were to be given to hospitality (I Timothy 3:2 and Titus 1:8).

14. Howard W. Haggard, *The Doctor in History* (New Haven: Yale University Press, 1934), 19.

15. Garrison, *History of Medicine*, 118.

16. George Grant, *Third Time Around: A History of the Pro-Life Movement from the First Century to the Present* (Brentwood, TN: Wolgemuth and Hyatt, 1991), 19.

17. George E. Gask and John Todd, "The Origin of Hospitals," in *Medicine and History*, ed. E. Ashworth (New York: Arno Press, 1975), 129.

18. David Riesman, *The Story of Medicine in the Middle Ages* (New York: Harper and Brothers, 1936), 356.

19. Gask and Todd, "Origin of Hospitals," 130.

20. E. Natalli Rocco, "Hospitals, History of," *New Catholic Encyclopedia* (New York: McGraw-Hill, 1967), 3:160.

21. C. F. V. Smout, *The Story of the Progress of Medicine* (Bristol: John Wright and Sons, 1964), 40.

22. Garrison, *History of Medicine*, 118.

23. The Nestorians were a heretical Christian sect who denied that Mary, the mother of Jesus, was the mother of God (*theotokos*) and thus were formally excluded from orthodox Christianity in the late fifth century.

24. Cyril Glasse, *The Concise Encyclopedia of Islam* (New York: HarperSanFrancisco, 1989), 265.

25. Howard R. Turner, *Science in Early Islam* (Austin: University of Texas Press, 1995), 133.

26. Haggard, *Doctor in History*, 138.

27. Ernle Bradford, *The Sword and the Scimitar: The Saga of the Crusades* (New York: G. P. Putnam's Sons, 1974), 128.

28. Mary Risley, *House of Healing: The Story of the Hospital* (Garden City, NY: Doubleday, 1961), 106.

29. Faxon, *Hospital in Contemporary Life*, 10.

30. Edgar Erskine Hume, *Medical Work of the Knights Hospitallers of Saint John of Jerusalem* (Baltimore: John Hopkins, 1940), 1.

31. Nasalli-Rocca, "Hospitals," 161.

32. R. M. McGuinness, "Blind and Visually Handicapped," *New Catholic Encyclopedia* (San Francisco: McGraw-Hill, 1967), 2:615.

33. Max Meyerhof, "Science and Medicine," in *The Legacy of Islam*, eds. Sir Thomas Arnold and Alfred Guillaume (London: Oxford University Press, 1931), 350.

34. "The Muslim Concept of Charity," http://home.att.net/~a.f.aly/charity.htm (accessed November 28, 2003).

35. Ibid., xliii.

36. Ibid., xliii, 179. For example, Muslims must give at least 2.5 percent of the funds that an individual donor has accumulated at the end of the year. On secondary income (bonuses, inheritance money, financial awards, stocks, and bonds) the *zakat* rate increases to 20 percent. There are further explicit instructions based on whether one is a farmer or a gardener;

for example, if one owns cattle and has 30 cows, he must give one cow as *zakat.*

37. Ibid., 36.

38. Ibid., 35.

39. John E.Booty, "Christian Socialism," *Academic American Encyclopedia* (Danbury, CT: Grolier, 1996), 4:412.

40. Fyodor Mikhaylovich Dostoyevsky, *The Brothers Karamazov,* trans. Constance Garrett (Chicago: Encyclopedia Britannica, 1952), 32.

41. Marvin Olasky, *The Tragedy of American Compassion* (Washington, DC: Regnery Gateway, 1992), 6.

42. Ibid., 7.

43. Alex de Tocqueville, *Democracy in America,* trans. Henry Reeve and rev. by Francis Bowen (New York: Vintage Books, 1945), 2:185.

44. Gunnar Myrdal, *An American Dilemma: The Negro Problem and Modern Democracy* (New York: Harper and Row, 1944), 11.

45. Ibid.

46. V. Hodgkinson and M. Weitzman, *Giving and Volunteering in the United States* (Washington, DC: Independent Sector, 1992), 1.

47. Eileen W. Lindner, *Yearbook of American and Canadian Churches, 1998* (Nashville: Abingdon, 1998), 14.

48. Amos Warner, *American Charities: A Study in Philosophy and Economics* (New York: Thomas C. Crowell, 1894), 316.

49. Dean R. Hoge, et al., "Giving in Five Denominations," in Mark Chaves and Sharon I. Miller, eds., *Financing American Religion* (Walnut Creek, CA, 1999), 3.

50. Sharon I. Miller, "Financing Parachurch Organizations," in *Financing American Religion*, eds. Mark Chaves and Sharon I. Miller (Waluut Creek, CA: Alternate Press, 1999), 120.

51. Ibid., 122.

52. "Religious Construction on the Rise," *World*, June 12, 1999.

53. Ibid.

54. Cited in Martin Gumpert, *Dunant: The Story of the Red Cross* (New York: Oxford University Press, 1938), 63.

55. D. James Kennedy and Jerry Newcombe, *What If Jesus Had Never Been Born?* (Nashville: Thomas Nelson, 1994), 152.

56. Cited in Gumpert, *Dunant*, 300.

57. Kennedy and Newcombe, *What If Jesus*, 152.

58. Gumpert, *Dunant*, 102–103.

59. Ibid.

304

60. Cited in Robert Spencer, *Islam Unveiled: Disturbing Questions About the World's Fastest Growing Faith* (San Francisco: Encounter Books, 202), 159.

61. "Minarets in Oxford," http://www.balkanarchive.org.yu/kosta/islam/Mina

retsinOxford.2.html (accessed February 25, 2004).

62. Christopher H. Schmitt and Joshua Kurlantzick, "When Charity Goes Awry," *U.S. News and World Report*, October 29, 2001, 35.

63. Ibid.

64. Edward T. Pound and Lisa Griffin, "A Charity's Odd Ties," *U.S. News and World Report*, November 12, 2001, 34.

65. Schmitt and Kurlantzick, "Charity Goes Awry," 35.

66. "Shutting Down Terrorist Financial Networks: Whitehouse Fact Sheet on Hamas," (http://usinfo.state.gov/topical/pol/terror/01120409.htm), (accessed February 5, 2004).

67. Naraj Warikoo, "Cleric Makes Case for Freedom," Detroit Free Press, October 2, 2002. Cited by Robert Spencer, *Onward Muslim Soldiers* (Washington, D.C: Regnery, 2003), 48.

68. Yusuf al-Qardawi, *Fiqh az-Zakat: A Comparative Study* (London: Dar Al Taqwa, 1999), 447.

CHAPTER 6

1. Thomas F. Madden, *A Concise History of the Crusades* (Lanham, MD: Rowman and Littlefield, 1999), 1.

2. Ibid.

3. Thomas F. Madden, "Crusade Propaganda: The Abuse of Christianity's Holy War," www.nationalreview.com (August 18, 2003).

4. For further discussion, see Paul Fregosi, *Jihad in the West: Muslim Conquests from the 7th to the 21st Centuries* (Amherst, NY: Prometheus Books, 1998).

5. Serge Trifkovic, *The Sword of the Prophet: Islam, History, Theology, Impact on the World* (Boston: Regina Orthodox Press, 2002), 97.

6. Raymond H. Schmandt, *The Crusades: Origin of an Ecumenical Problem* (Houston: University of Saint Thomas Press, 1967), 16.

7. Kenneth Scott Latourette, *The Thousand Years of Uncertainty, A.D. 500–A.D.1500* (New York: Harper and Brothers, 1938), 317.

8. Bernard Lewis, "The Roots of the Muslim Rage," *Atlantic Monthly*, September 1990, 49.

9. Roland Armour, *Islam, Christianity, and the West* (Maryknoll, NY: Orbis Books, 2002), 64.

10. W. Montgomery Watt, *The Majesty That Was Islam: The Islamic World, 661–1100* (New York: Praeger, 1974), 247.

11. Bernard Lewis, *Islam and the West* (New York: Oxford University Press, 1993), 12.

12. Ibid.

13. Robert Irwin, "Islam and the Crusades, 1096–1699," in *The Oxford Illustrated History of the Crusades*, ed. Jonathan Riley-Smith (New York: Oxford University Press, 1995), 259.

14. Madden, "Crusade Propaganda."

15. Paul Johnson, "Relentlessly and Thoroughly," *National Review*, October 15, 2001, 20.

16. Guenter B. Risse, *Mending Bodies, Saving Souls* (New York: Oxford University Press, 1999), 139.

17. Oriana Fallaci, *The Rage and the Pride* (New York: Rizzoli, 2002), 82.

18. Tomas Dixon, "An Apology, 900 Years in the Making," *Christianity Today*, September 6, 1999.

19. Jonathan Riley-Smith, *What Were the Crusades?* (Totowa, NJ: Rowman and Littlefield, 1977), 18.

20. Sandra Schaam, "Legacy of the Crusades," *Archaeology* (September/October 2002), 27.

21. Madden, "Crusade Propaganda."

22. Martin Luther, "On War Against the Turk," in *Luther's Works: The Christian in Society*, ed. Robert C. Schultz and Helmut T. Lehmann (Philadelphia: Fortress Press, 1967), 46:161–205.

23. Carl Limbacher and NewsMax.com Staff, "Bush Appointee Critical of President," *NewsMax.com* (November 29, 2003).

24. Ernest Barker, "The Crusades," in *The Legacy of Islam*, ed. Sir Thomas Arnold and Alfred Guillaume (London: Oxford University Press, 1931), 57–65.

CHAPTER 7

1. Portions of the present chapter that pertain to the Judeo and Christian influence on liberty and justice in the West are excerpted from Chapter 10 in my book: *Under the Influence: How Christianity Transformed Civilization* (Grand Rapids: Zondervan, 2001).

2. Augustine, *The City of God Against the Pagans* (Cambridge: Harvard University Press, 1963), 2:272.

3. See a copy of the Magna Carta in J. C. Holt, *Magna Carta* (Cambridge: Harvard University Press, 1965), 317–337.

4. Ibid., 317.

5. As church historians know all too well, this was not the first or the last time that a pope contradicted Christian values. Throughout the Middle Ages there were occasions when, despite the opposition of the pope, Christians "let their light shine" as Jesus had commanded them.

6. Leon McKenzie, *Pagan Resurrection Myths and the Resurrection of Jesus* (Charlottesville: Bookwrights, 1997), 49.

7. Martin Luther, "Against the Heavenly Prophets in the Matter of Images and Sacraments," in *Luther's Works,* trans. Bernard Erling, ed. Conrad Bergendoff (Philadelphia: Muhlenberg, 1958), 40:98.

8. Gary T. Amos, *Defending the Declaration: How the Bible and Christianity Influenced the Writing of the Declaration of Independence* (Brentwood, TN: Wolgemuth and Hyatt, 1989), 42.

9. Ellis Sandoz, *A Government of Laws: Political Theory, Religion, and the American Founding* (Baton Rouge: Louisiana State University Press, 1990), 94.

10. Thomas Jefferson, in Bernard Mayo, ed., *Jefferson Himself: The Personal Narratives of a Many-Sided American* (Charlottesville: University of Virginia Press, 1970), 322.

11. Amos, *Defending the Declaration,* 78.

12. John Locke, *The Second Treatise of Government* ((Indianapolis: Bobbs-Merrill, 1952), 14.

13. Amos, *Defending the Declaration,* 56.

14. Robert Wernick, "The Godfather of the American Constitution," *Smithsonian* (September 1989), 183.

15. James Madison, in Robert A. Rutland, ed., *The Papers of James Madison* (Chicago: University of Chicago Press, 1977), 10–98.

16. Baron de Montesquieu, *The Spirit of Laws,* trans. Thomas Nugent (Cincinnati: Robert Clarke, 1886), 2:134.

17. Ibid., 2:121.

18. Ibid., 2:122.

19. Ibid., 2:124.

20. Ibid., 1:174.

21. Sandoz, *Government of Laws,* 13.

22. C. F. Adams, ed., *The Works of John Adams* (Boston: Charles C. Little and James Brown, 1851), 4:293.

23. Balint Vazsonyi, *America's 30 Years War* (Washington, DC: Regnery Gateway, 1998), 79.

24. Malcolm Muggeridge, *The End of Christendom* (Grand Rapids: Eerdmans, 1980), 19.

25. F. A. Hayek, *The Road to Serfdom* (Chicago: University of Chicago Press, [1944], 1994), 19.

26. Kenneth Cragg, *Counsels in Contemporary Islam* (Edinburgh: At the University Press, 1965), 74.

27. Alex de Tocqueville, *Democracy in America* (New York: Vintage Books, 1945), 1:5.

28. James Bryce, *Modern Democracies* (New York: Macmillan, 1921), 1:28.

29. Tocqueville, *Democracy*, 1:6–7.

30. Ibid., 1:6.

31. Ibid., 2:100.

32. Ibid.

33. "The Covenant of Medina," (http://www.iifr.com/Research?IHR Documents/TheCovenantofMedina.htm), (accessed December 25, 2003).

34. A. Guillaume, *The Life of Muhammad: A Translation of Ishaq's Sirat Rassul Allah* (London: Oxford University Press, 1955), 232.

35. Irshad Manji, *The Trouble With Islam: A Muslim's Call for Reform in Her Faith* (New York: St. Martin's, 2003), 34.

36. Abdulrahman A. Al-Sheba, "Misconceptions on Human Rights in Islam," trans. Mohammad Said Dabas, www.islamcall.com/rights_misco .htm (accessed December 18, 2003).

37. Milton Viorst, *In the Shadow of the Prophet* (Boulder: Westview Press, 2000), 142.

38. Paul Lunde, *Islam* (New York: Dorling Kindersley, 2002), 35.

39. Susie Steiner, "Sharia Law," *The Guardian Review Online,* August 20, 2002, http://www.guardian.co.uk/theissues/article/0,6512,777972,00.html, (accessed December, 19, 2003).

40. Ibid.

41. "Bashir Vows Sharia Punishment for Armed Robbery," *Middle East Times*, (http://www.metimes.com/2K1/issue2001-26/reg/bashir_vows_ sharia.htm), (accessed December 18, 2003). In February 2001, it was reported that in January of the same year five Sudanese men who committed robbery each had his right hand and his left foot amputated (known as cross amputation). This took place while they were in Khartoum's Kober prison. The report also stated that another 19 were awaiting the same fate.

42. "The Religion of Peace: Eyewitness to Stoning Woman in Saudi Arabia for Adultery," http://www.liddyshow.usliddyfile35.php, (accessed February 5, 2004).

43. The International Society of Human Rights (Germany), "Stoning as a Form of Punishment under Sharia Law," March 2003, (http://ishr.org/activities/stoning /ishr_position_paper.htm), (accessed December 19, 2003).

44. "Stoning to Death in Iran: A Crime Against Humanity Carried Out by the Mullahs' Regime," http://www.vibrani.com/stoning.htm, (accessed December 18, 2003).

45. Ibid.

46. Paul Marshall, "Extreme Sharia Punishments Live on in Africa," *National Review On-line* (September 29, 2003), 1.

47. Ibid.

48. Daniel Somerville, "Sodomite Sentenced to be Stoned to Death," http://www.mask.org.za/Sections/AfricaPerCountry/ABC/nigeria/nigeria_3.htm,(accessed December 19, 2003).

49. Steiner, "Sharia Law."

50. The International Society of Human Rights, "Stoning."

51. Amnesty International, "Yemen: Death by Stoning and Flogging," http://web.amnesty.org/library/Index/ENGMDE3100622002?open&of=ENG-YEM, (accessed December 19, 2003).

52. Ibn Warraq, *Leaving Islam: Apostates Speak Out* (Amherst, NY: Prometheus Books, 2003), 34-35.

53. Barnabas Fund, "Where Conversion Means Death," http://www.barnabasfund.org/Apostasy/Conversion_Means_Death.htm, (accessed December 21, 2003).

54. Ibid.

55. Uwe Siemon-Netto, "Iranian Converts Pray for Homeland," United Press International E-Mail Report (December 29, 2003).

56. Neville Kyrke-Smith, "Pakistan: The Oppression of Christians," http://members4.boardhost.com/acnaus/msg/1597.html, (accessed January 30, 2004).

57. "Religious and Ahmadi-specific Laws," *The Gazette of Pakistan*, April 26, 1984, http://www.thepersecution.org/50years/paklaw.html (accessed January 30, 2004).

58. Robert Spencer, *Onward Muslim Soldiers: How the Jihad Still Threatens America and the West* (Washington, DC: Regnery, 2003), 206.

59. Patrick Sookhdeo, *A People Betrayed: The Impact of Islamization on the Christian Community in Pakistan* (Fearn, Scotland: Christian Focus, 2002), 180–182, 215–220.

60. Ibid., 231–232. "A Christian student of science at the Islamia College in Karachi was forbidden by his fellow students to drink from the tap. Five Christian schoolgirls from St. Mary's School, Gujrat, who were taking a Home Economics practical examination on 25 February, 1997, found that the Muslim examiner would not test or mark the food they cooked. She ordered the Christians' food to be put in the dustbin, but tested the food of their eight Muslim classmates in the normal way."

61. " 'Jew, Fight Fair,' " http://www.omdurman.org/jew.html (accessed February 25, 2004).

62. Ibid.

63. Middle East Media Research Institute, "Friday Sermons in Saudi Mosques: Review and Analysis," MEMRI Special Report No. 10, September 26, 2002, www.memri.org, (accessed December 25, 2003).

64. Spencer, *Onward Muslim Soldiers*, 196.

65. Middle East Media Research Institute, "A Friday Sermon on PA TV: 'We Must Educate our Children on the Love of Jihad,' " MEMRI Special Dispatch No. 240, July 11, 2002, www.memri.org, (accessed December 25, 2003).

66. *Reliance of the Traveller* (Beltsville, MD: Amana, 1994), o11.6.

67. Ibid, o11.7.

68. R. V. C. Bodley, *The Messenger: The Life of Mohammad* (Garden City, NJ: Double Day, 1946), 234.

69. Serge Trifkovic, *The Sword of the Prophet: Islam History, Theology, Impact on the World* (Boston: Regina Orthodox Press, 2002), 200.

CHAPTER 8

1. Some portions of the present chapter pertaining to Christianity's influence on development of science are excerpted from Chapter 9 in my book: *Under the Influence: How Christianity Transformed Civilization* (Grand Rapids: Zondervan, 2001). The brief summaries of various scientists, who were influenced by Christianity, are also taken from chapter 9 of this book (see Appendix B).

2. Alfred North Whitehead, *Science and the Modern World* (New York: Macmillan, 1926), 19.

3. Rodney Stark, *For the Glory of God: How Monotheism Led To Reformations, Science, Witch-Hunts, And The End Of Slavery* (Princeton: Princeton University Press, 2003), 147.

4. Lynn T White, "The Significance of Medieval Christianity," in *The Vitality of the Christian Tradition*, ed. George F. Thomas (New York: Harper and Brothers, 1945), 96.

5. Ernst Mach, *Science of Mechanics*, trans. Thomas J. McCormick (La Salle, IL: Open Court, 1960), 549.

6. Whitehead, *Science*, 18.

7. Thomas Goldstein, *Dawn of Modern Science: From the Arabs to Leonardo da Vinci* (Boston: Houghton Mifflin, 1980), 171.

8. Roger Bacon, *Opus majus,* trans. Robert Belle Burke (New York: Russell and Russell, 1962), 584.

9. Brian Clegg, *The First Scientist: A Life of Roger Bacon* (New York: Carroll and Graf, 2003).

10. Magnus Magnusson, ed., "Bacon, Francis, Baron Verulam of Verulam, Viscount St. Albans," in *Cambridge Biographical Dictionary* (New York: Cambridge University Press, 1990), 88.

11. Herbert Butterfield, *The Origins of Modern Science, 1300–1800* (London: G. Bell and Sons, 1951), 79.

12. Stanley I. Jaki, *The Savior of Science* (Edinburgh: Scottish Academic, 1990), 41.

13. Butterfield, *Origins*, 7–8.

14. Richard Fletcher, *Moorish Spain* (New York: Henry Holt, 1992), 153.

15. Tarif Khalidi, *Classical Arab Islam: The Culture and the Heritage of the Golden Age* (Princeton: Princeton University Press, 1985), 96.

16. Ibid.

17. Howard R. Turner, *Science in Medieval Islam* (Austin: University of Texas Press, 1995), 28.

18. Dick Teresi, *Lost Discoveries: The Ancient Roots of Modern Science—From the Babylonians to the Maya* (New York: Simon and Schuster, 2002), 221.

19. Max Meyerhof, "Science and Medicine," in *The Legacy of Islam*, ed. Thomas Arnold and Alfred Guillaume, (New York: Oxford University Press, 1931), 322.

20. Eugene A. Myers, *Arabic Thought and the Western World* (New York: Frederick Ungar, 1964), 76.

21. Ibid., 9.

22. Ibid., 8.

23. George Sarton, *Introduction to the History of Science: From Rabbi Ben Ezra to Roger Bacon* (Baltimore: Carnegie Institution of Washington, 1931), 2:144.

24. Caesar E. Farah, *Islam: Beliefs and Observances* (Woodbury, NY: Barron's Educational Series, 1970), 198.

25. Teresi, *Lost Discoveries*, 86.

26. Ibid.

27. Turner, *Science*, 47.

28. Charles Singer, *A Short History of Scientific Ideas to 1900* (Oxford: At the Clarendon Press, 1959), 149.

29. Ibid.

30. Ibid.

31. F. Sherwood Taylor, *A Short History of Science and Scientific Thought* (New York: W. W. Norton, 1949), 56.

32. H. D. Anthony, *Science And Its Background* (London: Macmillan, 1948), 93.

33. Stark, *Glory of God*, 131.

34. Myers, *Arabic Thought*, 77.

35. S. D. Goitein, *Studies in Islamic History and Institutions* (Leiden: E. J. Brill, 1996), 47.

36. Taylor, *Short History*, 56.

37. Turner, *Science*, 66.

38. Florian Cajori, *A History of Mathematics* (New York: Chelsea, 1980), 100.

39. Bernard Lewis, *The Muslim Discovery of Europe* (New York: W. W. Norton, 1982), 229.

40. Wilhelm Windelband, *A History of Philosophy*, trans. James H. Tufts (New York: Macmillan, 1926), 317.

41. Ernest Barker, "The Crusades," in *The Legacy of Islam*, ed. Sir Thomas Arnold and Alfred Guillaume (London: Oxford University Press, 1931), 56.

42. Windelband, *History of Philosophy*, 317.

43. Lewis, *Muslim Discovery*, 229.

44. Pervez Hoodbhoy, *Islam and Science: Religious Orthodoxy and The Battle for Rationality* (London: Zed Books, 1991), 77.

45. Meyerhof, "Science and Medicine," 327.

46. A. C. Crombis, *Medieval And Early Modern Science* (Garden City, NJ: Doubleday, 1959), 132.

47. Singer, *Short History*, 145.

48. Meyerhof, "Science and Medicine," 320.

312

49. Ibid.

50. Thomas Goldstein, *Dawn of Modern Science* (Boston: Houghton Mifflin, 1980), 100.

51. Meyerhof, "Science and Medicine," 323.

52. Ibid., 344.

53. Singer, *Short History*, 147.

54. Meyerhof, "Science and Medicine," 344.

55. Ibid., 337.

56. Aaron Segal, "Why Does the Muslim World Lag in Science?" *Middle East Quarterly* (June 1996), 61.

57. Ibid.

58. Ibid., 64.

59. George Sarton, *Introduction to the History of Science* (Baltimore: Carnegie Institution of Washington, 1931), 2:61.

60. Meyerhof, "Science and Medicine," 337.

61. David C. Lindberg, *The Beginnings of Western Science* (Chicago: University of Chicago Press, 1992), 173.

62. Bernard Lewis, *Islam and the West* (New York: Oxford University Press, 1993), 183.

63. Lindberg, *Beginnings of Western Science*, 344.

64. Haggard, *Doctor in History*, 272.

65. Ibid., 345.

66. Lindberg, *Beginnings of Western Science*, 151.

CHAPTER 9

1. Rachel 7, "What If Islam Ruled America?" http://www.freeman.org /m_online/nov98/islam.htm, (accessed December 18, 2003).

2. Some portions of the present chapter's discussion regarding the separation of church and state are excerpted from Chapter 10 in my book: *Under the Influence: How Christianity Transformed Civilization* (Grand Rapids: Zondervan, 2001),

3. Bernard Lewis, *Islam and the West* (New York: Oxford University Press, 1993), 135.

4. "Hosius to Constantius the Emperor," *Athanasius,* in *The Nicene and Post-Nicene Fathers of the Christian Church* (Grand Rapids: Eerdmans, 1980), 4:286.

5. Robert Wilken, *The Christians as the Romans Saw Them* (New Haven: Yale University Press, 1984), 124–125. Recently, Robert Kolb has

argued that the English word "religion" is derived from *religere* (to regard with awe), not *religare* (to bind together). However, he still says religion "indeed does function as that which binds together all aspects of life." See his "Nothing But Christ Crucified: The Autobiography of a Cross-Cultural Communicator," in *The Theology of the Cross for the 21st Century*, ed. Alberto L. Garcis and A.R. Victor Raj (St. Louis: Concordia, 2002), 53.

6. Martin Luther, "Temporal Authority: To What Extent It Should Be Obeyed," in *Luther's Works*, ed. Walter I. Brandt and Helmut T. Lehmann (Philadelphia: Muhlenberg, 1963), 45:111.

7. Benjamin Hart, *Faith and Freedom: The Christian Roots of American Liberty* (Dallas: Lewis and Stanley, 1988), 349.

8. Robert Cord, *Separation of Church and State* (New York: Lambeth, 1982), 41.

9. John Locke, *Treatise of Civil Government and A Letter Concerning Toleration*, ed. Charles Sherman (New York: Appleton Century Crofts, 1937), 175.

10. Michael M. Smith, *The History of Christianity* (Herts, England: Lion, 1977), 142.

11. Jacques Chabanes, *St. Augustine*, trans. Julie Kernan (New York: Doubleday, 1962), 164.

12. Martin Luther, "Letter to the Princes of Saxony Concerning the Rebellious Spirit," in *Luther's Works*, trans. Bernard Erling, ed. Conrad Bergendof (Philadelphia: Muhlenberg, 1958), 40:58.

13. Thomas Bailey, *The American Pageant* (Lexington, MA: D.C. Heath, 1975), 3.

14. Lewis, *Islam*, 37.

15. Maryam Jameela, *Islam and the West* (Delhi, India: Kitab Bhavan, 1969), 73.

16. Ibid., 42.

17. Lewis, *Islam*, 184.

18. Majid Fakhry, "Philosophy and Theology: From the Eighth Century C.E. To The Present," in *The Oxford History of Islam*, ed. John L. Esposito (New York: Oxford University Press, 1999), 299.

19. Mohamed Elhachmi Hamdi, "Islam and Democracy: The Limits of the Western Model," *Journal of Democracy* (April 1996), 84.

20. Bernard Lewis, *What Went Wrong? Western Impact and Middle East Response* (New York: Oxford University Press, 2002), 101.

21. Cited by Bernard Lewis, *Islam in History: Ideas, People, and Events in the Middle East* (Chicago: Open Court, 1993), 262.

22. Bernard Lewis, "Islam and Liberal Democracy: A Historical Overview," *Journal of Democracy* (April 1996), 61.

23. Bernard Lewis, *The Emergence of Modern Turkey* (New York: Oxford University Press, 1961), 271.

24. Lewis, *Islam*, 38.

25. Peter Balakian, *The Burning Tigris: The Armenian Genocide and America's Response* (New York: HarperCollins, 2003), 368.

26. Jameela, *Islam*, 38.

27. Robert Spencer, *Onward Muslim Soldiers* (Washington, DC: Regnery, 2003), 110.

28. Bernard Lewis, *The Muslim Discovery of Europe* (New York: W. W. Norton, 1982).

29. Robert Spencer, *Islam Unveiled: Disturbing Questions About The World's Fastest-Growing Faith* (San Francisco: Encounter Books, 2002), 110.

30. Uwe Siemon-Netto, "Europe—Hostage to Its Muslims?" United Press International E-Mail Report (July 10, 2003). Furthermore, in July 2003, Uwe Siemon-Netto, reporter for United Press International, wrote that the media in Germany had reported that secret Shariah courts are meting out "justice" in Italy, where a man, known to Muslims as a sex fiend, recently appeared with a hand missing. It was apparently amputated in accordance with Shariah law. The report also noted that Italian physicians have recently been treating women who have been lashed, the consequence of another Shariah law.

CHAPTER 10

1. Bernard Lewis, *Islam in History: Ideas, People, and Events in the Middle East* (Chicago: Open Court, 1993), 366.

2. Bernard Lewis, *The Muslim Discovery of Europe* (New York: W. W. Norton, 1982), 66.

3. John Kaltner, *Islam: What Non-Muslims Should Know* (Minneapolis: Fortress, 2003), 121.

4. Ibid.

5. Cyril Glasse, *The Concise Encyclopedia of Islam* (New York: Harper San Francisco, 1991), 209.

6. Bernard Lewis, "Jihad vs. Crusade," *The Wall Street Journal*, September 27, 2001, A8.

7. Lewis, op. cit., 372, 373.

8. Cited in Daniel Pipes and Mimi Stillman, "The United States Government: Islam's Patron?" *Middle East Quarterly* (Winter 2002), 27.

9. Ibid., 28.

10. President George W. Bush, "Islam is Peace," http://www.whitehouse .gov/news/releases/2001/09/20010917-11.html, (accessed February 14, 2004).

11. Colin Powell, "Powell Hosts the State Department Iftaar November 5," http://usembassymalaysia.org.my/wf/wfl105_powell_iftaar.html (accessed February 14, 2004).

12. Cited in Pipes and Stillman, "United States," 31.

13. BBC News, "Stop Islam Stereotypes—Blair" (February 23, 1999), http://news.bbc.co.uk_politics/nesid_284000/284455.stm (accessed February 21, 2004).

14. Irshad Manji, *The Trouble With Islam: A Muslim's Call for Reform in Her Faith* (New York: St. Martin's, 2003), 28–29.

15. Oriana Fallaci, *The Rage and the Pride* (New York: Rizzoli, 2002), 28–29.

16. Reza F. Safa, "Foreword" to *Secrets of the Koran*, by Don Richardson (Ventura, CA: Regal Books, 2003), 11.

17. George Sale, *The Koran* (New York: A. L. Burt, 1894), 43.

18. Edward Gibbon, *History of the Decline and Fall of the Roman Empire* (Chicago: Encyclopedia Britannica, 1952), 2:231.

19. Glasse, *Concise Encyclopedia*, 231.

20. Gene Edward Veith, "Conflict of Religions," *World* (April 19, 2003), 18.

21. C. Iqbal, "We Moderate Muslims Must Stop Living in Denial," http://www.danielpipes.org/comments/4506, (accessed February 14, 2004).

22. Don Richardson, *Secrets of the Koran* (Ventura, CA: Regal Books, 2003), 109.

23. Daniel Pipes, "Who Is The Enemy?" *Commentary* (January 2002), 23.

24. Guy Chazan, "Hamas Is Broadening Its Appeal," *The Wall Street Journal*, January 15, 2004.

25. Robin Lustig, Martin Bailey, Simon de Bruxelles, and Ian Mather, "War of the Word," http://books.guardian.co.uk/Observer/race/story /0,11255,603760,00.html (accessed February 16, 2004).

26. "The Peace Encyclopedia: Blasphemy," http://www.yahoodi.com /peace/blasphemy.html, (accessed February 16, 2004).

27. Oriana Fallaci, *Rage and the Pride*, 29.

28. Ibid., 105.

29. Don Feder, "A Time for Truth – 9/11 and Islam" (http://www .donfeder.com/filecabinet/911Islam091101.txt), accessed December 27, 2003.

CHAPTER 11

1. Ibn al-Rawandi, "Origins of Islam: A Critical Look at the Sources," in *The Quest for the Historical Muhammad*, ed. Ibn Warraq (Amherst, NY: Prometheus Books, 2000), 106.

2. Al Sina, "How Islam Became the Darling of the Western Apologists," http://www.faithfreedom.org/oped/sina3114.htm, (accessed December 18, 2003).

3. Daniel Pipes, *Militant Islam Reaches America* (New York: W. W. Norton, 2000), 108.

4. Caesar E. Farah, *Islam Beliefs and Observances* (New York: Barron's Educational Series, 1970), 76.

5. "Raymond Lull: First Christian Missionary to the Muslims," *The Voice of the Martyrs*, May 2002, 10.

6. Riccoldo de Montre Croce, "Vorrede Bruder Richards," in Martin Luther, *Sammtliche Schriften*, Joh, Georg Walch edition (St. Louis: Concordia, nd.), 20:2222. My translation. Interested readers may read a recent English translation of Riccoldo's publication in Riccoldo de Montre Croce and Martin Luther, *Islam in the Crucible: Can It Pass the Test?* trans. Thomas C. Pfotenhauer (Kearney, NE: Morris, 2002).

7. Rollin Armour, Sr., *Islam, Christianity, and the West: A Troubled History* (Maryknoll, NY: Orbis Books, 2003), 119.

8. Martin Luther, "Bruder Richards Verlegung des Alkoran," in Martin Luther, *Sammtliche Schriften,* Joh, Georg Walch edition (St. Louis: Concordia, nd.), 22:2220. My translation.

9. Riccoldo de Montecroce and Martin Luther, *Islam in the Crucible: Can It Pass The Test?* trans. Thomas C. Pfotenhauer (Kearney, NE: Morris, 2002).

10. George Sale, *The Koran* (New York: A. L. Burt, 1894), 41.

11. Edward Augustus Freeman, *The History of Conquests of the Saracens* (London, 1877), 53.

12. Edward Gibbon, *The Decline and the Fall of the Roman Empire* (Chicago: Encyclopedia Britannica, 1952), 2:229.

13. Ibid., 245.

14. Bernard Lewis, *Islam and the West* (New York: Oxford University Press, 1993), 98.

15. Tor Andrae, *Mohammed: The Man and His Faith,* trans. Theophil Menzel (London: George Allen and Unwin, 1956), 155.

16. Ibid., 176.

17. Arthur Gilman, *The Story of the Saracens* (New York: G. P. Putman's Sons, 1896), 211.

18. Ibid., 212.

19. John Bagot Glubb, *The Life and Times of Muhammad* (New York: Stein and Day, 1970), 195.

20. James A. Michener, "Islam: The Misunderstood Religion," *Readers' Digest*, May, 1955, 72..

21. Robert Morey, *Islamic Invasion: Confronting the World's Fastest Growing Religion* (Eugene, OR: Harvest House, 1992), 87.

22. Ali Dashti, *Twenty Three Years: A Study of the Prophetic Career of Muhammad,* trans. F. R. C. Bagley (London: George Allen and Unwin, 1985), 129.

23. Desmond Stewart, *Early Islam* (New York: Time, 1967), 20.

24. Muhammad Husayn Haykal, *The Life of Muhammad*, trans. Ismail Ragi A. al Faruqi (North American Trust Publications, 1976), 183.

25. Sue Penney, *Islam* (Chicago: Heinemann Library, 2001), 6.

26. John B. Christopher, *The Islamic Tradition* (New York: Harper and Row, 1972), 25.

27. Robert Payne, *The Holy Sword: The Story of Islam from Muhammad to the Present* (New York: Collier Books, 1962), 65.

28. Tor Andrae, *Mohammad: The Man and His Faith* (New York: Barnes and Noble, 1956), 155–56.

29. Serge Trifkovic, *The Sword of the Prophet* (Boston: Regina Orthodox Press, 2002), 12.

30. Ibn Warraq, "Studies on Muhammad and the Rise of Islam," in *The Quest for the Historical Muhammad*, ed. Ibn Warraq (Amherst, NY: Prometheus Books, 2000), 21.

31. Agape Press, December 22, 2003, cited in "Teaching Islam in School Ok'd by Court," *AFA Journal* (March, 2004), 10.

32. "No Separation of Mosque and State," www.baptistpillar.com /bd0460.htm, (accessed February 5, 2004).

33. Ibid.

34. Editorial, "Mandating the Koran," *Wall Street Journal*, August 13, 2002, A20.

35. Armour, Sr., op. cit., xiii.

318

36. Sean D. Hamill, "Willow Creek Welcomes Muslim Imam," *The Chicago Tribune* (October 12, 2001), Metro Page 8.

37. J. Muehleisen Arnold, *Ishmael: A Natural History of Islamism and Its Relation to Christianity* (London: Rivington, Waterloo Place, 1859), 189.

38. A.H. Strong, *Systematic Theology,* 389, cited in Francis Pieper, *Christian Dogmatics* (St. Louis: Concordia Publishing House, 1951), 2:335.

39. Armour, *Troubled History*, 51

40. Rodney Stark, *For the Glory of God: How Monotheism Led To Reformations, Science, Witch-Hunts, and the End of Slavery* (Princeton: Princeton University Press, 2003), 49.

41. Alan Dershowitz, *The Case for Israel* (Hoboken, NJ: John Wiley and Sons, 2003), 72.

42. Pipes, *Militant Islam*, 212.

43. Daniel Pipes, "American Muslims Against America's Jews," *Commentary*, May 1999, 35.

44. Ibid.

45. Cited in Ze'ev Schiff and Ehud Ya'ari, *Intifada: The Inside Story of the Palestinian Uprising that Changed the Middle East Equation,* trans. Ina Friedman (New York: Simon and Schuster, 1989), 235.

46. Tom White, "Trust in the Law," *The Voice of the Martyrs*, November 2003, 8.

47. Patrick Goodenough, "Australian Embassy Deals With Concerns About Religious Vilification Case," http://ms101.mysearch.com/jsp /GGcres.jsp?id=unJDXkhj&su=http%3A//ms101.myse. (accessed January 22, 2004).

48. Ibid.

49. Daniel Pipes, "How Dare You Defame Islam," *Commentary*, November 1999, 43.

50. Ibid.

51. Pipes, "How Dare You Defame Islam," 41–45.

52. Cited in Fred Halliday, "The Fundamentalist Lesson of the Fatwa," *New Statesman and Society*, February 12, 1993.

53. Cited in Ibid.

54. Ibid.

55. Ibid.

56. Cited in John Leo, "In Search of the Middle Ground" *U.S. News and World Report*, March 6, 1989.

57. Andrew Loung, "The Fatwa Continues: The Salman Rushdie Affair After Ten Years," http://varsity.utoronto.ca.16080/archives/119/nov23 /feature/fatwa.html, (accessed February 16, 2004).

58. Ibid.

59. Pipes, *Militant Islam Reaches America,* 177.

60. For this and following examples, see Pipes, *Militant Islam Reaches America.*

61. Stephen Schwartz, *The Two Faces of Islam* (New York: Doubleday, 2002), 240.

62. Robert Spencer, *Islam Unveiled: Disturbing Questions About the World's Fastest-Growing Faith* (San Francisco: Encounter Books, 2002), 14.

63. Stephen L. Carter, *Civility* (New York The Free Press, 1998), 213.

64. "The Peace Encyclopedia: Blasphemy," http://www.yahoo.com /peace/blasphemy.html, (accessed February 16, 2004).

65. Tor Eigelanc, "Granada's New Convivencia," *Saudi Aramco World* (September–October, 2003), 16.

66. Uwe Siemon-Netto, "Europe—Hostage to its Muslims?" United Press International E-Mail Report, July 10, 2003.

67. Ibid.

68. Burton Bollag, "Muslims Worry French Universities," *The Chronicle of Higher Education*, December 12, 2003.

69. John Rossant, "Is France's Center Coming Unglued?" *Business Week*, February 23, 2004.

70. Cited in Daniel Pipes, "The Danger Within Militant Islam in America," *Commentary*, November 2001, 23.

71. Henri Astier, "Secular France Mulls Mosque Subsidies," *BBC NEWS World Edition*, http;//ms101.mysearch.com/jspCCcres.jsp?id=ywCw PuVJgmoJ&su=http%3A//ms101.mys, (accessed February 2, 2004).

72. Ibid.

73. Anne Beamish, "MIT/AKPIA Fall Lecture Series: New Mosques in Germany," http://ms101.mysearch.com/jspGGcres.jsp?id=mFmJWHVc8 zcJ&su=http%3A//ms101.my, (accessed February 2, 2004).

74. Mark Walsh and Detlef Siebert, "Salman Rushdie: Between the Devil and Deep Blue Sea," *Filmmakers Library: Arts and Literature*, http://www.filmakerrs.com/indivs/SalmanRushdie.htm, (accessed February 10, 2004).

75. Stephen Schwartz, *Two Faces*, 240.

76. Ibid., 227–231.

77. Cited in "Number of American Mosques Grows by 25 Percent," http://www.arabicnews.com/ansub/Daily/Day/010428/2001042825.html, (accessed January 29, 2004).

78. Marvin Olasky, "What We Don't Know Can Hurt Us," *World*, March 8, 2003, 25.

79. Robert Payne, *The Holy Sword: The Story of Islam from Muhammad to the Present* (New York: Collier Books, 1959), 323.

80. Ibid.

81. Ibid., 199.

82. Robert Morey, *Islamic Invasion* (Eugene, OR: Harvest House, 1992), 22.

83. Shamin A. Siddiqi, *Methodology of Dawah Ilallah in American Perspective* (Brentwood, MD: International Graphic, 1989), 109.

84. Ibid., 118.

85. Ibid.

APPENDIX B

1. Thomas Goldstein, *Dawn of Modern Science: From Arabs to Leonardo da Vinci* (Boston: Houghton Mifflin, 1980), 206.

2. Herbert Butterfield, *The Origins of Modern Science, 1300–1800* (London: G. Bell and Sons, 1951), 39.

3. Howard W. Haggard, *The Doctor in History* (New York: Yale University Press, 1934), 215.

4. Agatha Young, *Scalpel: Men Who Made Surgery* (New York: Random House, 1956), 20.

5. Cited in Haggard, *Doctor in History*, 244.

6. Henry Morris, *Men of Science—Men of God* (San Diego: Creation Life, 1982), 80.

7. Arthur Koestler, *The Sleep Walkers: A History of Man's Changing Vision of the Universe* (New York: Macmillan, 1959), 117.

8. Werner Elert, *The Structure of Lutheranism,* trans. Walter A. Hansen (St. Louis: Concordia, 1962), 423.

9. Cited in W. Montgomery Watt, *The Majesty That Was Islam: The Islamic World, 666–1100* (New York: Praeger, 1974), 99.

10. Owen Gingrich, *The Eye of Heaven: Ptolemy, Copernicus, Kepler* (New York: American Institute of Physics, 1993), 333.

11. Koestler, *Sleep Walkers*, 394.

12. Ibid., 259.

13. Stanley I. Jaki, *The Savior of Science*, (Edinburgh: Scottish Academic, 1990), 90.

14. Koestler, *Sleep Walkers*, 410.

15. Ibid., 397.

16. Max Caspar, *Johannes Kepler* (Stuttgart: W. Kohlhammer Verlag, 1948), 73.

17. Cited in Koestler, *Sleep Walkers*, 315.

18. Cited in Caspar, *Johannes Kepler*, 430.

19. Cited in Gingrich, *Eye of Heaven*, 307.

20. Cited in Casper, *Johannes Kepler*, 93; my translation.

21. Butterfield, *Origins of Modern Science*, 50–51.

22. Hal Hellman, *Great Feuds in Science* (New York: John Wiley and Sons, 1998), 15.

23. Koestler, *Sleep Walkers*, 279.

24. Eric Temple Bell, "Newton, Isaac, Sir," in *The World Book Encyclopedia* (Chicago: Field Enterprises Educational, 1958), 12:5619.

25. Isaac Newton, "God and Natural Philosophy," in *Newton's Philosophy of Nature: Selections from His Writings*, ed. H.S. Thayer (New York: Hafner, 1953), 66–67.

26. Michael Drosnin, *The Bible Code* (New York: Simon and Schuster, 1997), 21.

27. Blaise Pascal, *Pensees*, in *Great Books of the Western World*, ed. Mortimer Adler (Chicago: Encyclopedia Britannica, 1996), 267.

28. Ibid., 278.

29. G. W. Leibnitz, Theodicy: Essays on the Goodness of God, the Freedom of Man, and the Origin of God, trans. E. M. Haggard (La Salle, IL: Open Court, 1985), 67.

30. Karl A. Kneller, *Christianity and the Leaders of Modern Science,* trans. T. M. Kettle (Fraser, MI: Real-View Books, 1995), 118.

31. Ibid., 132.

32. Ibid., 123.

33. Geoffery Cantor, et al., *Michael Faraday* (Atlantic Highlands, NJ: Humanities Press, 1996), 18.

34. Kneller, *Christianity*, 38.

35. L. L. Laudan, "Boyle, Robert," in *The Encyclopedia Americana* (Danbury, CT: Grolier, 2002), 4:390.

36. Ibid., 391.

37. Ibid.

38. Philip Schaff, "Robert Boyle," in *The New Schaff-Herzog Encyclopedia of Religious Knowledge* (Grand Rapids: Baker Book House, 1977), 2:244.

39. Morris, *Men of Science*, 71.

40. Kneller, *Christianity*, 180.

41. Morris, *Men of Science*, 104–105.

42. Walter Addison Jayne, *The Healing Gods of Ancient Civilizations* (New York: University Books, 1962), 285.

43. Gabriel Compayre, *Abelard and the Origin of Early Universities* (New York: Charles Scribner's Sons, 1899), 243.

44. Ibid., 245.

45. Haggard, *Doctor in History*, 128.

46. Carl Joseph von Hefele, *Conciliengeschichte* (Freiburg: Herder'sche Verlagshandlung, 1886), 5:441.

47. Howard R. Haggard, *Devils, Drugs, and Doctors* (New York: Harper and Brothers, 1929), 147.

48. Rodney Stark, *For the Glory of God: How Monotheism Led to Reformations, Science, Witch-Hunts, and the End of Slavery* (Princeton: Princeton University Press, 2003), 143.

49. Cited in Henry M. Pachter, *Magic into Science: The Story of Paracelsus* (New York: Henry Schuman, 1951), 93.

50. David Riesman, *The Story of Medicine in the Middle Ages* (New York: Harper and Row, 1936), 341.

51. J. F. C. Hecker, *The Epidemics of the Middle Ages* (London: Trubner, 1859), 92.

52. Ibid.

53. Haggard, *Devils, Drugs, and Doctors*, 194.

54. Frances E. Crecher, "Pare, Ambroise," in *The World Book Encyclopedia* (Chicago: Field Enterprises Educational, 1958), 13:6104.

55. Samuel Evans Massengill, *A Sketch of Medicine and Pharmacy* (Bristol, TN: S. E. Massengill, 1943), 257.

56. Haggard, *Devils, Drugs, and Doctors*, 225–26.

57. Ibid.

58. Morris, *Men of Science*, 84.

59. Rene Vallery Rador, *The Life of Pasteur* (Garden City, NJ: Doubleday, Page, 1923), 464.

60. Haggard, *Devils, Drugs, and Doctors*, 117.

61. Morris, *Men of Science*, 69.

62. Herbert Lockyer, *The Man Who Changed the World* (Grand Rapids: Zondervan, 1966), 1:177.

63. Massengil, *Sketch of Medicine*, 220.